Changing Lives, Changing Drug Journeys

This book describes how a group of young people make decisions about drug taking. It charts the decision making process of recreational drug takers and non-drug takers as they mature from adolescence into young adulthood. With a focus upon their perceptions of different drugs, it situates their decision making within the context of their everyday lives.

Changing Lives, Changing Drug Journeys presents qualitative longitudinal data collected from interviewees at age 17, 22 and 28 and tracks the onset of drug journeys, their persistence, change and desistance. The drug journeys and the decision making process which underpins them are analysed by drawing upon contemporary discourses of risk and life course criminology. In doing so, a new theoretical framework is developed to help us understand drug taking decision making in contemporary society. This framework highlights the pleasures and risks perceived when making decisions whether or not to take drugs. The ways in which drug journeys and life journeys intersect and how social relationships and transitions to adulthood facilitate or constrain the decision making process are also explored.

Qualitative longitudinal research of this kind is uncommon yet it provides an invaluable insight into the decision making process of individuals during the life course. The book will, therefore, be of interest to researchers and students from a variety of disciplines including qualitative research methods as well as sociology, criminology, cultural and health studies. It will also be an important resource for professionals working in health promotion, drugs education, harm reduction and treatment.

Lisa Williams is Lecturer in Criminology at the Centre for Criminology and Criminal Justice, University of Manchester, UK. For over a decade, she has undertaken research of both recreational and dependent forms of drug taking. Her research has focused upon recreational drug journeys during the life course, exploring onset, stability, change and desistance.

Routledge Advances in Ethnography

Edited by Dick Hobbs, University of Essex, and Geoffrey Pearson,
Goldsmiths College, University of London

Ethnography is a celebrated, if contested, research methodology that offers
unprecedented access to people's intimate lives, their often hidden social
worlds and the meanings they attach to these. The intensity of ethnographic
fieldwork often makes considerable personal and emotional demands on the
researcher, while the final product is a vivid human document with personal
resonance impossible to recreate by the application of any other social science
methodology. This series aims to highlight the best, most innovative ethnographic work available from both new and established scholars.

Changing Lives, Changing Drug Journeys

Drug taking decisions from adolescence to adulthood

Lisa Williams

Routledge
Taylor & Francis Group

LONDON AND NEW YORK

8/25/14
LN
$48.95

First published 2013
by Routledge
2 Park Square, Milton Park, Abingdon, Oxfordshire, OX14 4RN

Simultaneously published in the USA and Canada
by Routledge
711 Third Avenue, New York, NY 10017

First issued in paperback 2014

Routledge is an imprint of the Taylor and Francis Group, an informa business

British Library Cataloguing in Publication Data
A catalogue record for this book is available from the British Library

Library of Congress Cataloging in Publication Data
Williams, Lisa, 1970 Oct. 19-
Changing lives, changing drug journeys : drug taking decisions from adolescence to adulthood / Lisa Williams.
    p. cm. – (Routledge advances in ethnography)
    1. Youth–Drug use–Longitudinal studies. 2. Drug abuse–Longitudinal studies. 3. Risk-taking (Psychology) in adolescence–Longitudinal studies. I. Title.
    HV5824.Y68W554 2012
    616.8600835–dc23
                2012003343

ISBN 13: 978-1-84392-894-2 (hbk)
ISBN 13: 978-0-415-62351-3 (pbk)

Typeset in Times by
Taylor & Francis Books

Contents

List of tables

Acknowledgements

The project on which this book is based has been ongoing since 1991 and there are, therefore, many people who have contributed to it in various ways. I do my best to acknowledge the most important here.

I wish firstly to express my thanks to all the interviewees who took part in this research. They so willingly gave their time to me and openly discussed their lives. It was a pleasure to meet and interview them all. I am also grateful to the Economic and Social Research Council for funding my PhD research and earlier stages of the project, which allowed the project to continue to explore drug taking in young adulthood.

Special thanks are also due to some academics who supported and encouraged me during my PhD and in the writing of this book. Firstly, to my friend and PhD supervisor Judith Aldridge, who offered advice throughout the course of my PhD and always provided positive encouragement during the many highs and lows experienced in producing it. Her knowledge and experience of the North West England Longitudinal Study (NWELS) and ideas on how it could be developed were invaluable. Secondly, thanks also to Toby Seddon who became my supervisor during the final year of my PhD and has since continued to encourage and support me in producing this book. I am grateful for his constructive and positive comments on my draft manuscript. I am also indebted to some former colleagues who initiated and worked on earlier stages of the NWELS: Fiona Measham and Howard Parker.

I wish also to express my gratitude to my friends and family. Thanks, of course, to my Mum, Dad and sister, Tracey, for their continual encouragement, support and love. Thanks particularly to my Mum for travelling 'up North' to look after my daughter in the final stages of writing this book. My friends have been ever supportive too, continually asking how my work was progressing. Special thanks are due to Susan Batchelor, Nic Beck, 'Bob' Coates, Ange McGibbon and Tamara McNeill. Ange and Tamara deserve a special mention for providing childcare so that I could continue to write this book. Finally, and by no means the least, very special thanks are due to my partner Rob Ralphs and my children Ruby and Rafferty. Rob has been a constant, calming and encouraging support throughout and also provided valuable comments on my draft manuscript. Without him, his enduring love, willingness to put my work before his own and readiness to take on the majority of childcare during the writing of this book, it is unlikely this work would have reached completion. Thanks to Ruby for putting up with not spending as much time with me as I would have liked. And finally, thanks to Rafferty who kindly waited until I had just completed this manuscript before entering this world.

Lastly, thanks to Dick Hobbs and Geoff Pearson for their ongoing support and understanding when the manuscript was delayed by the birth of my children. Thanks also to Nicola Hartley and Tom Sutton at Routledge for their patience and support in delivering this book.

1 Understanding and researching drug taking

Lessons from the past

Introduction

The central focus of this book is about why and how decisions about recreational drug taking are made. It is important to note from the outset that it is not concerned with academic debates about changing prevalence, measures or definitions of drug taking (see, for example, Newcombe, 2007; Shiner, 2009). Even though the study on which this book is based has been developed from the North West England Longitudinal Study (NWELS), from which the normalization thesis of recreational drug use was formulated, it is not concerned with assessing or extending debates about the extent of normalization in contemporary society (see Aldridge et al., 2011; Parker et al., 1998, 2002).[1] Nor does the book attempt to provide an extensive commentary on and explanation of the development of drug policy in contemporary times (see Seddon et al., 2012). Rather, this book is about the experiences of young people growing up during the 1990s and into the millennium – a period of time in which undoubtedly the meaning and place of drugs changed in British society (South, 1999). The book attempts to capture the dynamics of young people's decision making process in relation to recreational drugs across the early part of the life course and contextualize it within their changing social, cultural and structural circumstances. It does not provide an account of decision making with regard to alcohol, however, it is recognized that, for many, consumption of legal and illegal substances goes hand in hand.[2] The purpose then is to follow the ethnographic tradition: to understand from the perspective of drug takers, and non-drug takers, how the process of growing up, or their transition to adulthood, in the late 1990s and into the millennium, interacts with the motivations for drug taking and the decision making process which underpins it. In this respect, interpersonal relationships with family, friends and intimate partners, and significant life course events which feature on the journey to adulthood, are explored.

The book has, at least in part, been inspired by my own life journey. I too 'grew up' during the 1990s and was presented with comparable circumstances to the sample in which decisions about drug taking were made. Regardless of drug decisions, as a young adult moving from Brighton, in the South, to

Sheffield, in the North of England, and from cities within the North, I came to realize how changes in location impacted upon my attitudes and behaviour. For instance, as new friendships and long-term intimate relationships were established in the new places I moved to, how I spent my leisure time changed. Initially, moving from a cosmopolitan southern city to a post-industrial northern city, clubbing became less of a past-time and pubbing became more prominent in my life. These changes, however, were not necessarily a result of the cultural opportunities available to me in the North; rather, they occurred because of the people I was now spending time with. A further move for work purposes to Manchester generated new friendships, a new long-term intimate relationship and a return to the clubbing scene. In this location, my transitions to adulthood have had the greatest impact upon my leisure time. As Shiner (2009) argues, the domestic transition appears to affect women the most. Since becoming a parent, my regular attendance at clubs or other similar events has reduced. Four factors underpin this change in behaviour: *changes in opportunities or situations*: my friends have made a similar transition and are not going out as often, therefore, I have fewer people I can go out with; *available social networks or relationships*: I only have a handful of babysitters I can call on to look after my children when I do go out; *changes in risk perceptions*: looking after two young children the day after clubbing is quite demanding and not something I want to repeat regularly; and *time constraints*: I want to spend some of my weekends with my children and, therefore, have less time to go clubbing regularly or spend weekends recovering from the effects of a club night. It is this interaction between adult transitions, opportunities and situations, social networks or relationships, and risk assessment which intrigues me and has largely been the driving force, at least for me, in shaping the direction of the NWELS. Indeed, my colleagues, who were authors of *Illegal Leisure* (Parker et al., 1998), predicted that transitions to adulthood would be significant for drug taking. However, even when our sample was aged 22, it was too early to assess how they might impact upon drug journeys (Williams and Parker, 2001). The data presented in this book reveals how the sample, who were aged 27/28 when data were last collected from them, manage the competing demands of life in young adulthood and how this influences their decisions about drug taking.

Most young people at some point during their lives will be faced with making decisions about drugs and many may decide to try them, even if they do not go on to take them regularly. The objective of this book is to understand the *why* and *how* of drug taking decisions, or, to put it another way, the meanings, motivations and social, cultural and structural situations which lead to decisions to take drugs, and also guide others to decisions not to take them, during the life course. The purpose then is twofold: to further understand why people choose to take drugs and others do not; and to describe how they make decisions about drug taking, or, in other words, what facilitates or constrains the decision making process.

It will be argued throughout this book that exploring life journeys and drug journeys can shed light on the relationship between agency, structure and culture. In this regard, the endeavour is to wrestle with the debate which has been a concern for social science inclined scholars for at least a century: the significance of structure, agency or culture. The aim, however, is to venture beyond orthodox explanations for drug taking provided by the sociology of deviance and cultural studies which offer causal explanations and outline motivations for drug taking, and to theorize the decision making process by drawing upon a relatively new body of work which has emerged from sociology and social anthropology, namely, risk theory. To this end, the theories most prominently developed by Ulrich Beck, Anthony Giddens and Mary Douglas are elucidated and applied to develop our understanding (see Chapter Two). In particular, Beck and Giddens emphasize the significance of agency when they argue we now live in riskier times and that we must carve out our own biographies and identity by assessing and avoiding risk (Beck, 1992; Giddens, 1991). In contrast, Douglas (1992) stresses the significance of the cultural dimensions of risk; the ways in which risk assessments are culturally located and influenced. Drug taking provides a suitable case study to understand how risk is assessed in contemporary life. With claims about the importance of risk avoidance or reduction made by Beck and Giddens, it appears almost counterintuitive that we have also witnessed an increasing trend in drug taking since the beginning of the 1990s, an activity which is normatively defined as risky and to be avoided, which has in recent times begun to plateau and slowly decline (Aldridge, 2008). The purpose then is to utilize theories of risk to develop a conceptual framework to explore how drug taking is perceived, assessed and managed or avoided in everyday life – essentially, to understand the meaning of drug taking for young people, how this may change across the life course and the process of or influences upon decision making. Such an enterprise allows us to appreciate how the detail of the 'big picture' accounts, which have materialized from sociology and social anthropology recently, play out at a micro level. In doing so, we can test the utility of these perspectives and acknowledge how they might need to be adjusted, revised and refined. Applying insights from these theories to drug taking decision making will appeal not only to academics and researchers within the drugs field, but scholars from various social science disciplines. The task, however, is not to dismiss what we can learn from past theories of drug taking, but to appreciate how these explanations may still remain valid and can be developed through the application of theories of risk.

The data presented in this book is largely qualitative. Although the NWELS collected quantitative and qualitative data, I took the opportunity to change the direction of the project for my PhD research and created a qualitative longitudinal dataset.[3] This type of methodology is not unique, however, it is uncommon. It permits us to appreciate the decision making process at a micro level over time. It is rare to be able to collect data from the same sample from adolescence into young adulthood. Drugs research is often cross-sectional and focuses on easy to access populations in schools or in particular settings, such as clubs. This study has collected data over a period of 15 years from a sample of young people, some of whom have never embarked upon a drugs journey, whilst others, who have, take recreational drugs in a variety of settings. The qualitative longitudinal data gathered reveals the ways in which life journeys and drug journeys intersect over time for different individuals. The interviewees' journeys are unique and diverse, however, there are also commonalities. This life course data facilitates the answering of why and how questions in relation to onset, continuity, change and desistance and, in doing so, provides an explanation not only for how decisions to take drugs are made, but how decisions to stop taking them are made and how drug abstinence is maintained across the life course. Hence, insights from life course criminology feature in the theoretical framework created in Chapter Two. This perspective offers both the prospect of explaining and understanding decision making over time and also exploring the interplay between structure, agency and changing situations.

In the remainder of this introductory chapter two matters will be discussed in more depth. Firstly, to prepare the ground for the conceptual framework created in Chapter Two, germane past theorizing from the sociology of deviance and cultural studies which facilitates an understanding of the meaning of drug taking and the decision making process which underlies it will be outlined. The development of concepts are traced over time and their significance for our understanding of drug taking are assessed. It will be argued that although there are insights which remain relevant today, risk theory permits us to focus in specifically on the process of decision making or risk assessment. Moreover, by applying perspectives on risk and from life course criminology, we can attempt to unpick or disentangle the relationship between agency, structure and culture, or changing situations, for decision making in contemporary times and, specifically, for drug taking decisions. Secondly, a summary of how the study has developed is provided together with a description of the sample for which the empirical data is presented, to elucidate the theoretical framework created in Chapter Two, in Chapters Three to Six. At the end of this chapter the structure of the book is outlined. An appreciation of past theories of drug taking now follows.

Theorizing drug taking decisions: an historical overview

When attempting to explain current prevalence and patterns of drug taking, it is argued we can learn a great deal from past theorizing. In his critique of the normalization thesis, Shiner (2009) accuses the authors, in their desire to reject previous theorizing which relied on individual pathology or social dysfunction, of being too hasty in dismissing other relevant theories and explanations for drug taking, namely, the sociology of deviance.[4] As Shiner notes, there are many insights from this perspective which remain relevant today (see also Measham and Shiner, 2009; Williams, 2007). The aim of this chapter is to outline and assess what past theories of drug taking from the disciplines of sociology *and* cultural studies can tell us about why and how decisions whether or not to take drugs are made. In doing so, it will be argued that perspectives on risk and life course criminology provide a more comprehensive framework for exploring motivations for drug taking and the processes which underpin decision making in contemporary society. In creating a theoretical framework in Chapter Two, these perspectives will be outlined and synthesized.

The sociology of deviance came to prominence during the 1960s in Britain and America. Its roots can be traced to earlier sociological theories exploring the relationship between 'deviant' and 'normal' behaviour, for example those developed by the Chicago School of Sociology and strain theory (Merton, 1938). The functionalist sociology of Merton, in the form of his strain theory, offered the first sociological attempt to explain drug taking behaviour. He observed how consensus to the American Dream to be successful and wealthy resulted in anomic or adaptive behaviour. For Merton, there is a disjunction between the culturally prescribed goal of success and the means to attain it, which induces structural strain for individuals. He conceptualizes drug takers as 'retreatists' from society who have personally failed. In doing so, they reject the goal to be successful and wealthy and the means available to them to achieve it. Over 20 years later, Cloward and Ohlin (1960) developed these ideas further to explain group behaviour. Drug taking, according to Cloward and Ohlin, is an outcome of 'retreatrist' subcultures available to lower class youths who fail to achieve the American Dream through legitimate or illegitimate means. Subcultures, therefore, provide a solution to structural pressures they experience. Applying the concept of 'differential association' (see Sutherland, 1939), they explain drug taking as a learned and shared cultural practice within the subculture. According to Cloward and Ohlin (1960), membership of a 'retreatist' subculture is a 'double failure': its members failed to achieve status through conventional means or through available 'criminal' or 'conflict' subcultures.

We can see then, from this body of work, three principal ideas developing about drug taking. Firstly, it is explained as a deviant activity which chimed with commonly held assumptions at the time about drug takers who were characterized as 'junkies' and 'freaks'. Secondly, it is a shared and learned practice within a subculture; the outcome of group membership and dynamics. Thirdly, the influence of structure upon behaviour is emphasized. In an attempt to challenge prevailing beliefs about drug takers, and to explore the significance of subcultures for drug taking, theories began to emerge from the sociology of deviance. In America, Howard Becker was a leading proponent, as was Jock Young in Britain. Their works have endured the test of time and are recognized as classics in the drugs field.

Becker (1963, 1973) provides the first detailed exploration of a particular form of drug taking: recreational cannabis (or marihuana) smoking. His research was carried out during the early 1950s in America with 50 predominantly jazz musicians. Explaining drug taking as a subcultural activity and solution to cannabis prohibition in America since 1937 was the focus of his study. He challenges the notion that drug taking is inherently deviant. Central to his thesis is the idea that crime and deviance are socially constructed behaviours and perceptions of what is criminal or deviant change over time and place. With the onset of deviant behaviour, Becker was concerned to understand why it continues, particularly in light of possible criminalization. He argues pleasure is significant for the continuity of drug taking and it is socially learnt: 'Enjoyment is introduced by the favourable definition of the experience one acquires from others. Without this, use will not continue, for marihuana will not be for the user an object he can use for pleasure' (Becker, 1973: 56). The importance of the group, rather than the individual experience, is emphasized in his work. Within the cannabis smoking subculture other smokers provide rationales and justifications for continued use which challenge conventional views. In this setting, effects which could initially be defined as unpleasurable, for instance altered perception, are redefined as pleasurable. Consequently, novice users learn to rationalize and justify their own drug taking and repudiate conventional attitudes. Over time, their identity shifts. According to Becker, the concept of 'societal reaction' is pivotal in determining a deviant identity and, in turn, persistence or desistance from drug taking. The negative reaction of others to deviant behaviour, particularly those not involved in a drug subculture, could lead to drug desistance. Desistance may also occur when smoking cannabis is no longer perceived as pleasurable. However, he notes this is dependent upon the extent to which a person is embedded within their subculture: frequent smokers are less likely to redefine their experiences as unpleasurable since they may receive reassurance from others in the subculture.

Young (1971) drew upon some of the ideas present in Becker's work. As Becker did, he rejects the notion that drug taking is inherently deviant. According to Young, our understanding of what constitutes deviance is dependent upon our relationship with or practice of the behaviour in question. He argues drug taking is largely ubiquitous in society, whether it involves the use of legal or illegal drugs. Drawing on the work of Matza and Sykes (1961), drug takers are seen to hold similar norms and values to the rest of society. He contends all members of society pursue 'subterranean values', for example, excitement, adventure and thrills. Yet, for most people, these are sought in socially acceptable ways, for instance by getting drunk rather than getting high. Similar to Becker, the meaning of drug taking for Young is provided within the subcultural setting. Drug taking is the result of an 'interaction between the physiological effects of the drug and the norms of the group of which the drugtaker is a member' (Young, 1971: 50). Developing the principle that subcultures provide a solution to problems associated with social positions, drugs are seen to be a problem solving tool used for relaxation or escapism. In this regard, his account of drug taking is set within broader structural processes and the political economy of the time.

Subterranean values are associated with play or recreation. In contrast, formal values in society are consistent with a work ethic. Young views these values as mutually dependent and what we now might conceptualize as a work-hard, play-hard ethos. Accordingly, hedonism is inextricably linked to and justified via production: we ultimately produce to consume and consume to produce.[5] Leisure is, therefore, an important component for stress relief and time out. However, the period of youth for Young is a time when the search for subterranean values can be legitimized without necessarily seeking a balance in terms of a work ethic. He argues the young, middle class hippies of the 1960s rejected work and demanded play. From Young's perspective, hedonism prevails in youth, however, with age, as structural factors such as work begin to take effect, play may be constrained.

The work of Becker and Young provides many insights into motivations for drug taking. They emphasize drug taking as meaningful and goal-oriented behaviour and how the norms and values present in drug subcultures, together with the effects of drugs, influence decision making. For Becker, pleasure is important for continued drug taking whilst Young connects continuity to the pursuit of subterranean values. Furthermore, in developing the idea of subcultures providing a solution to social problems, Young places emphasis on how choosing to take drugs is a form of escapism or relaxation in the context of contemporary society. In offering an explanation for both persistence of and desistance from drug taking, he suggests at particular stages of the life course subterranean play can either be legitimized or not. Desistance for Becker is linked to identity and the negative reaction of significant others beyond the subculture or it occurs when drug taking is no longer defined as pleasurable. These theories still remain relevant today for explaining why and how decisions about drugs are made. However, as we will see, the concept of subculture, group membership and the significance of structural influences began to be challenged during the 1990s. Before we consider this debate, we turn to accounts offered by British cultural studies commentators during the 1970s.

From the sociological explanations outlined so far, we can trace the origins of the concept of resistance as an explanation for drug taking. Young, for example, argued young, drug taking hippies rejected the dominant work ethic and prioritized the pursuit of subterranean values. In Britain, during the 1970s, academics at Birmingham's Centre for Contemporary Cultural Studies (CCCS) continued to explore many of the themes present in Young's account, particularly the concept of resistance. They deliberated about the relationship between class struggle, youthful rebellion and media representations of youth subcultures. Resistance was the order of the day and youth subcultures facilitated symbolic expressions of conflict or difference from those in power and capitalist ideology. The work of the CCCS culminated in the publication of *Resistance through Rituals* (Hall and Jefferson, 1976). From this perspective, drug taking is viewed as a normal subcultural activity for young Mods, Rastas and hippies of the late 1960s and early 1970s. Their cultural practices are conceptualized as an act of rebellion subverting the values of the dominant culture. For instance, it is argued that consuming pharmaceutical pills for pleasure challenges the values of the medical profession (Hebdige, 1976). Similar to Young, Hebdige also emphasizes the relationship between consumption, subterranean values and structural positions. He explains one of the functions of taking amphetamines for Mods is:

> Amphetamine made life tolerable, 'blocked' one's sensory channels so that action and risk and excitement were possible, kept one going on the endless round of consumption, and confined one's attention to the search, the ideal, the goal, rather than the attainment of the goal – relief rather than release. [...] Speed suspended the disappointment when the search failed, inevitably to turn up anything substantial and gave one the energy to pick up and start again.
>
> (Hebdige, 1976: 91–92)

Taking drugs, therefore, makes life 'tolerable', but also psychologically defends against risks and provides energy to get on with life in an imaginary sense. In line with Young, this body of work highlights how decisions to take drugs are an act and expression of resistance. In addition, they function as a form of escapism or self medication, temporarily providing relief from everyday life.

During the 1990s there was a renaissance in subcultural theory in Britain. With the rise of rave culture, researchers began to describe this behaviour as a new form of (sub)cultural expression. This body of work became known as post-subcultural theory (see, for example, Malbon, 1999; Muggleton, 2000; Redhead, 1993; Thornton, 1995). Many of the concepts and explanations already offered by the sociology of deviance and cultural studies dominated this new body of work and some were also contested.

Firstly, a number of researchers discussed how rave culture, as other drug subcultures before it, was significant for identity construction. Thornton (1995), for example, focuses upon the media's role in creating, defining and amplifying drug taking and how subcultures are important sources of identity. From this perspective, rave culture is seen to express and validate identity (see also Muggleton, 2000; Redhead, 1993). Drawing on Bourdieu's (1984) work, she suggests it endows young people with 'subcultural capital' and, in doing so, a valued identity. Secondly, as previous theories had suggested, this new subcultural form was characterized as challenging dominant political ideology. However, Redhead (1993) argues early subcultural theory failed to acknowledge the complexities of youth culture and the central role of the media in influencing youth cultural practices. Media discourses on drugs are seen to frame youth culture as problematic in contemporary times. Rave culture was, therefore, viewed as at the 'cutting edge of "politics" and deviance' (Redhead, 1993: 5) and defying dominant power structures through illegal parties and drug taking. Thirdly, pleasure and hedonism continued to prevail as significant motivations for drug taking (see, for example, Redhead, 1993). Fourthly, continuing to explore the significance of escapism as a function of drug taking, some commentators emphasized the ongoing influence of structural and political processes. Taking drugs was seen to relieve the boredom and uncertainty of young people's everyday lives (Cohen and Taylor, 1992; Jones and Martin, 1997; Sobel, 1991) and distract them from their powerlessness (Cote and Allahar, 1996; Taylor, 1999). As earlier subcultural theorists had argued, the choice to take drugs is conceptualized as a solution to structural positions. For example, the rise in the consumption of some drugs during the 1990s, such as ecstasy, has been explained in relation to their anti-depressant qualities (Keane, 1997) and young people's increasing alienation in contemporary life (Fox, 1999).

Whilst many of the concepts present in previous theorizing were initially applied in a similar way, as the post-subcultural debate progressed throughout the 1990s, some began to question the concept of group political resistance as a motivation for drug taking and rave culture. Here, then, we see the beginning of a paradigm shift which moves the focus from structural to individual processes. Notably, this shift in theorizing occurred at the same time as theories about the individualization of risk were being developed (see Beck, 1992; Giddens, 1991). Melechi (1993), in his observations of Acid House subculture,[6] argues that to explain it as a political expression is missing the point; it provides an escape from identity and a loss of the self through intoxication (see also Rietveld, 1998). In addition, the absence of everyday identities in clubs where drugs are consumed is seen to create a sense of belonging: 'A place where nobody is, but everybody belongs' (Melechi, 1993: 37). As such, drug taking becomes a source of resistance in contemporary society at the level of the individual rather than a collective expression of political opposition:

> ... resistance on a micro-level, on the level of everyday life, where the unspoken is that which binds the group together, where the desire to be with others is manifested, and differences are addressed. ... in taking Ecstasy (in not taking Ecstasy), in dressing in a certain way, in the emotional and empathetic effects of close proximity to hundreds of others, not necessarily like yourself, but sharing, at the very least, a desire to be right there, right now. This is the resistance found through losing yourself, paradoxically to find yourself.
>
> (Malbon, 1999: 280–81)

We can see, then, how the function or meaning of subcultural membership is developed and challenged by accounts like these. Others were also beginning to dispute the relevance of the concept of subculture in our fragmented and diverse contemporary world and, in doing so, questioned the continuing significance of structure. Traditional structures, for example class, gender and ethnicity, were no longer viewed as important in determining subcultural membership. Instead, it was argued, we are presented with a variety of subcultures from which to choose; from rave, to drum and bass, to grunge: all were seen to be accessible to all social groups (Calcutt, 1998). This led many to assert that subcultures are dead. Bennett (2000) and Miles (2000) are particularly critical of the concept and seek to replace it with the notion of lifestyle. Emphasizing the importance of agency, they argue that through consumerism we can construct our own individualistic lifestyles and identity. In this respect, it has been noted in our consumer society, today's drug markets are now more widespread, accessible and diverse (Taylor, 1999).

The post-subcultural perspective affirms and develops some of the explanations provided by the sociology of deviance and early cultural studies commentators. It similarly emphasizes the significance of identity, resistance, pleasure and, initially, structural positions. However, we can witness the origins of accounts which begin to shift the focus from collective to individual processes as explanations for drug taking: concepts of political resistance, subculture and the significance of structure are scrutinized. The normalization thesis also challenged our understanding of drug taking on these grounds. An outline of this perspective which offers an explanation for changing prevalence in drug taking during the 1990s and into the new millennium follows.

By the end of the 1990s, what has been described as a 'new academic orthodoxy' (Shiner, 2009) began to emerge. This statement may somewhat overstate the case, however, the normalization thesis (Aldridge et al., 2011; Parker et al., 1998, 2002) conceived from the NWELS has provoked intense debate since it was first proposed. The principle aim of the thesis was to offer an explanation for unprecedented rates of drug taking which materialized during the 1990s. In doing so, it challenges the view of drug taking as a deviant, subcultural and rebellious activity by a minority of the population and questions the continuing relevance of the concept of subculture. A further key objective was to situate the increasing trend in drug taking within the context of social change, particularly in relation to the effects of globalization on illegal drug importation, the processes of individualization (Beck, 1992) or the project of the self (Giddens, 1991), and the impact of extended youth transitions (see Coles, 1995; Furlong and Cartmel, 1997; MacDonald et al., 2001; Wallace, 1987). To consider the value of the thesis for our understanding of why and how decisions about drug taking are made, each of these aims and objectives will be addressed in turn.

The thesis mounts a challenge to the notion of drug taking as a subcultural activity in three ways. Firstly, it argues, because of increasing rates of drug taking during the 1990s, it moved 'from the margins to the centre of youth culture' (Parker et al., 1998: 152). The authors of the thesis are clear this does not mean it is 'normal' to take drugs or that most people will become drug users, however, the increasing trend in drug taking indicated a shift in young people's behaviour and willingness to try drugs. Secondly, they argue there has been a change in attitudes towards drug taking. The youth of the 1990s are described as drug-wise insomuch as drug abstainers, as well as drug takers, have friends who are drug experienced. Moreover, drug taking is socially accommodated by drug abstainers: they express tolerant attitudes towards it, particularly cannabis, and many are willing to permit the consumption of it in their company. A shift in cultural attitudes was also discerned: during the 1990s drugs were being discussed more openly and with less condemnation in society. Thirdly, it is argued we witnessed an upsurge in the availability of drugs in Britain throughout the 1990s. The reasons for this are linked to globalization and evidence is provided from a growth in drug seizure rates and the falling street price of drugs. At the same time, the NWELS sample reported their access to drugs also increased, whether they were drug takers or not. As they became older, many discussed how a range of drugs were easily accessible to them via their social relationships. The authors, therefore, conclude that drug taking can no longer be described as a subcultural activity; it pervades all sections of society irrespective of experience with drugs.

Focusing in on the decision making process, the authors of the thesis drew upon theories of risk put forward by Beck (1992) and Giddens (1991). In their accounts, as we will see in Chapter Two, agency and a rational, cognitive risk assessment is pivotal. It was similarly argued decisions to take drugs involve a rational, cognitive cost-benefit analysis in which the positive effects are assessed against the negative effects (see Parker et al., 1998). Following Beck and Giddens, the decision making process was viewed as agential, and structural factors, such as class, gender and ethnicity, were seen to hold less purchase for drug taking and decision making. In a reassessment of the thesis (see Aldridge et al., 2011), it is suggested that despite, at the time, quantitative data supporting an agential perspective, the significance of structural factors was perhaps downplayed too much. Indeed, a critique emerged in response to the initial thesis, which sought to emphasize the continuing importance of structural factors (see MacDonald and Marsh, 2002; Shildrick, 2002). Further data collection and analysis of qualitative data from the NWELS reveals the ongoing impact of structure upon drug journeys (see Aldridge et al., 2011; Measham et al., 2011; Williams, 2007). Moreover, it is noted how: 'In our desire to project the rational cost-benefit analysis and general reasonableness of young people, some of the compulsions, cravings, passions, pleasures, irrational consumption and simple utter "caning" was lost' (Aldridge et al., 2011: 23). Here, then, we see how the decision making process may not always involve a rational, cognitive cost-benefit assessment, as initially suggested, and is contingent upon many other factors.

In *Illegal Leisure* (Parker et al., 1998), a stated objective was to explore the influence of extended youth transitions upon drug taking. However, at this stage of the study, when the cohort were aged 18, this objective was premature. Indeed, even when they were age 22, due to transitions to adulthood generally being delayed, it was difficult to be certain how their extension had affected drug taking or the accomplishment of them might affect it in the future (Williams and Parker, 2001). Subsequent analysis of data collected from the cohort in their twenties reveals how transitions to adulthood, for many, brought with it a change in priorities which influenced their decision making and led some to moderate the frequency of their drug taking or to curtail their drug journeys (see Aldridge et al., 2011; Williams, 2007). In regard to employing a cost-benefit assessment when making decisions about drugs, it is argued in some cases continuing to take drugs is perceived as a risk to certain adult roles (Aldridge et al., 2011). Nevertheless, some interviewees were still willing to accommodate drug taking into their lives despite accomplishing various adult transitions, indicating the ways in which drug taking continues to be normalized in young adulthood (see Aldridge et al., 2011; Measham et al., 2011; Williams, 2007).

The response to the normalization thesis has been mixed, with some offering support for it (Hammersley et al., 2003; Pearson, 2001; Wibberley and Price, 2000) and others arguing it has been exaggerated (Ramsay and Partridge, 1999; Shiner, 2009; Shiner and Newburn, 1997, 1999). The latter criticisms relate to the extent to which there has been a monumental shift in drug prevalence in recent times and need not detain us here. Instead, we are concerned with the insights the thesis can provide for why and how decisions about drugs are made. There are, as Measham and Shiner (2009) note, some clear parallels between previous theorizing and the conclusions reached in the thesis. The idea of drug taking as a deviant activity is rejected. Rather, it is conceptualized as meaningful, pleasurable and goal-oriented behaviour. The concept of subculture is contested by the assertion that drug taking, in terms of behaviour, generally tolerant attitudes and the availability of drugs, permeates all corners of society. Moving the debate on from the cultural studies perspective which began to emphasize agency in decision making, we gain a picture of how decisions about drugs are made. Initially, they are conceptualized as a rational, individualized cost-benefit analysis. However, more recently, this assertion has been reconsidered and the ongoing significance of structure is also emphasized. Finally, transitions to adulthood are contemplated and noted as important for decisions about drugs.

The purpose of this section of the chapter has been to highlight, rather than dismiss, some of the insights from previous explanations about drug taking. As Shiner (2009) argues, there is much continuity in theorizing about drugs. Conversely, we can also trace notable differences as debates develop. Initial explanations placed emphasis upon the significance of structure for drug taking. These theories, however, were gender, ethnicity and class blind with their focus on male, white, working class groups, and, with the exception of Young, did not attempt to explain the drug taking behaviour of other social groups. Connected to this debate is the continuing relevance of the concept of subculture. The work of Becker and Young conceptualized subcultural membership as a solution to structural or social circumstances and, therefore, drug taking as a subcultural activity. Given the lower prevalence of drug taking, and attitudes towards it at the time, such assertions were correct. However, in recent times it has been argued drug taking diffuses many features of contemporary life and is accessible to all social groups. Consequently, commentators assert it can longer be defined as a deviant or subcultural activity associated with 'drop outs' or rebellious youth. This not only contests the political motivations associated with subcultures, but the ways in which the meaning of or motivations for drug taking are provided within subcultural groups. In this regard, researchers from the sociology of deviance assert drug taking is culturally and socially learnt. Whilst there is patent value in such claims, there is also a sense that decisions about drug taking largely occur in a vacuum: within or by reference to the subcultural setting alone. Moreover, a drug taking identity is privileged above and beyond other possible identities. These accounts are now somewhat dated given explanations which note we may now belong to multiple cultural groups and create plural identities which influence our behaviour in different spatial and temporal locations (see Beck, 1992; Giddens, 1991).

Thinking about the influence of significant others upon decision making, Becker observed how members within a subculture provide rationales for drug taking. The authors of *Illegal Leisure* developed the concept of social accommodation to explain how macro level attitudes towards drug taking had become more tolerant. Here, they missed an opportunity to consider how this concept impacts upon decision making at a micro level. In my PhD thesis (see Williams, 2007 and also Aldridge et al., 2011), I explored the ways in which drug taking is socially accommodated within interpersonal relationships and affects decisions about drugs. These ideas reflect what Pennay and Moore (2010) have since described as the politics of micro-normalization: how the attitudes of others influence our own behaviour. Indeed, they are also reminiscent of some of the conclusions reached by Becker about 'societal reaction' and, as we will see in Chapter Two, theories of risk which explain decisions about risk as a process of accountability to others (see Douglas, 1992).

With the emphasis placed upon agency in recent theorizing, we have also witnessed the emergence of accounts which attempt to explain the decision making process as an individual, rational cost-benefit assessment. It will be argued throughout this book that a focus on agency and rationality only provides a partial explanation and, as we have seen, commentators have latterly emphasized the continuing influence of structures. In this regard, Young's account of the significance of the relationship between work, play and escapism, and the journey to adulthood, is astute and remains relevant today. Nevertheless, there is scope to develop and extend his ideas. Although he notes how the freedom associated with youth facilitates drug taking and how work in adulthood constrains it, he neglects to consider other important life events experienced on the journey to adulthood, for example, becoming a parent or owning a home, which may also constrain decisions about drug taking. It is argued in Chapter Two, life course criminology offers further insights about the significance of transitions to adulthood which can be applied to decisions about drug taking.

Whilst the structure and agency debate provides the context or backcloth against which decision making occurs, culture is also significant for this process. As we have seen, the meaning of drug taking is acquired within (sub)cultural groups, yet others outside this setting may also be influential. Subcultural and cultural perspectives have attempted to focus in on the specific meanings individuals attach to their behaviour and emphasize pleasure and hedonism as significant. Latterly, researchers conceptualizing decisions about drugs as a cost-benefit analysis have catalogued the various benefits associated with it (see Boys et al., 1999, 2001; Measham et al., 2001; Parker et al., 1998). However, there has been a tendency to focus on risks rather than pleasures. In Chapter Two, it will be argued that cultural theories of risk acknowledge the hermeneutic dimensions of risk and pleasure.

A central aim then of this book is to reconsider, expand and extend some of the concepts and ideas which have emerged from previous theorizing about drug taking. In particular, insights about the processes which underlie decision making and the meaning of drug taking will be explored and developed. It is argued in the following chapter that creating a conceptual framework drawing on theories of risk from sociology and social anthropology, and theorizing from life course criminology, provides a comprehensive perspective which allows us to better understand why and how decisions about drug taking are made. The different standpoints on risk and conclusions reached by life course criminologists can reveal the relationship between agency, culture or changing situations, and structure for decision making in contemporary times. In addition, theories of risk that focus on how risk is evaluated permit us to zoom in on the mechanisms or processes of decision making: how risk is perceived and assessed and why decisions to take so-called 'risks', in this case drugs, are made. The overarching objective throughout this book is to grapple with the age-old debate about the significance of structure versus agency and the importance of culture. In this regard, it will be argued that agential decisions about drug taking are framed within cultural and structural circumstances or locations. Before completing this chapter, an outline of the study upon which this theoretical explanation is formulated is provided.

Collecting drug taking data from adolescence to young adulthood

The study on which this book is based emerged from the NWELS which commenced in 1991. Originated by Howard Parker and colleagues at the Department of Applied Social Science, University of Manchester, the research team in the early years consisted of Judith Aldridge, Fiona Measham and Russell Newcombe. I became part of the team in 1999. The aim of the study was to assess how young people growing up in the 1990s developed attitudes and behaviour in relation to drugs and, as they became older, to assess the impact of entry into young adulthood upon their behaviour (see Aldridge et al., 2011; Parker et al., 1998, 2002). Using an age cohort, quantitative and qualitative data was collected at various discrete time intervals. At the beginning of the study several hundred young people were surveyed when they were age 14 (N=776) in 1991. Questionnaires were administered annually until the sample were age 18 (n=529) in 1995. A further survey was undertaken when they were age 22 (n=465) in 1999. In addition, qualitative data was collected by interviewing 86 of the sample when they were 17 and a further 86 respondents when they were 22. The study has generated a wealth of data about attitudes and behaviour in relation to drug taking, and experiences with regard to education, employment, housing, family, friends, intimate relationships and parenthood.

The original sample was drawn from eight co-educational state secondary schools in two boroughs of North-West England, which included suburban and inner-city areas. These boroughs were selected to represent middle and working class areas, different ethnic groups and young people in the North-West of England. Longitudinal research is subject to many problems, the main being sample attrition (Aldridge et al., 2011; Dale and Davies, 1994; Hakim, 2000).[7] Over time, it becomes more difficult to keep in contact with a sample or to trace them and they are also more likely to drop out of a study the longer it progresses. Consequently, the remaining sample are unlikely to be representative of the original sample. At the beginning of the study, 776 respondents completed questionnaires. By Year 9, when the sample were aged 22 in 1999, 465 respondents returned a completed questionnaire. Attrition particularly affected the sample at Year 3, when they were aged 16 and a large number of respondents left school (see Table 1.1). Mainly males, working class and Asian and black respondents were lost at this stage. Some of these respondents had reported early episodes of drug taking and a smaller number were drug abstainers from mainly Muslim backgrounds.

Despite attrition being minimized during later years of the study, the sample has still become more female, middle class and white, and there are fewer drug takers. Because attrition reduced the proportion of male and working class respondents in the sample who were also drug takers, it is likely drug prevalence rates would have been higher if attrition had not affected the sample.

Table 1.1 A comparison of gender, class and ethnicity at key stages of attrition

	Year 1 (N=776)*	Year 3 (n=523)**	Year 9 (n=465)
	%	%	%
Male	53.7	43.0	42.4
Female	46.3	57.0	57.6
Middle class	52.3	68.7	68.8
Working class	47.7	31.3	31.2
Asian	7.8	4.7	3.7
Black	4.0	2.3	1.3
White	86.9	91.7	93.8
Other	1.3	1.4	1.3

* Three respondents did not indicate their gender and 46 did not indicate their ethnic background
** Three respondents did not indicate their ethnic background

When I joined the research team, the sample were at an age when their transitions to adulthood were starting to bed in. However, it was too early at age 22 to assess the full impact of adult transitions upon drug taking. Given the plethora of available data and the interest and commitment of respondents to the project, I was motivated to collect further data from the sample for my PhD research.

This was an interesting study to develop not only because we rarely have the opportunity to collect longitudinal data on drug taking over such a period of time, but also because it gathers data from drug takers and non-drug takers. Drugs research often collects data from drug takers and neglects to explore how non-drug takers maintain a drug free status. Moreover, at times, drugs research has a tendency to focus on what critics of subcultural theory might describe as spectacular forms of drug taking, for instance, the consumption of dance drugs in clubs (see, for example, Jackson, 2004; Malbon, 1999; Measham *et al.*, 2001). Whilst this endeavour is enlightening and has its place, projects like the NWELS collect data on all forms of recreational drug taking, involving a variety of drugs which are taken in different settings. In doing so, it helps us to appreciate why some people begin drug journeys and others do not. In addition, drugs research samples are typically drawn from young adults in their early to mid twenties and much younger, or specific groups, for instance, offenders (Hammersley et al., 2003) or university students (Ashton and Kamali, 1995; Makhoul et al., 1998). The NWELS has followed a group of 'ordinary' young people from age 14 until age 28. The aim then in developing the project was to explore drug taking decisions across the early part of the life course. Central research questions included: Why and how are decisions to take drugs made? What are the perceived costs and benefits? What impact do major life events, for instance leaving school, going to university, starting full-time employment, beginning or ending an intimate relationship or becoming a parent, have upon decision making?

In autumn 2004, a questionnaire was sent to the entire sample, when they were age 27, for whom contact details were held (n=765). The primary aim of administering a further questionnaire was to obtain a snapshot of the sample some five years since they had last completed a survey to assess their current attitudes and behaviour towards drugs and their position with regard to transitions to adulthood. A further aim was to inform interview sampling decisions (see Hakim, 2000). A full sweep of the NWELS involving several reminders to respondents to encourage them to complete and return the questionnaire was beyond the scope of my PhD research.[8] By Christmas 2004, after receiving the initial letter enclosing the questionnaire, 217 respondents had returned it completed. Given five years had elapsed since they were last surveyed, the number of questionnaires returned was quite remarkable.[9] Indeed, at this stage of the life course, respondents were less likely to be living at the last address provided. Table 1.2 compares the sample at age 22 and 27. The composition of the sample at age 27 is largely similar to age 22. There have been very small increases in respect of key demographics. The gender

Table 1.2 A comparison of gender, class and ethnicity at age 22 and 27

	Age 22 (n=465)	Age 27 (n=217)
	%	%
Male	42.4	40.6
Female	57.6	59.4
Middle class	68.8	71.9
Working class	31.2	28.1
Asian	3.7	2.3
Black	1.3	1.8
White	93.8	95.4
Other	1.3	0.5

balance has slightly tipped again towards females (59.4 per cent). Likewise, there are now more middle class (71.9 per cent) and white respondents (95.4 per cent).

Initially, I had intended to analyse both quantitative and qualitative data which had been collected during the course of the NWELS to explore decisions about drug taking across the life course. However, after some preliminary analysis of the available quantitative data, I realized it was limited in what it could reveal and there were insufficient variables relating to all aspects of decision making which I wanted to explore. Given there had been two stages of qualitative data collection, I decided to develop the study by creating a qualitative longitudinal dataset. Qualitative longitudinal research is uncommon in social research, yet it can provide a rich and nuanced insight into attitudes and behaviour over time at a micro level. The task was to understand, from the perspective of the interviewees, the meanings which underlie their actions or behaviour and the ways in which cultural and structural circumstances impact upon their decision making. Adopting this approach facilitated an exploration of their complex life journeys and drug journeys, and continuity and change in this respect over time. In-depth interviews with the sample at age 17 and 22 had collected data pertaining to initial and ongoing decisions about drug taking and major life events.

The questionnaire sample at age 27 provided a sampling frame to create the qualitative longitudinal dataset and select respondents for interview. The purposive sampling technique entailed several criteria. Firstly, only respondents who had been interviewed at least once before and who had consented to be interviewed again were selected for further interview. A majority of respondents (n=154) consented to be contacted for interview, however, only 32 per cent had been interviewed previously. In total, there were 49 potential interviewees. Secondly, from the number of available interviewees, the sample were selected on the basis of their drug status, that is, whether they were a drug abstainer, drug desister or current drug taker.[10] Rather than selecting only current drug takers, the objective was to collect data from drug desisters and drug abstainers to also explore their decisions about drug taking. Thirdly, the interview sample were further selected on the basis of age of onset of drug taking.[11] The aim of these last two elements of the sampling technique was to obtain an interview sample with a range of drug statuses and drug taking onset that reflected the overall sample at age 27. Applying these criteria, 20 respondents were initially selected to be contacted for interview.[12] In total, 19 respondents were interviewed.[13] Six interviewees had been interviewed twice before and eleven once before. Although I had undertaken a large amount of interviewing when the sample was age 22, there were only two interviewees selected at age 27 whom I had previously interviewed. The interview sample at age 27 is relatively small, however, the creation of a qualitative longitudinal dataset consisting of interview data from the present study and from earlier stages of the NWELS generated 42 interview transcripts to be analysed.

The final interview sample consists of seven current drug takers, seven drug desisters and five drug abstainers (see the Appendix for profiles of the

Table 1.3 Characteristics of the interview sample at age 27*

	Age 27 (n=19)
	%
Female	63.2
Male	36.8
Asian	0.0
Black	5.3
White	94.8
Employed full-time	73.7
Employed part-time	15.8
In further/higher education	15.8
Looking after children or a relative full-time	10.5
Other	5.3
Living with parents	10.5
Living in own/jointly owned mortgaged home	63.2
Living in rented accommodation	21.1
Other	5.3
Living with a partner	42.1
Married	36.8
'Seeing or going out with someone'	21.1
Single	5.3
A parent	46.6

* Note that not all categories for the variables are listed; therefore, not all add to 100 per cent

interviewees which describe their life journeys and drug journeys).[14] These drug status categories were created using the quantitative data collected at age 27. Drug abstainers are respondents who have never tried a drug in their lifetime, drug desisters are respondents who have not taken a drug in the past year when they were surveyed at age 27 and current drug takers are respondents who have taken a drug in the past year.[15] The main characteristics of the interview sample are contained in Table 1.3. The majority are female, white, employed full-time, living in a home they own and with a partner whom they are married to or cohabiting with. Almost half are also parents. Their modal age at the time of interview is 28. Previously, school catchment area has been used as a measure of social class for the study. However, over ten years has elapsed since the sample left school. Their current income provides a more accurate measure of socio-economic status. The mean net income per month for interviewees is £1,427.89 (median=£1,400, range= £100.00–£4,000.00, SD=£926.22). This indicates that a number of the interviewees are economically secure and are not of a low socio-economic status. Nevertheless, there are a few interviewees who could be described as such.

The survey data collected at age 27 provides a picture of the interview sample's drug profiles (see Tables 1.4 and 1.5). Almost three-quarters of interviewees have tried a drug. Just under half have taken a drug in the past year and two-fifths in the past month.

Commensurate with the overall sample, cannabis is the main drug interviewees have tried. This is followed by amphetamines, cocaine powder, ecstasy and LSD. A different pattern of prevalence emerges when we examine more recent rates of drug taking. Whilst cannabis is still the drug most likely to be consumed in the past year or month, it is followed by cocaine, ecstasy and amphetamines. LSD is not a drug the sample have taken recently which suggests their patterns of drug taking have changed over time. It is, therefore,

Table 1.4 Lifetime prevalence of drug taking for the interview sample at age 27

Drugs tried	Age 27 (n=19)
	%
Amphetamines	52.6
Cannabis	73.7
Cocaine powder	52.6
Crack cocaine	5.3
Ecstasy	47.4
Heroin	5.3
LSD	22.2
Magic mushrooms	5.3
Solvents	5.3
Tranquillizers	10.5
At least one drug	73.7

Table 1.5 Prevalence of recent drug taking for key drugs for the interview sample at age 27

Drugs tried	Past year (n=19)	Past month (n=19)
	%	%
Amphetamines	10.5	5.3
Cannabis	36.8	31.6
Cocaine	31.6	21.1
Ecstasy	26.3	10.5
At least one drug	47.1	41.2

important to explore the reasons for this and the decision making which underpins this process.

Although the previous interview transcripts were to be reanalysed, the interview technique employed with the sample at age 28 drew upon life and oral history research with an oral history method being employed.[16] The aim was to obtain a full picture of decisions about drug taking over time from onset to desistance. As Laub and Sampson (2003: 58) observe in relation to life histories: '[they] expose human agency and reveal how conceptions of self and others change over time'. These methods can uncover both the details of a person's life, complex patterns of continuity and change, and set their journeys in context. Indeed, MacDonald and Marsh (2002) argue that the biographical approach can contextualize drug careers. The task, then, was to set drug journeys in the wider context of life journeys. In doing so, this addresses criticisms directed at some risk perspectives for failing to explore the cultural and contextual aspects of risk (Mitchell et al., 2001; Mythen, 2004). Adopting the oral history method, the objective was to focus upon the interviewees' process of decision making in relation to drug taking across the life course, during one in-depth interview. Employing this technique permitted an exploration of how different interviewees respond to similar life events, for instance leaving home, starting full-time employment, becoming a parent and so on, and which became, for some, turning points in their drug journeys.

The interview technique associated with the oral history method is an informal or focused interview. The purpose is to allow the interviewee to discuss what they see as relevant, guided by specific themes pertinent to the research focus (Berg, 2001; Byrne, 2004). With this in mind, an aide-mémoire rather than a semi-structured interview schedule was used. The process of interviewing began in October 2005 and was completed by January 2006. Most interviews took place at the interviewees' homes. Interviews varied in length from 35 minutes to three hours. The majority were between one and two hours, however, five also exceeded two hours.

All 19 interviews at age 28 were transcribed in full. Analysis of the qualitative data drew upon elements of grounded theory (Glaser and Strauss, 1967). This approach permits not only a description of behaviour, but an explanation too. The analysis proceeded by reading the transcripts from the latest set of interviews and identifying themes within each interviewee's transcript. *Atlas-ti*, a qualitative data analysis software package, was used to manage this process. Emergent themes were grouped or linked together to form main themes (see Ritchie et al., 2003). As the analysis progressed, themes were added, adjusted and reorganized. Each of the transcripts from earlier stages of the NWELS was analysed applying the themes developed from the interviewees' transcripts at age 28 and creating new themes which had not been identified. In Chapters Three to Five, a cross-sectional analysis with a longitudinal element is presented. Chapter Six presents a longitudinal analysis of four case studies. Pseudonyms have been given to all interviewees and other people, for example, partners, children and friends, who were also mentioned during the interviews. Furthermore, when discussing their employment status in the following chapters, specific details relating to interviewees' occupations have been changed, as have details about where interviewees live who have moved away from the North West.

Before completing this section, it is worth clarifying some definitions and terms which are used in this book. The project has largely generated data on recreational drug taking involving all types of drugs from cannabis to amphetamines to ecstasy, taken in different settings, from the home, to pubs or bars and clubs. For the purpose of this book, recreational drug taking is defined as the consumption of a drug or variety of drugs in the context of leisure time; for instance, ecstasy is typically taken at weekends with friends when clubbing.[17] At times in this book, the collective term stimulant drugs is used; this refers to amphetamines, cocaine, ecstasy, ketamine and MDMA powder or crystal. It is also important to define frequency of drug taking. This can vary for different drugs. Cannabis, for instance, is more likely to be consumed daily than, for example, ecstasy which is often confined to the weekend. Daily, weekly or fortnightly cannabis consumption is defined as regular drug taking, for the purpose of this book. If it is consumed once a month or less, it is defined as occasional consumption. With regard to stimulant or hallucinogenic drugs, such as amphetamines, ecstasy, MDMA powder or crystal, cocaine, ketamine and LSD, regular consumption entails taking any one of these drugs at least every weekend to once every two months and occasional consumption is less than once every two months.

Outline of the book

The remainder of this book is organized as follows. Chapter Two creates a theoretical framework drawing upon risk theory and life course criminology, which is applied to the empirical chapters which follow. The purpose is to provide the apparatus for explaining why and how decisions about drug taking are made across the life course. The first of a quartet of empirical chapters begins with Chapter Three. This chapter illustrates the agential cost-benefit approach to decision making and highlights the risks to health and well-being identified by interviewees. In Chapter Four, a cultural perspective is employed which emphasizes the ways in which the meaning of risk is shaped by social and cultural influences, for example, the attitudes and behaviours of significant others. In addition, the subjective meaning of risk is further highlighted and the pleasures associated with drug taking are understood within their cultural context. Chapter Five places emphasis upon the continuing influence of structure upon behaviour. It explores how transitions to adulthood impact upon the decision making process, at times facilitating or constraining drug taking decisions. The ways in which new adult identities affect drug journeys are also explored. The final chapter which presents empirical data is Chapter Six. Here, a case study approach is adopted. The purpose is twofold: to demonstrate how the themes explored in the previous chapters play out at a micro level, and the benefits of a qualitative longitudinal approach. Finally, Chapter Seven reconsiders the value of past theorizing on drugs and evaluates the utility of the theoretical framework created in this book, not only in relation to developing these theories of risk, but also what it tells us about drug taking decision making in contemporary times. This chapter also contemplates the implications the findings of this study have for drug policy and suggests future directions for research.

2 Theorizing decisions about drug taking

Introduction

In Chapter One pertinent insights from past theorizing on drug taking were outlined. Whilst it was noted that the different perspectives provide a range of reasons and motivations for drug taking and offer explanations for the decision making process, it was argued risk theory can provide a framework to explore the mechanisms of decision making in finer detail. Interwoven with insights from life course criminology, this permits us to examine the relationship between agency, structure and culture or changing situations. Furthermore, a task of this book is not only to reassess the value of past theorizing, but to appreciate how the grand theories on risk operate to explain behaviour at a micro level. This body of literature will now be sketched out and evaluated to create a theoretical framework which can help us to understand why and how decisions about drug taking are made across the life course.

The conceptual framework created in this chapter draws upon a recent collection of academic theorizing which has emerged from sociology and social anthropology, namely, the study of 'risk' by the eminent scholars Ulrich Beck, Mary Douglas and Anthony Giddens.[1] It is argued by Beck (1992) and Giddens (1991) that recent social change has altered the meaning and conduct of contemporary life. It is now characterized by making diverse choices involving an individual assessment of various risks with the ultimate aim of preventing or minimizing harm. Decisions about drugs provide an interesting case study because they are normatively defined as 'risky', yet in recent decades the trend in drug taking has generally been upward. This raises the following questions: Why have so many young people in Britain in the past two decades or so decided to take drugs? How do they make these decisions? What influences the decision making process?

In explaining how risk is assessed, Beck and Giddens conceptualize it as a rational and agential process informed by 'expert' knowledge. Portraying decision making in this way fits well with the cost-benefit approach which has recently emerged and formed part of the normalization thesis (Parker et al., 1998) to account for why and how people make decisions about drugs. Accordingly, decision making involves individuals weighing up the perceived costs and benefits. In contrast, Douglas (1992) emphasizes the cultural dimensions of risk assessment: the ways in which decision making is the product of intersubjective relations or, as others might put it, culturally situated 'lay' knowledge, and the subjective meaning of risk. This mirrors the debate about drug taking as a shared and learned cultural practice developed by the sociology of deviance (see Chapter One). A further body of work in relation to risk and/or drugs, which will be outlined in this chapter and was touched on in Chapter One, has sought to foreground the continuing impact of structure upon the decision making process.

Blackman (2004: 145) accuses the authors of the normalization thesis of 'lack of clarity' regarding their position in relation to theories of risk. In recognition of this critique, the task here is to demonstrate how, through the lens of risk, we can apply various concepts developed by these theorists to explore why and how decisions about drug taking are made. In creating a theoretical framework, it is argued that our understanding of the decision making process in respect of drug taking is better developed through a synthesis of all three approaches which attempt to explain our relationship with risk and that this can illuminate the interplay between agency, structure and culture. To this end, the exceptional work of life course criminologists Laub and Sampson (2003) also forms part of the theoretical framework to further appreciate this relationship and to explore the impact of intersecting drug journeys and life course journeys.

The main body of this chapter is structured as follows. It begins by outlining key features and concepts of Beck's and Giddens' theorizing and goes on to assess and critique its relevance for decisions about drug taking. Continuing the evaluation of their work, Douglas' approach is described and applied to the drug taking decision making process. This is followed by a consideration of the significance of structure when choosing how to act. Finally, to illustrate how these approaches can be further synthesized, insights from the work of Laub and Sampson are sketched out to appreciate the ways in which agency, structure and culture interact and the life course journey provides the context in which decision making occurs.

The agential decision maker

The distinctive risk theses presented by Beck and Giddens are framed within a broader understanding of the impact of recent social change. They contend that the modernization process which has occurred in recent decades has changed the character of contemporary life. For instance, technological developments have led to changes in the constitution, and also the fragmentation, of traditional institutions, such as employment or family. In turn, the fragmentation of society has created uncertainty: jobs or intimate relationships are no longer secure or for life and risks are, therefore, ubiquitous. Because traditional institutions like these are no longer secure or certain, and other sources which were previously considered important for identity construction, such as class and gender, are believed to have less significance, it is argued we have become more responsible for creating our own identity and life trajectories in a variety of ways: '[individuals] must produce their own biographies themselves, in the absence of fixed, obligatory and traditional norms and certainties and the emergence of new ways of life that are continually subject to change' (Beck, 1994: 13). The message is clear: we are living in uncertain times and the modernization process has led to a greater proliferation of risks and the requirement to assess and manage them individually throughout the life course. Our everyday experience is, therefore, focused upon an ongoing negotiation with risk. With fewer traditional norms and institutions to turn to, risk and risk management have seeped into everyday life. The fundamental problem of western societies, according to Beck and Giddens, is the prevention or minimization of harm. As Massumi (1993: 10) notes, there is an apparent feeling of: 'imminent disaster … Even pleasure no longer felt the same. Smoking was the insidious onset of a fatal ailment. Food becomes a foretaste of heart disease.' What was once pleasurable and considered harmless is now subject to the discourse of risk and requires risk assessment. Our concern about risk in everyday life, according to Beck (1992), is also founded upon an increasing awareness of global risks in recent times.

It is within the context of recent social change that Beck and Giddens develop their theses about how we assess and manage risk. As noted, they emphasize the agential nature of contemporary society: as social actors we are all responsible for shaping our own destinies and identity, and for the decisions which accompany this. Beck refers to this process as one of 'individualization' whilst Giddens describes it as the 'project of the self'. The ultimate goal is to reach our full potential accomplished by minimizing risk and maximizing personal opportunities. Reflexive decision making is essential to achieve this. They argue the process of reflexivity involves a self critique of potential behaviour and the consequences of it. Beck's characterization of the risk society includes a growth in technologies for identifying risk: risks are scientifically detectable, measurable and controllable. As individuals, we must draw on information provided by scientific 'experts' when making decisions about risk. From perspectives like these, risk is viewed as an objective danger or hazard, scientifically measured and observed within the positivist tradition, however, our understanding of it is mediated through social and cultural processes, for example, the media. Giddens develops the reflexivity process, further noting the importance of trust. He maintains we must trust in what 'experts', whom we will never meet, tell us is good for us or not. Without trust, we cannot engage in the 'leap of faith' that is required in dealing with 'expert' knowledge systems which are often presented in unfamiliar technical language. Trust, therefore, enables us to get on with our everyday lives keeping risk at bay.

Beck and Giddens acknowledge the problem in contemporary times is that we are presented with a myriad of competing and conflicting 'expert' knowledges. This, in turn, produces what Giddens describes as 'ontological insecurity': our belief in the continuity of the self becomes fragile. We do not know what to believe or what might be good for us. We may arrive at the conclusion that so-called 'experts' do not really know what is best for us and nothing is certain. Because 'expert' knowledges are often conflicting or constantly being revised, there are more choices to be made: 'the self, like the broader institutional contexts in which it exists, has to be reflexively made. Yet this task has to be accomplished amid a puzzling diversity of options and possibilities' (Giddens, 1991: 3). These competing and conflicting knowledges, it is claimed, only further entrench feelings of uncertainty. Beck and Giddens conclude that, as a consequence of social change, increasingly more aspects of life are considered to be subject to human agency. Paradoxically, however, the contemporary self is placed in a position of making choices about countless aspects of life, such that: 'Choosing is the inescapable fate of our time ... with an apparent openness of lifestyle comes additional burdens, including the assumption of all the risks that go with decision making' (Melucci, 1996: 44). Ostensibly, the dilemma of contemporary life, when faced with various choices and decisions to make, is how to act (Reith, 2004).

What does all this mean for the explanatory framework being created here? How can this theorizing illuminate the *why* and *how* which underlie decisions about drug taking?[2] The main thrust of Beck's and Giddens' argument is that the assessment of risk is an individual process. It follows that decisions about drug taking are also made at an individual level. Further, they argue decision making involves risk assessment. This perspective typifies the cost-benefit approach which has emerged within drugs research in recent decades. Researchers have conceptualized drug takers as rational, individual calculators weighing up the perceived costs or harms against the perceived benefits or pleasures associated with drugs before deciding how to act (Coffield and Gofton, 1994; Measham et al., 2001; Parker et al., 1998).[3] Similarly, from an economics perspective, a theory of rational addiction has been advanced by Becker and Murphy (1988). It characterizes drug takers as rational beings who assess the future impact of their current drug taking behaviour and, in doing so, aim to maximize its utility over time. These approaches draw attention to the agential and reasoned nature of decisions about drug taking. Indeed, as Measham and Shiner (2009: 505) remind us: 'a cost-benefit analysis of illicit drug use prioritizes individual "choice" and agency in the context of a consumer society which increasingly emphasizes the individualisation of both risk and responsibility.' From Beck's and Giddens' standpoint, we can conclude that decisions about drug taking entail a rational, cognitive and agential process. Whilst there is value in this viewpoint, as it will become clear in the remainder of this chapter, it provides only a partial answer to how decisions about drug taking are made; cultures and structures also determine responses to risk.

When explaining how we assess risk, Beck and Giddens extol and prioritize scientific 'expert' knowledges above all other sources of knowledge. In this regard, the knowledge of medical 'experts' would be considered as important for decisions about drug taking. Frequently, they construct drug taking as a harmful activity and often highlight how it is problematic leading to a variety of objectively measured harms, for instance, addiction (Cami and Farre, 2003; Hall and Babor, 2000; Robbins and Everitt, 1999) or cognitive and psychological disorders involving memory loss or paranoia (Dafters et al., 2004; Fergusson et al., 2002; Parrott et al., 2002). Beck's and Giddens' assumption regarding the significance of 'expert' knowledges and their importance for the process of reflexivity becomes questionable when considered against the general upward trend in drug taking in recent decades. The implication of their theses is that 'expert' knowledges about the harms associated with certain behaviours or activities will lead to decisions to avoid risk, and in this case, not to take drugs. Further, as noted earlier by Measham and Shiner (2009), the responsibility for risk behaviour, and the negative consequences of it, are placed firmly upon the individual. Consequently, from this perspective, 'risk takers', or in this case drug takers, are held responsible or blamed for making flawed decisions, or are portrayed as ignorant. Given the availability of 'expert' knowledges via, for example, government initiatives such as *Talk to Frank*,[4] it becomes difficult to sustain these claims. It is important, therefore, to consider the significance of 'expert' knowledges and other sources of knowledge when making decisions about drug taking. As we will see, a cultural perspective permits an understanding of both the subjective meaning of drug taking and the significance of culturally situated sources of knowledge about drugs.

Perhaps, however, Giddens (1991) has a valid argument to make with the concept of ontological insecurity and the problem of contradictory 'expert' knowledges. 'Expert' knowledges in relation to drugs are frequently being revised. Pearson (2001), for example, analysed reports in *The Lancet* about the long-term effects of smoking cannabis and noted how they changed within a few years. Initially, it was claimed the long-term consumption of cannabis was not harmful to health. Three years later, this was qualified to suggest moderate consumption of cannabis will not greatly affect health. In more recent times, 'expert' medical reports have connected the consumption of stronger forms of cannabis (skunk) with mental health problems, for instance, schizophrenia. Conflicting and contradictory 'expert' advice about the harms associated with drug taking can, as Giddens suggests, affect the decision making process and lead to young people not knowing what advice to believe. This may explain why so many young people decide to try drugs despite 'expert' and official discourses warning against the dangers of doing so.

The agential perspective offered by Beck and Giddens provides some conceptual insights into why and how decisions about drugs are made. However, it also raises several questions, some of which have been considered here; others will be discussed in relation to the alternative approaches to risk presented in this chapter. The following section outlines and considers the significance of the cultural dimensions of risk assessment for decisions about drug taking.

The cultural influences upon decision making

During the same period that Beck and Giddens were developing their theories about the significance of risk for contemporary life and how it is assessed, Douglas was advancing an entirely different explanation. Her cultural approach to risk challenges the objective, 'expert' scientific definitions of risk given precedence by Beck and Giddens. It highlights the importance of the social, cultural and subjective or 'lay' meanings of risk and, as will become apparent, proponents of this perspective question the extent to which risk assessment or reflexivity operates for some behaviours.

Although Beck and Giddens acknowledge our understanding of risk is filtered through social and cultural processes, Douglas (1992) places greater emphasis on the cultural and political aspects of risk.[5] The importance of 'lay' responses to and experiences with risk are underscored by this approach. It is argued they should be appreciated and understood within their particular cultural context. Douglas critically asserts that risk experts 'say practically nothing about intersubjectivity, consensus making, or social influences on decisions' (Douglas, 1992: 12). Risk perceptions and risk behaviour, she argues, can be understood as a 'culturally shared attitude' (Douglas, 1992: 44) with emotional, mutual or cultural accountability. It follows, when risk assessments and decisions to behave in a particular way are made, we use culturally learned assumptions. Similarities to the conclusions reached by proponents of the sociology of deviance discussed in the previous chapter are apparent here: decisions about drugs are influenced by the norms and values of members of a cultural group. As Tulloch and Lupton (2003: 9) contend: 'people construct their risk knowledges based on close observation of everyday phenomena and the behaviour of others around them'. Our perceptions of risk are, therefore, culturally conditioned: it is the cultures within which we are situated which can shape the dangers and harms we perceive. Douglas' cultural understanding of risk provides a vital counterbalance to the standpoint of Beck and Giddens. She emphasizes the significance of subjective meanings of risk and the ways in which intersubjective relations can influence risk assessments. These will now be explored in turn and assessed with regard to the explanatory framework being created in this chapter.

As Douglas contends, to fully understand risk behaviour an appreciation of its subjective meanings is required. Adopting this perspective contests the significance assigned to 'expert' knowledges and objective definitions for risk assessment. The subjective meanings of drug taking have been a focus of the sociology of deviance and cultural studies research since the groundbreaking work of Becker (1963). More recently, we have witnessed the emergence of research which explores how risk is understood and experienced by drug takers – as Rhodes (1997: 209) describes it: 'how individuals go about "doing" risk behaviour'. Exploring risk in this way, the negative portrayal of it as something to be avoided or minimized, as presented by Beck and Giddens, may also be questioned. A critique specifically directed at this aspect of their theorizing argues risk taking can be a voluntary and pleasurable activity (Lupton and Tulloch, 2002; Mythen, 2004; Tulloch and Lupton, 2003). Proponents advancing this perspective emphasize the hermeneutic dimensions of risk; the ways in which it is experienced, interpreted or perceived differently. Indeed, Mythen (2004: 182) asserts: 'one person's risk may constitute another person's pleasure'. In this respect, Lyng (1990, 2005), for instance, has observed how taking risks can be an exciting and pleasurable activity which pushes the self to the limits or the edge. Reith (2005) has applied these ideas to drug taking and, specifically, the extreme practices of Hunter S. Thompson. Whilst these insights highlight the subjective meanings and pleasures associated with risk taking, and remind us how they can differ from objective definitions, perhaps they are less able to explain recreational drug taking. It follows, from these accounts, that the pleasure in drug taking arises from continually perceiving it as a risky and potentially death defying activity which pushes the self to the edge. In turn, this makes taking drugs a thrilling activity. However, does every person who takes ecstasy at the weekend think they may be, quite literally, dancing with death? This is unlikely to be the case. Rather, they are likely to perceive different and perhaps less serious risks. Indeed, research with recreational drug takers (see, for example, Duff, 2008; Jackson, 2004; Malbon, 1999; Measham et al., 2001) has instead revealed how, subjectively, many of the effects and practices associated with drug taking are perceived as pleasurable which presents a challenge to objective definitions of risk.

Arriving at the conclusion that subjective meanings of risk differ from objective definitions, the concept of reflexivity and the significance of risk assessment can also be contested. Purported risky behaviour may subjectively be defined as quite mundane and normal and not necessitating risk assessment. The philosopher, sociologist and social anthropologist Bourdieu (1990) observes that some practices are so habitual, a result of the habitus, they do not require risk assessment. He defines the habitus as follows:

> The habitus, a product of history, produces individual and collective practices, more history, in accordance with the schemes generated by history. It ensures the active presence of past experiences which deposited in each organism in the form of schemes of perception, thought and action tend to guarantee the correctness of practices and their constancy over time more reliable than all formal rules and explicit norms.
>
> (Bourdieu, 1990: 54)

The habitus, formed from past experiences and practices, can supplant assessment of risk when certain behaviours are familiar and everyday. Moreover, Rhodes (1997: 217), in his analysis of risk theory, sex and drug taking, argues: 'Behaviours which are habitual do not demand risk assessment or calculation for their doing; they are simply done.'

Whilst it can be argued some drug takers do not assess or perceive risks when making decisions about drugs with which they are familiar and take regularly, for others, their risk perceptions may differ from normative definitions. It has already been argued that drug takers perceive drug taking as a pleasurable activity. It is also clear many do perceive risks associated with their behaviour. However, it has been suggested they are not particularly worried about the risks medical 'experts' identify (Shewan et al., 2000; Sumnall et al., 2004). Even if they are aware of these dangers, in the absence of problems, they may perceive the chances of experiencing them as low (Gamma et al., 2005). Moreover, familiarity with drugs and a desire for specific effects may eclipse 'expert' concerns about drug taking. Insights like these address criticisms directed at Beck and Giddens for failing to explore 'risk trade-offs': the acceptable risks we take in everyday life (Mythen, 2004). It is important, therefore, to gain an understanding of the various risks or negative effects which drug takers identify as significant when making decisions about drugs. Drugs researchers have explored how drug takers perceive, manage and negotiate risk in everyday life (Hutton, 2006; Measham et al., 2001; Parker et al., 1998; Plant and Plant, 1992; Shewan et al., 2000). Thinking about risk assessment and decision making in this way questions the assumption made by Beck and Giddens that so called risk takers are irrational, ignorant and flawed decision makers.

So far, then, we have seen how subjective meanings of risk are important to consider and can differ from objective, 'expert' definitions. Douglas' theorizing also calls attention to the ways in which understandings of risk are contingent upon intersubjective relations. This again challenges the assumptions made by Beck and Giddens, however, this time it questions the extent to which 'expert' knowledges are fundamental to risk assessments. According to Douglas, intersubjective relationships influence decision making or risk perceptions in two ways: through emotional, mutual or cultural accountability; and cultural or social learning. These will be addressed in turn.

With regard to drug taking, it has been argued decisions about drugs are made by reference to friends (Hunt et al., 2007; Pilkington, 2007), family (Abbott-Chapman and Denholm, 2001; Knowlton et al., 1998) or intimate relationships (Rhodes and Quirk, 1998). Social relationships, or the cultures in which individuals are embedded, can influence and hold them responsible or accountable for the decisions about drug taking they make. For example, abstainers may be challenged by family members or non-drug taking friends if they contemplate taking drugs. Alternatively, when drug taking is 'normalized' in a social group, decisions to take drugs can make sense (Crawshaw, 2004). Certain behaviours, therefore, possess a cultural logic within a social group. Considering further how decisions to take drugs are made, Douglas' work points to how understandings of risk emanate within cultural settings. Echoing the analysis of drug subcultures provided by Becker (1963) and Young (1971), the meaning of risk is learned from others within a particular cultural group.

There is, however, a danger of creating a dichotomy between the significance of 'expert' and 'lay' knowledges when making decisions about risk. It is apparent, greater value is placed upon 'expert' knowledges by Beck and

Giddens whilst Douglas venerates 'lay' knowledges. Perhaps there is a balance to be drawn between the importance of both knowledges when making choices about how to act. We may gather information about risk from 'experts' and a variety of other culturally situated sources (Reilly, 1999). In this regard, Reith (2004: 396) provides an insightful understanding of the function of risk assessment: 'Although it cannot make the future predictable or the world certain, it can create the means *for acting as though it were*' [emphasis in original]. Our assessments and perceptions of risk then can justify and rationalize our behaviour. Returning to consider the significance of different types of knowledges, 'expert' knowledges may be used to rationalize decisions not to take drugs whilst 'lay' knowledges may, dependent upon a cultural group's behaviour and attitudes, justify drug taking (see Chapters Three and Four).

The concept of risk perceptions and different sources of knowledge justifying and rationalizing behaviour is particularly useful in explaining not only current behaviour, but why risk perceptions may change over time. Transformations in risk perceptions can operate to justify or rationalize changes in behaviour. In a study of female ecstasy users, Hinchliff (2001) found they only became concerned about the risks of long-term harms related to their drug taking once they had begun to reduce their consumption. She concluded: 'It appears that the hazards involved in ecstasy use were considered with hindsight because perception of risk was pushed aside in order to subserve this life project' (Hinchliff, 2001: 464). An appreciation of changing risk perceptions emphasizes again the importance of subjective meanings and cultural influences when making decisions about drugs. In Hinchliff's research, a reduction in drug taking preceded changes in risk perceptions. It is likely with this decline in drug taking the participants were less involved with a drug taking culture and perhaps this shaped their changing attitudes towards drugs and subsequent risk assessments. No longer fully immersed in the culture their perceptions of risk changed. Similarly, Becker (1963) also observed how desistance was dependent upon the extent to which a person was embedded within a drug taking subculture.

The cultural perspective advanced by Douglas provides further insights into why and how decisions about drug taking are made. In contrast to Beck's and Giddens' theorizing, the emphasis is placed upon the importance of subjective meanings and intersubjective relations when deciding how to act. In the following section, the significance of structure for risk assessment and decisions about drug taking is outlined.

The structural influences upon decision making

The over-agential risk assessor portrayed in the accounts of contemporary life by Beck and Giddens has been further challenged by those emphasizing the continuing importance of structure and power relations for shaping behaviour and ultimately individualization or the project of the self. Variables which are argued to be essential to contemporary theorizing, including gender, socio-economic class and ethnicity, are said to condition our responses to risk. It has been noted in the field of drugs research that the shift to counter earlier theories explaining drug taking by way of individual pathology and social dysfunction, and to emphasize agency and rationality, neglected to consider the structural influences upon drug taking (Measham and Shiner, 2009). Recently, however, there has been a move towards emphasizing and reassessing the significance of structure (see Aldridge et al., 2011; MacDonald and Marsh, 2002; Shildrick, 2002). This anthology of work, which focuses upon the continuing significance of structures, will now be summarized.

It was in response to Beck's assertion that risk has now superseded class conflict that much of this theorizing in sociology emerged.[6] The main thrust of his argument is that structural factors have weakened in contemporary times and are far less significant for the process of individualization. Whilst risks may have a differential impact upon social groups, he contends the threat from global risks are ubiquitous. Lash (1994) is particularly critical of Beck's work and maintains many do not have the resources, for instance, access to income or information, available to them to engage in reflexivity and individualization. Similar conclusions about the continuing significance of structure for limiting the process of individualization or the course of life trajectories have been reached in the field of youth transitions research. This body of work explores how structures affect the process of becoming an adult. The three main transitions young people are required to negotiate, and make decisions about, are the transition from school to work, from parental home to the housing market, and from family of origin to family of destination (Coles, 1995; Furlong and Cartmel, 1997, 2007; MacDonald et al., 2001). It is argued that the process of becoming an adult is now fraught with difficulty because social change, over the past half a century, has undermined this journey. Adult transitions are no longer considered to be linear or straightforward; they are often delayed or protracted (Coles, 1995; Furlong and Cartmel, 1997, 2007; MacDonald et al., 2001; Roberts, 1995). Moreover, they are further complicated by the influence of structural factors. Roberts et al. (1994) conceptualize the journey to adulthood as one involving 'structured individualization': the process of individualization is constrained by gender, location, family background and educational attainment. Similar structural forces at play are identified by Furlong and Cartmel (1997, 2007) who also note how employment and socio-economic class may shape the pathway to adulthood. Structural factors are, therefore, viewed as having considerable purchase in contemporary society and continuing to restrict the process of individualization, the decision making which goes with it and ultimately the behaviour arising from it.

Whilst many of these critiques have arisen in direct response to Beck's and Giddens' theorizing, there has been a similar debate surfacing amongst drugs researchers focusing attention on fundamental postmodern variables and the ways in which they may determine drug journeys or decisions about drugs. In short, many have explored the meaning of socio-economic class, gender and ethnicity for drug taking. In undertaking this task, the perspectives of drug takers have been privileged. Initially, the normalization thesis, influenced by the theorizing of Beck and Giddens, in its most comprehensive form (Parker et al., 1998) concluded, mostly from statistical data analysis, that class, gender and ethnicity were not significant indicators of involvement in drug taking. Recently, some of the original contributors to the thesis have acknowledged that agency and rational choice making was over-emphasized (Aldridge et al., 2011). The consequence of their original conclusion, however, was a growing critique aimed at developing the thesis through an assessment of the ways in which structures continue to shape drug taking. Shildrick (2002) and Mac-Donald and Marsh (2002), for example, re-conceptualized normalization to allow for how social class impacts upon drug journeys and decision making. They identified this process as 'differentiated normalization'. In Shildrick's study, social disadvantage was linked to frequent use, use of a wider range of drugs, and, in some cases, problematic drug taking episodes. The potential relationship between social exclusion and problematic drug use was acknowledged in MacDonald and Marsh's research. These studies concluded structural factors remain important for explaining drug taking.

Others, although not in response to the conclusions reached in the original normalization thesis, have sought to foreground the influence of gender or ethnicity upon motivations for drug taking. Recently, the similarities between male and female drug taking have been emphasized: women have been characterized as active and equal consumers of drugs compared with men (Henderson, 1999; Hinchliff, 2001; Hutton, 2006). The parity in male and female drug taking, at least in terms of being active consumers, if not in respect of prevalence rates, has led to an exploration of the ways in which drug taking is accommodated in young women's lives (see Measham et al., 2011). The significance of gender for Measham (2002) is in how drug taking, for women, and the scene associated with it, can accomplish femininity. Much of this work has resulted in calls for a gender-sensitive approach to further our understanding of female drug taking (Ettore, 2004; Measham et al., 2011). In regard to ethnicity, prevalence data in Britain points to lower rates of drug taking amongst ethnic minority groups. Explanations provided for this often revolve around cultural and religious constraints (see White, 2001). However, when involvement in drug taking is compared across different ethnic minority groups, cultural deficiency, or essentially lack of values constraining drug taking in some groups (Dorn and Murji, 1992), has been offered as an explanation for differential rates of drug taking. In this regard, it has been argued discussions of ethnicity and drug taking are inextricably linked to debates about racism: typified as a war on drugs against specific ethnic minority groups (see Miller, 1996; Murji, 1999). Hence, we find certain drugs, and images of drug takers, have become coupled with specific ethnic groups, for example, crack cocaine with Black African-Caribbeans and cannabis with Rastafarians. Murji (1999: 50) asserts, when considering the relationship between 'race' and drugs: 'it is difficult to impute any essential traits to racial groups'. Indeed, the disentangling or identification of any one variable, social class, gender or ethnicity as significant for decisions about drugs is a demanding task. Hence, some have argued we cannot ascribe the effect of any single social or structural variable to drug taking (see Ettore, 2004; Murji, 1999).

It is worth pausing to consider the relevance of this perspective, and the other two outlined in this chapter so far, for the framework being created. The main conclusion we can draw from this body of work is that individual risk assessments or decisions about drug taking continue to be constrained by structural factors. However, they must be understood as the result of the interplay of different social and structural variables, rather than any one variable, which will have greater significance at certain times or in particular settings. Assessing all three perspectives, it is argued to adopt any one approach for the theoretical framework would be too deterministic. Whilst Beck and Giddens can be accused of being over-agential, the other perspectives outlined are equally deterministic and too cultural or structural. To fully understand why and how decisions about drug taking are made a synthesis of insights from all three perspectives is necessary. As Measham and Shiner (2009: 505) suggest: 'a perspective which recognises the role of agency and pleasure, but locates them within a broader structural framework' is required. To this, the cultural dimensions of drug taking must be added both in terms of the hermeneutic, subjective meanings and how the decision making process is influenced by cultural locations or situations. Relatively new theorizing from life course criminology emphasizes the reciprocal relationship between agency and structure which may lead to changes in cultural situations. This perspective and its relevance to the theoretical framework will now be considered.

The influence of structure, agency and culture or changing situations upon decision making

It is argued, in this chapter, that to fully appreciate the decision making process in relation to drug taking, we must assess the ways in which agency, structure and culture interact. The reciprocal relationship between structure and agency has been outlined by Giddens (1984) in his theory of structuration. Social structures are said to make social action possible but are also reproduced through social action. In addition, it is argued here, culture or situations can also be seen to intersect with this relationship. As noted earlier, 'lay' or subjective meanings of risk acquired within a specific cultural group are important for the decision making process and behaviour which arises from it. Choosing how to act can, therefore, be understood as an outcome of agency facilitated or constrained within the context of structural and cultural locations. The interplay of structure and agency upon behaviour and the cultural situations produced is commendably articulated within life course criminology and the work of John Laub and Robert Sampson. Theorizing of this kind presents a challenge to the agential and decontextualized accounts of Beck and Giddens. As Lupton (1999) argues, 'lay' risk assessments and risk behaviours are often appropriate in the context of a person's life. It is against a backcloth of life course journeys or current locations within the life course that we should appreciate and attempt to understand the decision making process. Insights from life course criminology can, therefore, set drug journeys and the decision making that is inextricably linked to them in context.

Life course criminology, as the term implies, is concerned with studying the development of deviant or criminal behaviour over time from onset, persistence to desistance and the impact of life events upon such behaviour. It draws largely on, and develops, control theories (see Gottfredson and Hirschi, 1990; Hirschi, 1969; Matza, 1964; Nye, 1958; Reckless, 1967; Sykes and Matza, 1957). Matza (1964) observes how most delinquent behaviour is episodic, short lived and does not continue into adulthood. With the onset of adulthood, he suggests delinquency largely desists. The importance of adult roles which may strengthen the social bond and invoke commitment to, involvement with, belief in and ultimately attachment to conventional institutions is believed to curtail deviant or criminal behaviour. Because of the sporadic nature of delinquency, many control theorists view deviant behaviour as adolescence-limited. Life course criminologists contend we must explore and understand behaviour beyond adolescence to gain a full understanding of crime and deviance (Caspi and Moffitt, 1995; Farrington, 2003; Laub and Sampson, 2003; Moffitt, 1993; Sampson and Laub, 1993; Thornberry, 1987). Whilst behaviour in adolescence is seen as an important influence on behaviour in adulthood, what occurs in adulthood is also considered significant for stability and change in behaviour. It is from this standpoint the groundbreaking work of Laub and Sampson begins.

Sampson and Laub (1993) and Laub and Sampson (2003) explore onset, continuity, change and desistance in male criminal behaviour using quantitative and qualitative data collected from a sample between the ages of 7 and 70.[7] They examine criminal behaviour in the context of three key social roles – marriage, employment and military service – and suggest individuals can change through interaction with key institutions, such as these, as they age. Desistance from crime is, therefore, viewed as a result of age graded informal social control. In their later work, they address a major shortcoming of control theory by emphasizing the significance of human agency. Criminal behaviour is seen to be purposeful, meaningful and exciting. Deterministic criminological explanations which focus solely upon the influence of structure on crime are challenged by exploring the relationship between agency, action, situations and structures over time. Agential processes (decisions to commit crime) are linked to situations (opportunities and social networks) and larger structural factors (marriage or full-time employment). It is suggested there is a reciprocal relationship between these elements: the latter two are partly determined by choice but simultaneously restrict choices: 'choices are always embedded in social structures' (Laub and Sampson, 2003: 282). Criminal behaviour is, therefore, conceptualized as a form of 'situated choice'. Because bonds with adults and institutions may be weakened in adolescence leading to delinquency or crime, with age, social bonds and social control can become more influential. In adulthood, new bonds may be formed through marriage or employment. Accordingly, desistance involves a combination of: 'structures, situations, and persons offer[ing] nurturing and informal social control' (Laub and Sampson, 2003: 279).

In further explaining desistance from crime, Laub and Sampson (2003) identify five stages. Firstly, structural turning points, such as marriage or employment, which occur by chance rather than exerting self control. Secondly, these structural events create social bonds and social capital which increase informal controls over offenders. Thirdly, an offender's daily routine changes and they begin to focus upon the responsibilities they have and associate less with their deviant peers. Fourthly, through these events an offender's life is changed and criminal activity is less likely as they are now invested in a new way of life. Finally, an offender can exert agency, or will, and resist opportunities to commit crime which acts as their continued motivation for desistance. Full-time employment, for example, can establish new social ties which may involve monitoring of behaviour, changes in routine activities and create a new sense of identity. Marriage may lead to: social support from, and strengthening of bonds to, another person; direct monitoring of behaviour; changes in lifestyles and routines through obligations to new family and friends; a change in living arrangements and a move to a different neighbourhood; and parenthood, which can also change perspectives on life and routines. The quality of attachment is, however, significant. Weak marital or employment attachments, for example modest commitment to a spouse or poor job security, increase the likelihood of criminal behaviour.

In contrast to emerging explanations noting the significance of cognitive transformations or identity shifts for desistance from crime (see Giordano et al., 2002; Maruna, 2001), Laub and Sampson (2003: 278) contend structural turning points act as 'catalysts for long-term behavioural change'. Desistance occurs by default rather than a commitment to turn away from crime or a cognitive or identity transformation. Taking advantage of structural or situational events is crucial: 'The majority of the men we interviewed desisted from crime largely because they were able to capitalize on key structural and situational circumstances' (Laub and Sampson, 2003: 279). Without realizing, many of the men invested themselves in a job or marriage. Thus, Laub and Sampson argue it is not the adoption of an adult role alone that will lead to desistance, but a person's commitment to that role. Hence, Giordano et al. (2002) conceptualize structural turning points as 'hooks for change': they make change and desistance possible, but subsequently a person must also act to change. The nature of relationships which transpire from structural turning points are, therefore, fundamental for explaining desistance from crime. In respect of marriage, Rutter (1996) notes desistance from crime is dependent upon whom we marry. However, Sampson and Laub (1993) argue strong marital attachments hamper crime and deviance irrespective of a partner's current criminal or deviant behaviour.

What, then, can this pioneering approach, combined with what has already been discussed in relation to risk assessments and agency, cultural and structural influences, tell us about drug journeys and the decisions and behaviour emanating from them? According to Laub and Sampson, the reciprocal relationship between agency, situations and structural factors is essential for explaining criminal behaviour. If we apply these ideas to drug taking, agential decisions about drug taking involving a cost-benefit analysis of the perceived pleasures and harms can be understood in the context of structural locations, for example employment, and the situations they produce. Drawing on control theories, Laub and Sampson emphasize the significance of key institutions associated with structural positions, and the people connected to them, which may exert informal social control. Thus, decisions about drugs, whether or not to take them, can also be interpreted as a product of informal social control (or lack of) stemming from different structural locations. Here, the journey to adulthood, or the adoption of adult roles, becomes highly significant. As Laub and Sampson note, it is the people attached to the key institutions associated with adulthood which may influence behaviour. Attachment and commitment to these life course positions, and the people associated with them, is also undoubtedly critical for the decision making associated with drug taking.

Earlier in this chapter, the value of youth transitions research was acknowledged in explaining how the journey to adulthood or the adoption of adult roles are constrained by structural factors. It is pertinent to return to this body of work now because it has identified how adult transitions in contemporary society have become fragmented and protracted and are no longer linear or certain. The restructuring of the labour market and the growth in post-compulsory education have been identified as responsible for these changes. Consequently, because of the delay in transitions to adulthood, some young people are postponing some key transitions, for example, cohabitation or marriage and parenthood, for even longer after they make other transitions, for instance, to employment, so they can enjoy some level of freedom before they enter 'full' adulthood (Arnett, 2004; Furlong and Cartmel, 2007). Laub and Sampson have pointed to the significance of adult roles for desistance from crime. In relation to motivations for drug taking or factors which facilitate it, Young (1971) acknowledges the expression of 'subterranean values' (getting high) is legitimized in youth and is not required to be balanced by formal values, such as a work ethic. According to Young, hedonism can prevail for teenagers and young adults, however, with age, as structural factors such as work begin to take effect, 'subterranean play' is constrained. If adult roles are being adopted by young people later than they were for previous generations, this will undoubtedly impact on criminal behaviour, or any other behaviour, like drug taking, influenced by such roles. It can, therefore, be argued that relatively recent social and structural changes which undermine or protract the journey to adulthood have led to greater opportunities for leisure and consequently drug taking. Indeed, Williams and Parker (2001) observe the period in which young people can take drugs has been extended, and rates of recent drug taking may also extend further into adulthood than they have in the past because the roles and responsibilities associated with adulthood are being delayed. Freedom from adult roles may not be the only explanation for drug taking in young adulthood. Young people's journey to adulthood is fraught with uncertainty, as is the whole life course journey, and in this context drug taking can function as a form of relaxation or escapism to defend against social positions (see Hebdige, 1976; Taylor, 1999; Young, 1971).

The relevance of life course criminology, and the roles adopted in adulthood, to explain prevalence and patterns in drug taking has been considered most comprehensively by Shiner (2009). He analysed data collected at one point in time by the British Crime Survey in 1998 and Youth Lifestyle Survey in 1998/9 from a sample of young people aged between 18 and 30. The impact of various life course indicators and age upon drug taking during young adulthood are explored. Accordingly, the transition to full-time work did not appear to significantly impact upon rates of recent drug taking: students and those in full-time employment are equally likely to be recent drug takers. However, recent drug taking is more prevalent amongst the unemployed and others excluded from the labour market. Shiner explains these findings in terms of the constraining effect of employment: the unemployed and others excluded from the labour market may have fewer commitments and, therefore, more freedom to take drugs when they choose. In contrast, the influence of the social bond or attachment is apparent when analysing drug taking and domestic circumstances. Recent drug taking is associated with being single or cohabiting, not being a parent and living in rented accommodation. Respondents who are married are less likely to be recent drug takers and more likely to be abstainers or ex-users. Rates of desistance increased for cohabitees if they were parents or home owners. With the end of a marriage, there appeared to be a return to drug taking and a single lifestyle. Domestic situations further influenced drug taking amongst single respondents: higher rates of recent drug taking were found amongst those living with parents or independently in rented accommodation and lower rates were present for those who had children or were buying a home. Shiner (2009: 156) emphasizes the significance of the domestic transition:

> Once stable relationships are formed and reinforced by external commitments, such as marriage and parenthood, then these spaces are squeezed and the domestic sphere becomes characterized less by the subterranean values of independence, spontaneity and ego-expressivity and more by connectedness and responsibility.

Domestic arrangements, then, appear to be of consequence when making decisions about drugs: 'settling down' can lead to desistance. Shiner also explores the gendered nature of transitions to explain the gender gap in recent drug taking which begins to emerge in young adulthood. Drawing on a similar explanation for gender differences in desistance from crime (see Graham and Bowling, 1995), he notes females are more likely to leave the family home and start their own families sooner than males. Their opportunities for drug taking are, therefore, limited earlier than males. In contrast, males are more likely to make these transitions at a later age.

Shiner concludes from his analysis of the data that drug taking can be understood as a form of 'situated choice': choice is constrained or influenced by structural determinants in the form of adult transitions (see also Measham and Shiner, 2009). Other drugs research also supports the idea that drug taking declines with greater responsibilities in life. For instance, lower rates of drug taking are associated with marriage (Bachman et al., 1997), full-time employment or parenthood (Vervaeke and Korf, 2006). Using prevalence data, Shiner points to how drug taking declines or begins to desist around the mid-twenties precisely at the time when adult transitions are starting to bed in. He concludes, similar to Young (1971), that younger adults have the freedom to pursue hedonistic lifestyles without being restricted by adult roles.

The findings which emerge from Shiner's work are compelling and important for theorizing the meaning of drug taking and the decision making process which underpins it. They demonstrate the influence of key transitions to adulthood, or as Laub and Sampson put it, structural turning points, and the ways in which they limit opportunities for engagement in 'subterranean play' or drug taking. However, there are some shortcomings, which are generally methodological or analytical, that are worth outlining here. Shiner's analysis largely presents either a comparison of type and frequency of drug taking with age or different adult transitions. Conclusions reached from this are that drug taking is principally a young person's leisure pursuit and the domestic transition is most significant for desistance. There are, however, problems with this kind of analysis. By identifying the average age of onset and the average age where drug taking begins to decline or desist, we lose sight of what happens in between – in other words, the ways in which drug journeys can slow down, even halt temporarily, or become more intense and frequent at different points in time. Similarly, statistical comparisons of adult transitions and drug taking rates can only show when specific transitions have been accomplished and their relationship to current drug taking status. Yet, as we know, becoming independent and an 'adult' is by no means straightforward and may involve, for instance, a return to dependence on family.[8] The twisting and (re)turning nature of this journey, and its effect on drug taking, is largely absent from an analysis like this. Longitudinal data collected over a period of time which extends beyond the orthodox notion of when drug taking ceases may uncover individuals who have returned to drug taking, yet who appeared to have previously made transitions to adulthood which curtailed their drug journeys. Moreover, as Shiner acknowledges, quantitative data cannot tell us what it is about the nature of adult transitions which facilitates or constrains drug taking or the ways in which they impact on drug journeys; for example, does drug taking suddenly stop or slowly decline?

On the whole, Shiner presents an analysis which independently assesses the effect of age *or* adult transitions upon rates of drug taking yet often reaches conclusions about the simultaneous effect of both. Unfortunately, the most interesting analysis of both the domestic transition *and* the cumulative effect of age is only briefly explored. A further problem relates to the use of cross-sectional data. Shiner compares the behaviour of younger members of the samples with older respondents to draw conclusions about changes in behaviour at different stages of the life course, however, data like these cannot assess within-individual changes. In this regard, the heterogeneity created by quantitative analysis is problematic. In addition, if the journey to adulthood is significant for drug journeys, it makes sense to explore the ways in which these complex journeys intertwine and how they do so at the level of the individual.

A final problem relates to the data used to develop analytical concepts. As noted at the beginning of this section, decisions about drug taking involve the interaction of agency, structure and culture. An understanding of the relationship between structural turning points, situational circumstances, agency and behaviour, which is present in the work of Laub and Sampson, is lacking in Shiner's analysis. A partial explanation is offered focusing largely upon indicators of behaviour and structure to the detriment of illustrating agential processes. Indeed, agency, perhaps correctly, is viewed as implicit in behaviour. Drug taking behaviour is described as meaningful and goal-oriented and evidence for this is connected to participation in other leisure related behaviour, for example alcohol consumption and tobacco smoking, and the night-time economy, which are presented as forming part of a hedonistic lifestyle. Further evidence for the meaningful nature of drug taking is ascribed to the higher rates of recent drug taking amongst younger adults aged 22 and under. However, from this age onwards, it is argued that the freedom to take drugs becomes constrained by adult roles and responsibilities, and the implication is that agency is also restricted. Unfortunately, because of the nature of the data, no evidence is provided specifically in relation to agential processes or, to put it another way, the decision making which underpins these changes in behaviour. Despite emphasizing the meaningful nature of drug taking, we are left with a rather superficial gloss offering statistical associations between types and frequency of drug taking and other behaviours seen to embody subterranean values which become less prevalent with age and the accomplishment of adult transitions. What is missing is an understanding of the subjective meaning of drug taking in the context of life journeys. Despite these criticisms, Shiner's work still provides some valuable insights into the significance of adult transitions for drug journeys. The qualitative longitudinal methodological approach adopted in this study, however, begins to address some of the shortcomings outlined above and the conclusions which can be reached with a solely quantitative approach.

It should, by now, be apparent that the theoretical framework developed in this chapter emphasizes the role of agency, structure and culture or changing situations when deciding how to act. The overarching argument is agential decisions about drug taking should be explored and understood in their cultural and structural circumstances. Agency is, therefore, culturally and structurally situated. Life course criminology calls attention to the value of approaches which explore the relationship between structure, agency and culture. In this respect, the agential and reflexive process of decision making is appreciated in the context of structural locations and the situations they produce. Moreover, the ways in which structural positions change during the life course, and act as turning points leading to changes in cultural circumstances, are emphasized. The theoretical framework, therefore, sets drug journeys and the decision making which accompanies them within the context of life journeys.

Summary

The purpose of this chapter has been to create a theoretical framework to further our understanding of risk and decisions about drug taking. Risk theory is developed in two ways: by arguing that we can better understand risk assessment through a synthesis of approaches which appreciate the role of agency, structure and culture; and by setting risk assessment or decision making in the context of life course journeys. The remainder of this book provides a case study for this framework. Drug taking, normatively defined as a risky activity, offers an insight into the way risk is perceived, assessed and managed in everyday life. The framework created here provides the conceptual tools to develop our understanding of why decisions to take drugs are made and how this process operates. Whilst this suggests a focus upon drug takers' decision making, the following chapters also consider why and how decisions not to take drugs are made by drug abstainers.

The conceptual framework provided in this chapter also structures the following three chapters. Chapter Three fits well with the agential perspective offered by Beck and Giddens. It outlines the costs and benefits to health and well-being – frequently these are the risks emphasized by 'experts' – which form part of the assessment of drug taking. However, it also begins to develop a cultural perspective which challenges objective definitions of risk and highlights the subjective meaning of risk and pleasure. Chapter Four further explores the cultural and subjective dimensions of risk assessment and provides an illustration of Douglas' theorizing. The final chapter in this trilogy, Chapter Five, considers the significance of structure for decision making and examines the ways in which life course events and the situations they produce further determine decisions about drug taking. Chapter Six, the final empirical chapter, contains four case studies which exemplify the explanatory framework and the themes outlined in the previous three chapters. The first of these empirical chapters now follows.

3 A balancing act? Weighing up the costs and benefits to health and well-being

... I never really thought, 'Ooh, I don't want to do this again'. You know, when you drink too much and think, 'Oh, I'm never drinking again', the next day or whatever, and I know you always do. But, it was just a kind of a given that if you had a good night [taking drugs] you were going to feel like crap the next day. But, you knew that. You didn't really mind.

(Vicky, interview at age 28)

Introduction

The aim of this chapter is to begin to develop empirically the theoretical framework outlined in Chapter Two. In doing so, both the *why* and *how* decisions about drug taking will be explored. Beck and Giddens present the risk assessment process as an individual, rational and cognitive appraisal of 'expert' scientific knowledge: one which involves assessing 'expert' advice about risk and acting upon it to prevent or minimize harm. The cost-benefit approach which has been offered as an explanation for how decisions about drugs are made (see Coffield and Gofton, 1994; Measham et al., 2001; Parker et al., 1998) similarly emphasizes an agential and rational evaluation. In relation to decisions about drug taking, the type of 'expert' knowledge which corresponds with Beck's and Giddens' theorizing, and which predominantly informs policy discourse, is that of medical 'experts' who identify a range of physical, cognitive and psychological harms, in sum, the ways in which drug taking damages health and well-being. An objective of this chapter is to begin to assess the significance of the individualised rational, cost-benefit approach for decisions about drug taking. In this regard, the different risks to health and well-being perceived by all interviewees when making decisions about drug taking will be outlined[1] and the significance of objective 'expert' knowledge evaluated. Additionally, the reflexive decision making process will be summarized for all interviewees in respect of perceiving risks, and for drug takers in regard to how they accept, manage and avoid certain risks. A consideration of changing risk perceptions during the life course and how they act to validate current behaviour (see Reith, 2004) will further illustrate the process of reflexivity.

An additional aim of this chapter is to counter the negative portrayal of risk as something to be avoided or minimized, present in the work of Beck and Giddens. Here, we begin to observe the subjective and hermeneutic meanings of risk through a consideration of the pleasurable effects drug takers perceive in respect of different drugs and their significance for decision making. In recent years, a criticism directed at the cost-benefit approach adopted in the drugs field has been its focus upon risks at the expense of defining and outlining benefits (Aldridge et al., 2011; Duff, 2008; Measham, 2002; Williams, 2007). Attention is paid to both elements of the equation in this chapter.

The chapter is divided into four core sections. It begins by exploring the main physiological and psychological effects perceived by most drug takers and their significance for the decision making process. Following this, principal risks and negative effects to health and well-being which were emphasized in the interviews with drug abstainers are outlined. Some of these risk perceptions were also discussed by drug takers and their views are provided as an alternative perspective. The following section details the risks and harms to health and well-being described by drug takers. These were a different set of risks and dangers which drug abstainers did not acknowledge. A detailed discussion of the ways in which perceived risks are evaluated and acted upon is provided in the final section of this chapter.

Perceived physiological and psychological effects of different drugs and their significance for decision making

As was noted in Chapter Two, an appreciation of the perceived effects drug takers associate with specific drugs is vital to understand why decisions about drug taking are made. The effects outlined here comprise two categories: physiological and psychological. Physiological effects were experienced as sensations or causing some kind of change, albeit temporary, in the body. The most common described by interviewees were: the 'buzz', increased energy and weight loss. In addition, various effects perceived after taking drugs which impacted upon psychological well-being were discussed. Predominantly, the majority of drug takers identified the following effects: increased confidence and lowered inhibitions, and feeling relaxed.

Physiological effects: the buzz, increased energy and weight loss

An effect associated with many stimulant drugs is a physical sensation experienced throughout the body and sometimes described as a 'buzz' (Aldridge et al., 2011; Duff, 2008; Jackson, 2004; Malbon, 1999). A similar feeling was expressed by interviewees who had taken these drugs. They talked of a pleasurable physical 'buzz', 'rush' or 'tingly' feeling through the body. These sensations were particularly experienced during the initial stage of a drug taking episode; what most drug takers describe as the 'coming up' phase. Enthusiasm for these effects was apparent in interviewees' accounts:

'it's that feeling that you get, you can't stop that feeling. It's amazing, it's unbelievable!' (Stacey, interview at age 28). Kate, who at the time of interview was taking amphetamines once or twice a year, was also passionate about these effects: 'when you swallow it, and then give it 20 minutes say, and you get like, you just suddenly get this, it was that initial, "Oh my God, yeah, this is great, fantastic!"' (interview at age 28). As we will see later in this chapter, the perceived 'buzz' formed part of an interviewee's assessment of which drugs to continue to take or include in their drug taking repertoires.

In line with previous research (Aldridge et al., 2011; Boys et al., 1999, 2001; Duff, 2008; Hutton, 2006; Measham et al., 2001; Williams and Parker, 2001), an effect perceived by interviewees associated with taking stimulant drugs was increased energy, stamina or endurance. Many discussed enjoying these effects. Lindsay described how taking amphetamines when she was younger provided her with energy to dance: 'I had all this energy and I felt bloody great. And I could dance, I danced all weekend!' (interview at age 22).

In contrast, cocaine was described as a drug which provided a short rather than sustained burst of energy:

Yeah, I had some of that [cocaine] about two weeks ago.
Yeah.
Just one sniff. It was that night when I said I went out and I'd been smoking [cannabis] all afternoon. I went out …
Yeah.
And I thought, 'Fuck that!', I had a sniff of that and it perked me up a bit.
(Dean, interview at age 28)

Many interviewees, like Dean, identified cocaine as a drug which functioned as a short-lived 'pick-me-up' compared to other stimulant drugs.

A further effect discussed in relation to stimulant drugs, particularly amphetamines, which was a sole feature of the female drug takers' narratives, was weight loss. Many of these interviewees described weight loss in a positive light: 'I liked the weight loss, that was good. (Laughter) Come out like, all cheeks gone in' (Lindsay, interview at age 22). Stimulant drugs are believed to suppress appetites and, therefore, lead to weight loss (Boys et al., 2001; Hutton, 2006) – hence, the use of amphetamines as a key ingredient in some slimming aids. However, weight loss may also be facilitated by continual dancing for several hours when clubbing and consuming stimulant drugs. Interestingly, only one interviewee described this perceived effect as a purposeful function of her drug taking or key influence upon her decision making: 'I think the only reason why I took a bit of whizz [amphetamines] was because I was putting on weight, and I thought, "I'll take some of this and I'll lose some weight"' (Stacey, interview at age 17). Instead, most interviewees described weight loss as an added bonus or fringe benefit.

All the effects outlined in relation to drug taking so far relate to stimulant drugs and the ways in which they were described as producing a physiological effect upon the body. Interviewees also identified effects that were beneficial in terms of their psychological well-being. The following section considers two main effects discussed: increased confidence and lowered inhibitions, and feeling relaxed.

Psychological effects: increased confidence and lowered inhibitions, and feeling relaxed

Increased confidence and the lowering of inhibitions have been identified as functions of drug taking (Aldridge et al., 2011; Boys et al., 1999, 2001; Measham et al., 2001; Williams and Parker, 2001). Interviewees discussed how when they took stimulant drugs they felt more confident with friends or strangers. Vicky recalled how she felt after she took amphetamines: 'it kind of gives you a bit of confidence really as well, well for me it did anyway' (interview at age 28). Taking cocaine also made Lindsay feel more confident: 'Just the confidence, I think it does give you a boost. I mean I thought I was bloody Naomi Campbell!' (interview at age 22). In addition, inhibitions were perceived to have been lowered after taking drugs. Many noted, as we shall see in Chapter Four, how these perceived effects led to situations with others in which they felt at ease 'having a laugh', having fun, a banter or bonding with a variety of people. Smoking cannabis was also associated with this effect. Many recounted, for example, how when they first started smoking it they could not help laughing and they particularly enjoyed these effects: 'it made me giggle a lot, I like giggling' (Natalie, interview at age 22). The lowering of inhibitions was also identified in relation to ecstasy. Some interviewees described how they felt less repressed sexually when they had taken it (see Chapter Four). Drug takers discussed how sex, and the bodily sensations experienced, were enhanced and often more enjoyable when drugs, like ecstasy, were consumed (see also Boys et al., 2001). For these reasons, ecstasy had a specific function for some interviewees, to lower sexual inhibitions and heighten pleasure.

Cannabis, unsurprisingly, was described as a drug which produced relaxing effects. These effects are commonly acknowledged (see Aldridge et al., 2011; Boys et al., 2001; Williams and Parker, 2001). Most drug takers described how smoking cannabis helped them to feel more relaxed and less stressed. For instance, they discussed how it helped them to unwind after a day at work and forget about any concerns they had. Martin noted how smoking it made him feel 'a bit more relaxed and let your hair down a bit' (interview at age 28). Some interviewees reported how smoking it also helped them to sleep. These effects associated with smoking cannabis became, for many drug takers, purposeful reasons for continuing to smoke it (see Chapter Five). In addition, some interviewees identified one of the functions of their stimulant drug taking was to help them forget about their current concerns or to have time out at the weekend, which was described as a form of relaxation (see Chapter Five).

How perceived effects inform decisions about drug taking

It was apparent from the drug takers' accounts that there were a range of perceived pleasurable effects in respect of different drugs which formed an essential element of their decision making process and reasons for taking drugs. Rather than perceiving drug taking as a negative and risky activity, for many these effects made it enjoyable or functional. Some effects, for example feeling more relaxed after smoking cannabis, became key motivations for continued consumption. In addition, drug taking as an activity or past-time was perceived to provide time out or an escape from the reality of everyday life (see Hebdige, 1976; Taylor, 1999; Young, 1971). Taking drugs, therefore, was a form of escapism, albeit temporarily, which, as we will see in Chapters Four and Five, facilitated having fun or bonding with friends or strangers and provided reasons for continued consumption. Other effects, for instance, the 'buzz' or increased confidence and lowered inhibitions, were not generally described as main functions of drug taking, rather they were a pleasurable outcome or produced enjoyable situations which were still important for decision making (see Chapter Four). When decisions to take drugs were made, they could be based upon any one of the effects described by interviewees or a combination of all of them assessed against any potential negative effects and the setting in which they were to be taken.[2] Ecstasy, for instance, was associated with the 'buzz', increased energy and weight loss, as well as functioning as a form of escapism. Different drug takers placed greater emphasis or importance on different effects and associated functions when creating their own assessment of which drugs to take, for what purpose and in what setting.

Knowledge and experience of the effects of drugs also facilitated decisions about which drugs would become a regular feature of drug takers' repertoires, which to discard and which to take to manage the effects of other drugs. The interviewees were drugwise and could, in this sense, be described as pleasure seekers. For example, the 'buzz' perceived after taking stimulant drugs was important in determining which stimulant drugs to take regularly: ' ... whizz [amphetamines] you can feel, pills you can feel, ketamine you can most definitely feel! Coke I don't think you can feel' (Natasha, interview at age 28). Because some stimulant drugs were not perceived to produce such intense physical sensations in the body as others, they were taken less frequently. For instance, the shorter lasting effects of cocaine and its higher price compared to amphetamines and ecstasy, meant that some drug takers decided not take it as regularly.

Interviewees also discussed how the effects they perceived in respect of different drugs changed over time. For example, many described how they experienced the 'giggles' when they initially started to smoke cannabis, but regular and frequent smokers reported they no longer experienced this effect. In addition, the 'buzz' associated with stimulant drugs was reported by many interviewees as less intense with regular consumption:

But, I find now I'm not like, 'Oh wow!', you don't get like that tingly sort of feeling going through your body. And I don't get like that feel good sort of feeling any more. I just, I know it's there. It's completely different, it's as if it's different drugs all together. I just get more ... I don't get that, 'Ah, that feels nice' sort of thing.

(Kate, interview at age 28)

It is difficult to be certain why these pleasurable effects reduce with more frequent drug taking. It could be a consequence of various factors including increased tolerance, poor quality drugs or over-familiarity with the effects. Despite some interviewees lamenting how specific perceived effects diminished, none cited this as a reason for drug desistance. However, it may have been one of several reasons for changes in frequency and patterns of drug taking.

Knowledge about and experience of the effects of individual drugs was also important when deciding which drugs to take in combination. Many of the drug takers were poly-drug takers: they took more than one different type of drug per drug taking episode. Interviewees reported taking drugs in combination for two reasons: to intensify or sustain a 'high' or to minimize the effects of other drugs (see Boys et al., 2001). Natasha discovered that the pleasurable effects she perceived were heightened when she took ecstasy (aka pills) and ketamine at the same time:

... if you do a little bit [of ketamine] all the time then it can really enhance your pill, it really, really does.
[...]
So you say like it enhances your pill as well, so does it just sort of bring you back up?
Oh rushing, yeah, really good, but that's just like having what they call like a bump, like a key. Like you'd have a little bump of ketamine just on a key and that would be enough to like bring you up on your pill, especially if it was your first time on ketamine.

(interview at age 28)

For many drug takers, like Natasha, taking drugs concurrently functioned to enhance the effects and sensations they experienced. Amphetamines, for instance, were taken simultaneously with ecstasy to sustain a 'high' for longer. Interviewees were also knowledgeable about the order in which to take different drugs to achieve a desired effect. Some reported taking cocaine prior to taking ecstasy or amphetamines to give them a 'kick start'. Other interviewees, however, refused to take some drugs simultaneously. For instance, taking ecstasy and cocaine in combination was perceived to diminish the 'loved up' effects of ecstasy. Drug takers also discussed taking drugs concurrently to bring them down from the 'high'. They reported smoking cannabis or taking tranquillizers towards the end of a stimulant drug taking episode because they believed it would help them to 'chill out' and sleep.

Similarly, some interviewees discussed how they took cocaine to manage the effects of alcohol when they felt drunk:

> I need it [cocaine] when I'm bladdered [drunk], I mean to sober up. You know, it's just like walking round with carpet burns on me knees where I've fallen over in bars and things. (Laughs) That's when I need a line [of cocaine]!
>
> (Lindsay, interview at age 28)

One of the reported effects of taking cocaine when feeling drunk was that it facilitates further alcohol consumption (see Aldridge et al., 2011).

Knowledge about the various effects of drugs and how they work in combination demonstrate that rather than being irrational or ignorant decision makers, as Beck and Giddens might describe them, the drug takers possessed a detailed understanding of drugs and their effects that informed their decisions about which drugs to take for a specific purpose, which to take regularly and which to take in combination. Their knowledge of the effects of different drugs was largely grounded in their own experiences and perceptions. This experiential 'lay' knowledge was an important component and influence upon their decision making.

The perceived risks to health and well-being

The effects and functions associated with particular drugs which formed part of the drug takers' decision making process have been outlined. Conversely, the following section delineates the risks to health and well-being, and related harms or negative effects, that interviewees identified as important for their decisions about drug taking. Risks perceived by drug abstainers are distinguished from those perceived by drug takers. The most prominent in abstainers' accounts, when explaining their reasons for not taking drugs, were: addiction; feeling out of control; death; and the effect on general health. Drug takers' perceptions of these risks are also presented to illustrate how they informed their assessment of which drugs to take. The risk perceptions common to many of the drug takers' narratives, however, were more psychological, namely: the come down; feeling paranoid; and feeling unmotivated; and they are described in the final part of this section.

Risks to health and well-being predominantly perceived by drug abstainers: addiction, loss of control, death, and the effect on general health

The risk of addiction for dependent drug takers has been well documented by medical research. This potential risk is also often directed at recreational drug taking in that it is seen to lead to dependency in some cases. The perceived risk of addiction was common in the accounts of drug abstainers when they expressed their reasons for not taking drugs:

Even if I do take it [drugs] and think, 'Oh yeah, I like it' and then I'll get addicted, so why do it?

[...]

I've never found it appealing. I'm not scared of trying it, but I just wouldn't want to risk it just in case I do actually get addicted to it.

(Carl, interview at age 28)

Some, like Carl, adopted a deterministic, slippery slope perspective: once drug taking begins it will ultimately lead to addiction. Despite noting he might enjoy taking drugs, the potential for addiction was not a risk worth taking for Carl. Helen also thought taking drugs might lead to addiction: 'I'm just really glad that I haven't [taken drugs], you know, I'm really pleased. Because, you know, you hear of people that are addicted' (interview at age 28).

In contrast to the views of drug abstainers, it was less common for drug takers to perceive or discuss addiction as a potential risk from taking drugs which formed part of their decision making process. When they did talk about it, their perceptions were generally grounded in their own drug experiences. Some, for example, were critical of official messages and the general portrayal of illicit drugs as addictive. They perceived legal drugs they took, such as tobacco, to be more addictive than many illegal drugs. Drug takers, compared to drug abstainers, were also more able to describe in detail what the perceived risk of addiction meant to them and how it might occur. For instance, they thought it would be the outcome of prolonged and frequent consumption of drugs particularly amphetamines, cocaine, heroin and even cannabis. In contrast to the opinions of drug abstainers, addiction was viewed as a long-term risk arising from continuous drug taking rather than occurring after an initial or a few drug taking episodes. It was also perceived to cause various negative health effects, for example, weight loss, emaciated physical appearance or organ failure. Interestingly, however, although many drug takers did not discuss addiction as a potential risk which they needed to negotiate and manage during the course of their current drug journeys, some did reflect on their past experiences using terms such as 'addicted' or 'habit' to describe their former drug taking. These words were utilized to describe periods of time in which drugs were taken on a daily basis and, as we will see later in this chapter, provided justifications for their current, less frequent or non-drug taking behaviour.

Loss of control was identified as a perceived risk and reason not to take drugs by drug abstainers or not to take particular drugs by drug takers. Many drug abstainers were concerned about losing control if they took drugs. Frequently, they remarked that they did not want to take drugs because they perceived they would feel 'out of control' after taking them: 'I wouldn't like to feel so out of control. I'm not a controlling person, but I like to feel I'm in control. I imagine that you don't feel in control when you're taking drugs' (Michelle, interview at age 28). Feeling out of control was not a state many drug abstainers desired to be in or a risk they wanted to take. The concern most of these interviewees identified involved being able to manage or control how they might act and how they might perceive their environment after taking drugs. Many did not, however, distinguish between different types of drugs they believed would pose this risk.

In contrast, drug takers who did perceive this risk presented it as a reason not to take specific drugs. Some discussed it in relation to hallucinogenic drugs, particularly LSD (aka Acid):

> I think things that I've tried and I didn't like, I've not bothered with again. It's like Acid, we used to go trippy trailing, just in the countryside, because we used to go camping a lot. You know, a few of us, take a few tents, take a load of drugs, you'd end up building a camp fire, you know, as you do, have a bit of a dance, come whatever and one time we went trippy trailing.
> [...]
> And we were walking along there [a rocky outcrop] and then I ended up jumping into me fella's arms at the time because I thought there was spiders everywhere. It was weird, I've never experienced anything like that again and I never will. I've never had a trip since, it's completely put me off. (Laughs)
> [...]
> ... even the thought of it now, I can still remember it to this day, it absolutely scared the shit out of me. And I thought, 'Oh no, if that's what trips are all about you can forget it. (Laughs) Sod the hallucinations, you can forget it!'. So I've never, anything, yeah, that I've had a bad experience on, I've never touched again.
>
> (Kate, interview at age 28)

Narratives like Kate's offer support for the importance of pleasure when making decisions about drugs. She explained she did not enjoy the hallucinations she experienced and this became her primary reason not to take LSD again.

Other drugs were also perceived as risky by drug takers in terms of losing control. For example, this negative effect was associated with smoking cannabis and consuming alcohol. Many drug takers recalled how they had experienced what is commonly referred to as a 'whitey'. The symptoms involve feeling faint or passing out, and feeling nauseous or vomiting. Natalie recalled an occasion when she experienced this:

> ... one night at uni when I'd been drinking really heavily, I was really wasted, and we went back to someone's flat and smoked some pot [cannabis] and I just collapsed, completely collapsed and the next thing it was morning. Apparently, they carried me across the courtyard. I just can't remember a thing, the last thing I remember is smoking this joint ...
>
> (interview at age 22)

Interestingly, however, the risk of a potential whitey was not identified by drug takers as a reason not to take these drugs concurrently again. As we will see later in this chapter, strategies to manage risks like these may be adopted or such risks may be accepted as part and parcel of the drug taking experience.

The ultimate risk, death, associated with drug taking has received a disproportionate amount of media coverage in the past (Forsyth, 2001). Most recently in the UK, we have witnessed a 'moral panic' linking this risk with what was, at the time, a legal high known as mephedrone (Measham et al., 2010). Drug related death was a risk to health and well-being identified by many drug abstainers as a reason not to take drugs. With the exception of cannabis, they believed death could be a likely outcome from taking drugs. At age 17, Helen asserted one of the reasons she had not taken drugs was because: 'you can actually die from it'. Some drug takers whose drug repertoires extended only to cannabis also perceived this risk, as Natalie noted at age 22: '[drugs] can make you seriously ill and kill you'. More experienced drug takers were more likely to acknowledge this risk in relation to ecstasy and for this reason some had not tried it. Lindsay, who was drug experienced in terms of smoking cannabis and taking LSD, amphetamines and cocaine, was adamant that she would not try ecstasy because she felt strongly she could die: 'I still believe that ecstasy tablets could kill you, (Laughs) just one, so I don't take them' (interview at age 28). It is not surprising that many interviewees connected ecstasy with the potential risk of death from drug taking. It has been subject to intense media reporting (Aldridge et al., 2011; Critcher, 2000; Forsyth, 2001) and solely implicated in some drug-related deaths (Schifano et al., 2003). Many interviewees were familiar with the media reports in 1995 of the death of 18 year old Leah Betts after taking ecstasy, when they were also aged around 18.[3] This clearly influenced their risk perceptions. Lindsay's account above reflects the 'one pill can kill' and 'Sorted' anti-ecstasy campaigns which were dominant at the time. The potential risk of death was presented as a reason by most drug abstainers not to take drugs and some drug takers not to take specific drugs.

A further important risk to health and well-being which was a feature of drug abstainers' accounts when explaining why they did not take drugs was the potential negative effects drug taking may pose to their general health. Some less experienced drug takers also discussed this risk and presented it as a reason not to take some drugs: 'I don't think they're [drug takers] doing their bodies much good' (Natalie, interview at age 28). These interviewees explained and justified their perception of this risk in relation to their healthy lifestyles (see also Chapter Six). Similarly, more experienced drug takers also described how taking drugs may affect their general health. They connected being 'run down' from taking drugs regularly with minor illnesses, such as flu, tonsillitis or ear infections. However, these were not provided as reasons to stop taking drugs.

Risks to health and well-being predominantly perceived by drug takers: the come down, paranoia, and feeling unmotivated

The risks and associated harms to health and well-being which featured prominently in the narratives of drug abstainers when confirming why they did not take drugs have been outlined and compared with the perceptions and experiences of drug takers. The risks and negative effects to health and well-being which were a hallmark of many drug takers' narratives will now be sketched out. It was rare for drug abstainers to acknowledge or discuss these risks.

Research with drug takers has noted how the come down after taking stimulant drugs is a perceived risk (see Aldridge et al., 2011; Hinchliff, 2001; Hunt et al., 2007; Measham et al., 2001; Shewan et al., 2000). The generic term 'come down' is used to describe what studies have found to comprise of a number of facets including insomnia, lethargy, mood swings, inability to concentrate, and feelings of paranoia, anxiety and depression. The drug takers in this study also identified the come down as a significant risk to their health and well-being and described similar harms. It was often noted to occur after taking stimulant drugs, particularly ecstasy and amphetamines.[4] Interviewees explained how the come down could begin as the effects of stimulant drugs started to diminish and may continue for several days afterwards. All but one interviewee, who had tried stimulant drugs, discussed how they had experienced a come down to varying degrees.

Elements of the come down outlined by interviewees were both physiological and psychological. Vicky recounted what a come down after taking amphetamines felt like for her:

> Oh, it was horrible and you never wanted to eat or anything. It was so much worse than drinking. I mean I don't know what ecstasy come downs are like 'cos I never really had them.
> **Yeah.**
> But, it's just horrible. I just remember really I could never get to sleep for a start ...
>
> (interview at age 28)

Insomnia, a physiological aspect of the come down, was also discussed by other drug takers. Some viewed it as central to causing psychological symptoms which impacted upon how they felt during the days after taking stimulant drugs: ' ... tired and I don't want to do anything, not even talk. [...] just fucked up really' (Natasha, interview at age 22). As Natasha suggests, tiredness was perceived as affecting emotional well-being. Consequently, some described feeling irritable or tearful, whilst others felt paranoid or depressed during the days after taking stimulant drugs.

Stacey recalled how she frequently felt 'moody' the day after taking amphetamines. When she was interviewed at age 17, she was living at home with her family, and discussed how she would often argue with her mother the day after taking amphetamines. During her latest interview, she was still perceiving this risk, but in relation to ecstasy: 'It [taking drugs] means a lot of hassle basically cos it's just if you're losing out on your sleep you're getting very moody and it just messes your whole week up' (interview at age 28). Other drug takers recalled how they felt tearful during the come down. Lindsay maintained she often experienced this after taking cocaine, a drug most interviewees did not associate with a come down. She described an occasion when she attended parents' evening at her son's school:

> ... we'd done it [taken cocaine] that Sunday night, but finished at about, probably about two in the morning, gone to sleep about three, got up, taken Lloyd to school, and everything, and then gone to parents' evening. And I couldn't understand why, at parents' evening, why I couldn't stop crying. (Laughs) [...] And then afterwards I came out and it was like, I cried, and I know why I cried because I was coming down, fucking God Almighty!
>
> (interview at age 28)

These accounts indicate that lack of sleep brought on by the effects of stimulant drugs or by taking them into the early hours of the morning, rather than any specific pharmacological properties of drugs which influence emotional well-being, are a crucial determinant of the come down.

Feelings of paranoia were also identified as negative effects experienced during the come down. Interviewees, particularly female drug takers, discussed how they worried about their behaviour the day after they had taken drugs:

> And you just think, you know, it's embarrassing really. I used to wake up sometimes and think, 'Oh God, what did I say?' the next day. It's pretty bad really when you can't remember what you've said or you think, 'Why was I talking about that?' or 'Why did I tell someone that?' or you know, you just think, 'Oh God!'. I just can't bear that sinking feeling when you think, 'Oh My God, what did I do?' (Laughter).
>
> (Vicky, interview at age 28)

Paradoxically, these feelings of paranoia and embarrassment discussed by females may have been a result of the effects they perceived and experienced after taking drugs which they believed increased their confidence and lowered their inhibitions. Whilst the two male interviewees in the sample, Dean and Nigel, who had taken stimulant drugs before, also discussed how they felt paranoid during the come down, their concerns revolved around how others might perceive or judge them when they were experiencing a come down (see also Chapter Six).[5] Dean recalled how he felt paranoid when he returned home the morning after taking stimulant drugs:

... we've had some good times at clubs or some good times at people's houses thinking everything's great and then you walk down the street and you realize everything isn't great.

In what way isn't it great?

'Cos not everyone's on the same drug as you, you know. And they're going to work, you know like, and you've been up all night, you know. You see people going to work and you're still on drugs, I don't think it's the best feeling.

Yeah.

Some people can handle it differently, some people just happily walk down the street at eight in the morning full of ecstasy and walk past these people who are going to work and just not care, not bother. They seem to get on with it differently, I can't, I can't. I am a worrier, a worrier, paranoid individual.

(interview at age 28)

A further element of the come down described by drug takers was feeling depressed or 'low' in the days after taking stimulant drugs. Dean discussed how he could feel 'low' for up to five days after taking ecstasy:

And the come down's pretty hard.

Yeah.

It makes you, it keeps your feet on the ground anyway. The come down it makes you realize how insignificant you actually are (Laughter) 'cos you feel dead low about yourself and everything.

And would that happen the day after or a couple of days after?

The day after, the day after that, the day after that, probably two, three, four maybe five days, you know what I mean?

Yeah.

Until you've got, until you feel like you've got a level head again. I don't particularly like the feeling of ecstasy come downs.

(interview at age 28)

Despite the negative effects many drug takers connected to the come down, and the perceived risk of experiencing one, none of the drug takers identified it as a principal reason not to take stimulant drugs or for complete drug desistance.

Whilst many drug takers identified feeling paranoid as a feature of the come down, some also discussed how they perceived this negative effect when taking drugs. In her early twenties, for a period of a couple of months, Stacey took amphetamines most days of the week. She stated she suffered from paranoia when she took them. She also discussed, in her latest interview, how she could feel paranoid when she took ecstasy or cocaine, drugs she consumed less frequently: ' ... you see things a bit differently, like you'll think to yourself, "Is that girl talking about me?" or "Is she doing something that she's not?". But, you'll think she is because you're not with it, because you're getting paranoid' (interview at age 28). For other drug takers, feelings of paranoia were experienced when they smoked cannabis, as Dean's account illustrates:

> It was making me paranoid, I couldn't talk to people, do anything, I could only talk to me fellow weed smokers ...
>
> [...]
>
> I was thinking about things that didn't need to be thought about, you know what I mean? I was worrying about things that I didn't really need to worry about.
>
> **Yeah.**
>
> I was getting paranoid of the person sat right next to me [when I smoked cannabis], it weren't healthy I don't think.
>
> (interview at age 28)

Even though some drug takers had experienced or perceived this negative effect, generally they were willing to risk or accept it. They did not identify it as a main reason not to continue their drug journeys. However, in some cases, as Dean's narrative will illustrate later in this chapter, it may have been one of a number of negative effects which led to reducing the frequency of drug taking.

A further risk which many drug takers identified was feeling unmotivated when they had taken drugs (see Chapters Five and Six). This was particularly associated with, as Deehan and Saville (2003) have noted, smoking cannabis, but for some it was also linked to the come down. These feelings were experienced by some immediately after smoking cannabis whilst others felt smoking it or experiencing a come down had a more general effect upon their everyday levels of motivation. The following section outlines the ways in which the risks perceived by all interviewees informed the decision making process.

Perceiving, accepting, managing and avoiding drug taking risks

Perceiving drug taking risks

As elucidated above, there was a clear distinction between the risks perceived by drug abstainers and those identified by drug takers. Generally, drug abstainers were more likely to perceive serious and long-term risks and harms (see Aldridge et al., 2011; Williams, 2007). In contrast, drug takers were more likely to perceive risks and harms which could be described as less serious and more immediate or short-term (see Aldridge et al., 2011; Measham et al., 2001; Shewan et al., 2000; Williams, 2007). Drug takers with less extensive drug taking repertoires, for example, cannabis only, or less frequent experience were, however, more likely to identify with some of the risks discussed by drug abstainers. More experienced drug takers often challenged these perceptions or perceived these risks in respect of a specific drug they chose not to take or a particular form of drug taking, for example, dependent or intravenous use of heroin.

The perceived risks and harms outlined in this chapter were important for the interviewees' decision making process: they informed the practice of reflexivity. The negative effects identified by abstainers were presented as reasons for not taking drugs and avoiding risk. Some identified all of these risks, whilst others selected a few. They were also more likely to evaluate drug taking in a generic way and less able to identify how specific risks are linked to individual drugs. If they did distinguish between the harmfulness of particular drugs, it usually involved creating a hierarchy of two extremes in which cannabis was viewed as the least dangerous and drugs like (crack) cocaine or heroin as the most harmful (see Abbott-Chapman and Denholm, 2001; Green et al., 2000). Drug abstainers were also less likely to be aware of the benefits or positive effects of individual drugs, therefore, the negative effects they perceived substantially outweighed by far any potential pleasures and functions.

In contrast, drug takers assess each drug individually (Aldridge et al., 2011; Hunt et al., 2007; Shewan et al., 2000). The drug takers in this study may, for example, perceive a particular drug as risky and choose not to take it and another as far less risky, or not risky at all, and decide to take it. These attitudes towards risk point to important differences in perceptions not only between drug takers and non-drug takers but even amongst these groups. For instance, in respect of losing control, some drug takers perceived this as a negative effect associated with specific drugs, while others described hallucinations experienced after taking stimulant drugs as enjoyable and fun. Natasha enthused about the hallucinations (aka k-holes) she experienced when taking ketamine. It was clear she engaged with the encounter rather than finding it frightening or scary:

> In my first k-hole, on my own with Rick, there was, I can almost remember it now 'cos it kind of goes away from you, but it was like reliving a childhood memory and I remember something that was happening to me in my k-hole was like I'd done it before and it was all very familiar. And I knew what was going to happen, but I couldn't stop what was going to happen from happening and it was kind of like resigning to yourself that this is what's going to happen. And the next time I had a k-hole the same thing happened again. It's like I see musical notes and lines, you know when you see the bars on a piece of music?
> *Yeah.*
> And they did exactly the same dance and the room turned exactly the same and I knew exactly the way the chair was going to move and it was all going to come round and I was going to be sat here and 'doo doo doo doo doo' and that the same songs going through my head. And I thought 'No, I'm going to change it'. And so I stood up and it all totally changed and I was like 'Ooh this is different, ooh this is interesting' and I had a completely different experience.
>
> (interview at age 28)

For some interviewees, the risk of losing control was perceived as one not worth taking, whereas for others it was a positive effect associated with drug taking which they desired, relished and thoroughly enjoyed. Accounts like these clearly illustrate the subjective and hermeneutic meanings of risk; what is perceived as risky by one person may be perceived as pleasurable by another (see Mythen, 2004). Hence the different decisions made about drugs and different drug journeys which materialize amongst this sample and the general population.

Because drug takers assessed each drug individually, the risks and harms they perceived also impacted differentially on their decisions about each drug. In some cases, perceived or experienced negative effects and potential risks were acknowledged but appeared to be accepted as part and parcel of the drug taking experience. In other cases, their experiences and perceptions of risk led to risk management techniques, whilst for others, they resulted in changes in behaviour either involving reducing the frequency of drug taking or completely desisting from taking drugs or specific drugs. These differential responses to 'risk' further illuminate the decision making and reflexive process of drug takers. The ways in which drug takers accept, manage or avoid risk, or, in other words, the significance of their experiences and perceptions of risk for the decision making process, are summarized in the following three sections.

Accepting drug taking risks

It has been argued that some risks and harms are accepted by drug takers (Hunt et al., 2007; Shewan et al., 2000). This was also the case for the drug takers in this study. There were two principal negative effects which they perceived and accepted: the come down after taking stimulant drugs and the whitey associated with smoking cannabis. In addition, other potential risks identified by some drug takers, for example feeling paranoid after taking drugs, indicate a level of acceptance because many continued to take individual drugs without employing specific risk management techniques to ameliorate them.

The importance of drug, set and setting to explain why people choose to take drugs was first proposed by Zinberg (1984). Drawing on this work, Shewan et al. (2000) argue perceptions of risk are determined by what effects drug takers expect from a particular drug, their mindset and the context in which a drug is taken. The following account from Natasha highlights how drug takers expect to experience a come down to varying degrees after taking stimulant drugs:

> I don't want to say I don't have come downs, but I probably don't. I expect to feel shit because I've gone a whole night without sleep and not a lot of food so I expect to feel crap.
> [...]

I expect to feel shit in my body so I'm quite happy that I'll wake up on a Monday morning and I'll think, 'Yeah, I'm all right, I can deal with this'. As long as I've slept ...
Yeah.
... then, you know, I'm not really too fussed.
[...]
I feel shit that means I've had a wicked weekend!

(interview at age 28)

For Natasha, and other stimulant drug takers, the come down was a negative effect they expected to experience and many possessed a positive mindset towards it. It was an anticipated and accepted risk and recast as a measure of a good night out. In the earlier rounds of interviews, the come down was not identified as a reason not to take stimulant drugs. It was accepted in the same way as a hangover after consuming excessive amounts of alcohol. However, with age and the accomplishment of transitions to adulthood, some had begun to suggest the come down, along with other perceived risks, provided a motive for reducing the frequency of drug taking or even considering drug desistance (see also Aldridge et al., 2011; Williams, 2007).

In addition to the come down, the whitey also appeared to be accepted as a negative effect and potential risk when smoking cannabis and consuming alcohol concurrently. Earlier in this chapter, an account from Natalie described how she experienced a whitey, however, she did not identify it as a reason for her to stop smoking cannabis when she had also consumed alcohol. Interestingly, the whitey was discussed more frequently when drug takers were younger, suggesting that through their drug experiences they either began to accept this risk, managed it by not consuming excessive amounts of alcohol and cannabis or their levels of tolerance increased over time.

The narratives presented illustrate how drug takers are not ignorant of the potential risks associated with their behaviour, however, in some circumstances they are willing to accept or take these risks. Some risks then, as Mythen (2004) argues, are acceptable risks or risk trade-offs which we take in our daily lives.

Managing drug taking risks

Beck (1992) and Giddens (1991) argue our aim is to avoid risk or to minimize the harm we experience. There is evidence from the drug takers' narratives that they took steps to reduce the impact of specific negative effects. It has been noted how drug takers adopt various strategies to manage or minimize the harms or risks they perceive (Branigan and Wellings, 1998; Deehan and Saville, 2003; Hunt et al., 2007; Measham et al., 2001; Moore and Measham, 2008; Shewan et al., 2000). Although many drug takers appeared to accept the come down as a potential risk, some also adopted strategies to reduce its negative effects. Others took precautions to minimize the potential harm associated with taking adulterated drugs, a new substance or too many drugs on one occasion.

Various practices which drug takers adopt to ameliorate the symptoms of the come down have been identified, including sleeping or resting, exercise and taking other drugs (Deehan and Saville, 2003; Measham et al., 2001; Shewan et al., 2000). Many of the drug takers in this study also employed these techniques. Dean, for example, noted how playing sport the next day helped him to 'get me head straightened' (interview at age 28). It was apparent that many took steps to prepare in advance for the come down (see Shewan et al., 2000). Some discussed how they smoked cannabis or occasionally took Valium during the initial stages of the come down to help them sleep. These strategies required some preparation by ensuring certain drugs were available to take. Others also stated they booked the day off work to rest following a stimulant drug taking episode. After clubbing and taking stimulant drugs, Natasha normally attended post-club parties at friends' homes and took with her what she described as her 'party pack':

> I have a party pack: *Forehead*, 'cos you don't take paracetamol, face wipes, cleanser, toner, moisturizer, a face mask sometimes. That's great getting a bunch of gay guys in a room with their face masks on, that's really fun, that's fantastic! A real lot of fun that is. Minty face masks as well to keep you awake. Nasal, you know the *Vicks* inhaler, that, a bit of tiger balm as well for massaging your neck and *Deep Heat* for when people have got sore legs. And temazepams as well, if you can get hold of them, to help me sleep.
>
> (interview at age 28)

These purposeful strategies used by drug takers were presented as ways of minimizing the effects of the come down.

Earlier in this chapter, the views of drug abstainers and some drug takers were presented in respect of the identified risk of feeling out of control, as a reason for not taking either any drugs by drug abstainers or specific drugs by drug takers. This risk perception was reinforced for drug abstainers by what they believed was the unpredictable nature of the effects of drugs on the body:

> I wouldn't take anything, because I just think with drugs you don't necessarily know what's in them, you know? At least with alcohol, I mean, you know, you can stop when you get to a certain point. You can take some kind of drug and that's it then isn't it? You know, you can't take it back and you can't just have a bit really. So I just, I would just be petrified of what it would do to me.
>
> (Helen, interview at age 28)

Drug takers, however, adopted strategies to manage the risk of taking adulterated drugs or not knowing how a new drug might affect the body (see

Measham et al., 2001, 2011; Murnane et al., 2000; Shewan et al., 2000). Some of these techniques were also discussed in respect of managing the risk of death associated with ecstasy or the risk of feeling out of control. Firstly, as other research has found, they discussed how they rarely bought drugs from an unknown source. In doing so, the risk of buying adulterated drugs was believed to be reduced and there was some recourse to their source if a drug did not have the anticipated or desired effect. Secondly, the effects of new drugs were researched either by asking friends who had taken them or reading about them online or in books. Dean explained how he first learnt about ecstasy: 'Obviously you know it's around, you read things and you talk to people who've had them, blah, blah, blah' (interview at age 28). Thirdly, when initially taking a drug for the first time it was taken in small quantities. For example, when first trying ecstasy, many took half an ecstasy pill and monitored its effects before taking more. Dean tried ecstasy shortly after his interview at age 22. He described his initial pattern of consumption:

> Just one night I had half a pill, it didn't do anything at all really. And then another night I had a full one and then probably a week later I had two and a half and then three and a half and then after that I had six.
>
> (interview at age 28)

On each drug taking occasion, Dean increased the amount of ecstasy he took based upon how he had felt when he had taken it previously. Others also took precautions to reduce the risk of feeling out of control if they took too much of a drug. Vicky, for instance, noted that her preferred drug, amphetamines, was in powder form which was advantageous because 'you could dab a little tiny bit or you could have more' (interview at age 28). All these strategies helped the drug takers to manage the potential risk of feeling out of control when taking either too many drugs, adulterated drugs or a new substance.

The narratives presented suggest many were, at times, cautious when taking drugs or trying new drugs. Deehan and Saville (2003) have questioned the extent to which risk management practices translate into behaviour. Undoubtedly, there were times when these strategies were not implemented and, for example, more drugs were taken than intended or drugs were occasionally bought from unknown sources. Nevertheless, through their own experiences, and the experiences of others, drug takers learnt about the effects of different drugs and ultimately what drugs they preferred and would continue to take. In this sense, they can be described as 'chemically literate' (Jackson, 2004: 85). Some interviewees experienced negative effects when they first tried a drug and this became a reason not to take it again. Others, however, may not have found an initial drug taking encounter entirely pleasurable, or extremely negative, and persevered with trying a specific drug until they could maximize pleasure or because it had a particular function, for example, increasing energy. The following account from Natasha embodies the drug learning process and how to take drugs to enhance an activity:

You know what to expect, so when it happens you use it to your advantage as opposed to allowing it to consume you. Some people really allow, they'll go into their drugs and get very self-absorbed into it and kind of allow it to take over them. Whereas me, I use it, I kind of, it's like I put the reins on it, it's like horses. I suppose that's the image I've got in my head, and you're putting the reins on the horses and you're using them to take you somewhere as opposed to being thrown off the back of a horse and like 'Errrggghh!'

Yeah.

It's all about bridling it I suppose, and allowing it to enhance what you're doing.

(interview at age 28)

Over time, then, drug takers become familiar with the effects of different drugs. They learn what to expect and how to manage and control their drug taking for their benefit (see Jackson, 2004; Moore and Measham, 2008). This learning process is different from the social learning within a subculture emphasized by Becker (1963); it is individualized and based upon personal experiences rather than wholly influenced by group behaviour and attitudes. Control may be exerted through, drawing on Natasha's metaphor, 'bridling' drug taking and consuming what is required for pleasurable experiences. This is not to deny that pleasure may also be connected to feeling out of control or 'messy' after taking drugs. Drug takers essentially create a guide or manual of 'lay' knowledge about risk and pleasure, based on their experiences, the experiences of others and other available sources of information about drugs. As the effects of a drug become more familiar and predictable, the risks associated with them may be diminished, accepted or managed. It is unlikely, as Rhodes (1997) contends in relation to habitual drug taking, that assessment of risk does not operate for decisions about recreational drugs, however familiar the behaviour. Rather, recreational drug takers are likely to at least question, even fleetingly, whether they should take more of a drug, when they should take it, and so on, whilst at the same time assessing how they are feeling.

Avoiding or reducing drug taking risks

The picture painted so far is of drug takers who are knowledgeable about many health and well-being risks connected to and sometimes experienced when they take drugs. Their attitudes may involve accepting these risks or their perceptions and behaviour may provoke reflexivity and lead to strategies to manage them. In addition, the process of reflexivity was further illustrated when drug takers decided to avoid or reduce the incidence of certain risks by choosing not take some drugs or to moderate their drug taking. There were various negative effects some drug takers were not willing to risk, for instance, death, which was provided as a reason for not wanting to try ecstasy. Others were reflexive after an initial drug taking encounter in which they did not enjoy particular effects and, therefore, would not try a certain drug again. It has been argued that risk begins to outweigh pleasure when the positive effects reduce and the negative effects increase (Aldridge, 2008; Hunt et al., 2007)[6] and certain practices, therefore, become questionable. The following two accounts illustrate the ways in which risk begins to outweigh pleasure and the effect this has upon decision making.

Dean first tried cannabis in his late teens. He became a regular smoker and was smoking it most days of the week when he was interviewed at age 22. Over time, however, he began to perceive negative effects which he associated with smoking it. He felt paranoid and also began to feel unmotivated: 'it was stopping me from doing anything' (interview at age 28). Consequently, these negative effects were presented by Dean as risks he was not willing to take most days of the week. He decided to reduce the frequency of his cannabis consumption. When he was re-interviewed at age 28, he was smoking it on average once a week with friends and he was no longer buying his own supply. Although he reported he still felt paranoid and unmotivated at times when he smoked it, because he did so less often, it was a risk which he could accept and accommodate. Narratives like Dean's illustrate how a number of negative effects combine to provide reasons for moderating drug taking and reducing the frequency of it.[7]

When Kate talked about her drug taking, she described periods in her life when she felt she was 'addicted' to drugs. At age 16, she began smoking heroin occasionally at weekends but eventually progressed to daily use. For a period of 12 months, Kate was smoking approximately one bag of heroin per day.[8] When she stopped taking heroin daily, she noted her consumption of amphetamines began to gradually increase. She recalled how she became 'addicted' to amphetamines and took them frequently for three years in her late teens and early twenties. Towards the end of this period, she was consuming an ounce per week.[9] It was not until she was rushed to hospital after collapsing at work that she stopped taking amphetamines on a daily basis. Her decision was prompted by the health consequences she experienced at the time. At hospital, she was informed her drug taking had damaged two internal organs:

> And that was like at the hospital and they said, 'Right, you need to pack it in. If you carry on you're going to end up dead in another 12 months'. So I thought, 'Right yeah, you're right, I'm stupid'. So, you know, enough's enough.
>
> (interview at age 28)

It is clear how these negative health effects sparked reflexivity in Kate; she admonished herself as 'stupid'. We might expect that such serious and negative health problems would prompt complete desistance from drug taking or at least from taking particular drugs. Initially, Kate's experience was a key turning point in her drugs journey. She did not take any drugs for at least one to two years. Although she did recommence taking amphetamines, it was at a considerably lower frequency than in the past. When she was interviewed again at age 28, she was consuming no more than three ecstasy pills and/or a small amount of amphetamines per drug taking occasion. These drug taking episodes were restricted to a few times a year at music events or at home with her partner.

Deehan and Saville (2003) argue that negative health risks rarely trigger drug desistance. The narratives of the interviewees suggest the relationship between harmful health experiences and desistance is complex. In some cases, negative effects experienced when initially trying a drug, for instance LSD, did influence decisions not to take individual drugs again. However, when drug takers were experienced or familiar with a drug, and to some extent it was fundamental to their drug journeys or life, the road to desistance was less certain. In some cases, negative experiences were accepted as part and parcel of the drug taking experience or strategies were adopted to manage them. In others, over time, they led to a reduction in the frequency of drug taking or quantities consumed, whilst for others, harmful effects resulted in temporary desistance and a subsequent return to drug taking, albeit it, for some, at a slower pace or a switch to alternative drugs.

Risk perceptions: justifications and rationalizations of current behaviour

A striking feature of the interviewees' narratives was not only how their perceptions of risk differed from each other, but, as the qualitative longitudinal data revealed, how they also changed over time. Reith (2004) has argued perceptions of risk act to justify and rationalize current behaviour. The risk perceptions of all interviewees provided evidence to support this (see Aldridge et al., 2011; Williams, 2007). For instance, the risks perceived by abstainers tended to be more serious, such as death or addiction, which act to rationalize their choice not to take drugs, whereas the risks perceived by current drug takers, and identified as important to their decision making, were more immediate and short-term, and on the whole manageable or acceptable, therefore justifying their current behaviour. Whilst drug desisters may initially have possessed similar perceptions to current drug takers, these changed once they stopped taking drugs. They became concerned about the long-term health effects of past and future drug taking if they were to continue their drug journeys, which they provided as justifications for no longer taking drugs. Changes in risk perceptions were also evident in current drug takers' accounts. Their perceptions changed when they tried and became familiar with new drugs, reduced the frequency of their drug taking or stopped taking a particular drug.

As noted earlier, drug takers assessed each drug individually. Carroll (2000) argues risks perceived by drug takers differ from those perceived by non-drug takers. However, for drugs which drug takers did not want to try, and in support of Reith's contention above, they perceived similar risks to drug abstainers. For example, interviewees who had never tried ecstasy were more likely to attribute the risk of death to it and provide this as a reason for not wanting to take it. Nevertheless, over time, some interviewees became less resolute about this perceived risk. Stacey's narrative illustrates how her risk perceptions of ecstasy changed:

> ... people used to tell me, you have an ecstasy tablet, the first one, and you die. I think that's what kept me away from them really. I'd never touch them because I knew if I took one I'd die. Someone said you have a buzz for about five hours and then die.
>
> (interview at age 17)

When Stacey was a teenager, she clearly believed death was a possible outcome after taking ecstasy. Not long after this interview, Stacey did go on to try ecstasy with a friend and continued to take it occasionally when it was available to her. On one occasion, around the age of 21, after she had not taken it for 18 months, she had what she described as a negative experience which prompted her to stop taking it again. She declared: 'I thought that I was dying!' (interview at age 22). Although she cited this experience as her reason for no longer taking ecstasy, by the time she was interviewed at age 28, she had started taking it again in the past six months. During her latest interview, the risk of death when taking it was no longer discussed. Instead, she emphasized the positive effects she perceived. It was clear interviewees, like Stacey, adopted different positions towards risk during the life course. Perceptions of risk, therefore, are not static; they can alter throughout the life course. When interviewees were younger many perceived a risk of death associated with ecstasy, but in their twenties, knowing others who had tried it and trying it themselves, they no longer perceived this risk and were more likely to identify short-term risks, such as the come down, a less serious and more manageable risk, which rationalized their decision to continue taking it.

The narratives of interviewees who had become drug desisters by age 28 also provide further evidence of how risk perceptions change to justify and rationalize current behaviour. It has been noted how drug takers are rarely worried about the long-term health risks associated with taking drugs (Deehan and Saville, 2003; Gamma et al., 2005; Shewan et al., 2000; Sumnall et al., 2004). It was apparent from the interviewees' accounts that female drug desisters became concerned about the long-term impact past drug taking might have upon their current or future health[10] – a concern which had not been expressed in earlier interviews. As they reached their late twenties, the importance of maintaining and preserving their general health was now more apparent. Vicky began to assess the risks she associated with drug taking in the context of her other health risk perceptions and how they changed during the life course:

'Cos whereas like years ago we used to be more concerned with how much do you weigh, what do you look like and then how thin you are compared to everyone else or, you know?
Yeah.
Whereas now, it's like what is it that you're putting into your body and stuff. It doesn't matter if, you know, you don't look like that any more or it's just, you know, you just want to live as long as possible really, be as healthy as possible.

(interview at age 28)

Questioning what she consumed and how it might affect her health in the long-term was a primary justification for Vicky not to take drugs again.

Jan also voiced concern about the long-term health effects of drug taking. She was worried about how her past drug taking may have affected her current well-being. Interviewed at age 28, she appeared to have low self-esteem and lacked confidence, and was experiencing a variety of symptoms associated with this. Reflecting on her drug taking some years earlier, she believed smoking cannabis when she was younger had a detrimental effect upon her current psychological well-being:

> ... in hindsight, I think some days, you know, that's been quite damaging. Because, you know, I am a bit paranoid now, and I know that paranoia is one of the side effects of cannabis. [...] And I sometimes think, you know, 'God, I wonder whether that's had an effect on my, you know, mind?'

(interview at age 28)

In the past, Jan smoked a couple of cannabis joints a few times per week for a period of nine months. She connected her past consumption of cannabis to how she felt presently. It is possible she was searching for a reason to explain her current psychological state, especially in the context of her interview. However, perceiving paranoia as a long-term risk associated with drug taking – whether or not it actually had affected her current well-being – served to rationalize her decision not to smoke it again. Likewise, some current drug takers also became concerned about long-term or other serious risks when they stopped taking a particular drug or substantially reduced their consumption of it, even though they continued to take other drugs. For example, some began to perceive the risk of addiction once they stopped smoking cannabis or taking other drugs daily (see Chapter Six). The narratives of the female drug desisters and current drug takers illustrate how risk perceptions can change to justify behaviour. As Hinchliff (2001) argues, with hindsight, and changes in drug taking behaviour, risk perceptions alter. These interviewees began to discuss drug taking as a long-term or more serious risk to health and well-being: a risk they had not previously discussed or prioritized in their decision making. Narratives like these demonstrate how perceptions of risk are dynamic and fluid throughout the life course. More-over, they suggest that a policy focus which over-emphasizes risk associated with drug taking may be misplaced (see Chapter Seven). In Chapters Four and Five, other factors which can explain drug desistance will be outlined in relation to interpersonal relationships and transitions to adulthood.

Summary

The principal aim of this chapter has been to begin to develop empirically the theoretical framework proposed in Chapter Two. In this regard, the theorizing of Beck and Giddens has begun to be tested and evaluated. The accounts presented offer some support for an agential and rational view of the decision making process: one which involves weighing up positive and negative effects to health and well-being associated with different drugs. When considering the significance placed by Beck and Giddens on 'expert' knowledges for making decisions about risk, the narratives from drug abstainers generally support this. Their risk perceptions largely mirrored those of medical 'experts'. The meaning of risk is, however, contingent upon experiences and thus subjective. Drug abstainers admitted they knew little about drugs and, therefore, it is not surprising their views reflected normative or 'expert' opinions. In contrast, the meaning of risk for drug takers was premised upon their lived experiences of drugs. Generally, their risk perceptions differed from objective definitions and were more likely to be immediate, less serious and somewhat manageable or acceptable. However, for drugs they did not want to try or continue to take, risk perceptions were similar to those identified by medical 'experts'.

The view which emerges from the drug takers' accounts of their decision making is one which demonstrates an in-depth and critical understanding of risks associated with drug taking. In contrast to Beck's and Giddens' char-acterization of 'risk takers' as ignorant or negligent, they generally appeared to be competent risk managers (see Adams, 2003) and drugwise. These accounts highlight the complex relationship between risk, pleasure and desire which has failed to be considered by Beck and Giddens (Culpitt, 1999; Irwin et al., 2000). Not only were drug takers knowledgeable about the effects of different drugs and which to combine for a specific purpose, they also employed various strategies to reduce the negative effects which they per-ceived. The ways in which drug takers regulated their drug journeys involved a learning process contingent upon their own experiences, about which drugs to take, for what purpose, when and how to do so to maximize pleasure and minimize risk. As we will see in the following chapter, social relationships were also important for this learning process. For some, however, the risks perceived were not too threatening, so that they were accepted as part and parcel of the experience (Gamma et al., 2005; Shewan et al., 2000). As Hunt et al. (2007) argue, in these circumstances, pleasure outweighs risk.

It was apparent that decisions to reduce the frequency of drug taking or to completely desist from it involve a combination of different perceived risks to health and well-being. On the whole, the reflexive decision making process for drug takers was fluid and dynamic. Over time, their risk perceptions altered. It has been argued here that this served to justify current behaviour: risk perceptions changed as some interviewees started to take certain drugs and others stopped taking them. There was also evidence to suggest that even some of the less serious, but more immediate risks perceived by drug takers were beginning to outweigh pleasure and became reasons for reducing the frequency of drug taking. However, as it will be illuminated in Chapter Five, these risks were often assessed in relation to their current life journeys. If risk perceptions change and act to rationalize current behaviour, it suggests that a policy strategy that is focused upon emphasizing the negative effects of drug taking to current drug takers may be misplaced (see Chapter Seven). The narratives presented here indicate it is only in retrospect that drug takers and drug desisters begin to perceive more serious risks, once they have stopped taking drugs (see Hinchliff, 2001).

The central task of this chapter has been to evaluate the agential risk assessor portrayed in the accounts of Beck and Giddens. In part, decisions about drugs can be viewed as agential involving the weighing up of costs and benefits to health and well-being, and influenced by objective, 'expert' knowledges. This perspective largely explains why and how decisions not to take drugs are made. We have, however, also observed how for drug takers their decisions about drug taking are subjective and formed on their own drug experiences. In this regard, they create a 'lay' guide which informs their decisions about drugs based upon the positive and negative effects they experience. The following chapter continues to develop an approach which explores the subjective meaning of risk and pleasure by situating the decision making process within its cultural context. In this respect, the practice of pleasure and the influence of interpersonal relationship will be examined.

4 The meaning of pleasure and risk in a cultural context

... we were actually off our ... we had a few lines [of cocaine] while we were out and we just get silly, you know. And I had me chicken fillets [breast enhancers], you know, slapped over me eyes in a bar and I was just sat there like that, just with these two cheeky fellas. And it's like we don't give a toss who's around or ... we're just like in our own little mad bubble.

(Lindsay, interview at age 28)

I mean for me, it is definitely the people that I'm with.

(Vicky, interview at age 28)

Introduction

The reflexive individual presented in the work of Beck and Giddens cognitively assesses risk in a vacuum. Consequently, they have been accused of decontextualizing the process of reflexivity (Adams, 2003; Caplan, 2000; Lupton, 1999; Marris and Langford, 1996; Reilly, 1999; Tulloch and Lupton, 2003; Wynne, 1996).[1] A cultural perspective, following Douglas' lead and sketched out in Chapter Two, emphasizes the social and cultural influences upon decision making, the meaning of risk within its cultural context, and the importance of the experiences and opinions of friends, family, partners and colleagues when we make risk assessments. Building upon the analysis in the previous chapter and the theoretical framework outlined in Chapter Two, the aim in this chapter is to develop a cultural approach to understanding risk and decisions about drug taking. In this regard, it is important to explore the situated nature of the meaning of risk and pleasure, and, therefore, appreciate responses to risk and risk assessments within their cultural settings.

To develop a cultural understanding of the meaning of risk or drug taking, it is essential to analyse how risk is interpreted by drug takers themselves. This task began in Chapter Three, the subjective risk perceptions of drug takers and the pleasures they associated with drug taking, contrasted with objective 'expert' definitions. In this chapter, the meaning of risk, or the pleasures drug takers perceive in relation to drugs, are set within their cultural context. Researchers have observed for some time how pleasure is bound to the social context (see Hunt et al., 2007; Hutton, 2006; Measham et al., 2001). However, research undertaken by Duff (2008), Jackson (2004) and Malbon (1999) captures the essence of what Duff describes as 'pleasure in practice' and the lived experience of drug takers. This type of research emphasizes the ways in which pleasure is derived from the effects of drugs, enhanced by the environments in which they are consumed and the people they are taken with, and ultimately how drug taking can enrich lives. Drugs are 'consumed in order to facilitate or enhance some other activity like dancing, social interaction, conversation, sex and so on' (Duff, 2008: 387). Whilst the effects of stimulant drugs, as we have seen in Chapter Three, may be perceived to, for example, increase energy and produce physiological sensations in the body which are important to consider when making decisions about different drugs, pleasure is also derived from and intensified by harnessing these effects in an appropriate situation like dancing in a club and experiencing all the sensations which come with this, such as pumping music, flashing lights and hot bodies dancing closely together. Motivations for drug taking and decisions about drugs are, therefore, inextricably linked to the social and cultural settings in which they are consumed. This approach to understanding pleasure emphasizes the hermeneutic, sensual and transformative effects of drugs.

A cultural approach to understanding perceptions of risk and risk behaviour also demands we scrutinize the ways in which intersubjective relationships influence understandings of risk. Douglas has documented how risk perceptions are culturally determined. In this respect, social science research has found that everyday relationships with friends or intimate partners can expose individuals to risk *and* act as supports and sites of trust when making decisions about risk (Latkina et al., 2003; Miller and Neaigus, 2001; Pilkington, 2007; Rhodes and Quirk, 1998). As Rhodes and Quirk (1998: 166) astutely observe: 'The interpersonal social relationship is thus one of many social structures which fashion individuals' proximity to risk, their perceptions of what risk is, and how they act in response to it.' It is important, therefore, to encapsulate the social relations of risk as they are experienced by drug takers and non-drug takers. In doing so, the interactive dynamic relationship between social relationships and decisions about drug taking can be revealed. In the context of interpersonal relationships, decision making involves consensus, negotiation and disagreement (Pilkington, 2007), or what Douglas conceptualizes as emotional, mutual and cultural accountability. In this respect, the ways in which the attitudes and behaviour of others towards drug taking can influence decisions about drugs are explored. Pennay and Moore (2010) focus upon how the anti-drug discourses of significant others impact upon decision making in their study of the 'micro-politics of normalization'. In this chapter, the significance of pro- and anti-drugs attitudes *and* the drug taking behaviour of family, friends and partners for decision making is considered.

The chapter is divided into two halves. It begins by exploring the subjective meanings of risk, or, as we shall see, the practice of pleasure, associated with drugs, within its cultural context. To this end, the narratives of drug takers are presented. The significance of these cultural understandings of risk and pleasure are considered for decisions about drug taking. In doing so, a nuanced understanding of motivations for drug taking, and the decision making process, is offered which allows us to appreciate why some objectively defined risks may be worth taking. The following section turns to consider how interpersonal relationships expose individuals to risk, or opportunities for drug taking, yet are also important for developing an understanding of risk. Accounts of the decision making process are analysed from all interviewees. The significance of the attitudes, behaviours and drug status of significant others are examined to reveal the ways in which interpersonal relationships can facilitate and constrain decisions about drug taking.

The practice of pleasure: connecting and bonding with friends or strangers

The perception of pleasure, and how and where it is practised, or the context or setting in which drugs are taken form an essential element of the decision making process (see Shewan et al., 2000; Zinberg, 1984). Settings, and the people who are part of them, were crucial to the drug takers' decision making. For example, none discussed occasions when they decided to take ecstasy at home alone, however, many said they would choose to take it with friends when they were in a club. This section focuses on how some of the effects interviewees described in Chapter Three were important for making decisions about drugs in particular contexts. Drug taking and the practice of pleasure occurred in a variety of settings: at home, in clubs, pubs and bars. When drug takers discussed their reasons for taking, for instance, ecstasy, many reported how the pleasurable physiological sensations experienced after taking it are heightened in some of these more lively and vibrant environments. They also perceived transformative effects (see Duff, 2008) and described how increased energy facilitated dancing in a club until the following morning and how good nights out with friends taking ecstasy generated pleasurable emotional experiences and memories (see Malbon, 1999). Two main effects perceived after taking drugs, lowered inhibitions and increased confidence, and the pleasures associated with them are explored in this section.[2] These effects facilitated connecting or bonding with friends or strangers (see also Aldridge et al., 2011; Duff, 2008). Primarily, this was achieved through having a laugh, meaningful or 'fucked up' conversations, and flirting or sexual encounters.

Having a laugh

Drug takers described a whole host of occasions when they had a laugh with friends when taking drugs. These situations were associated with both stimulant drugs and smoking cannabis: drugs which were perceived to lower inhibitions and sometimes increase confidence. Natalie recounted a specific occasion which initiated laughter with her friends:

> ... when I was living with all those lads, we'd all been smoking cannabis and then suddenly one of them disappeared into the kitchen and he came back with a saucepan on his head pretending to be a Dalek, which was actually quite funny at the time. [...] it was so funny and of course it is not funny looking back on it now, but at the time we were just crying with laughter.
>
> (interview at age 22)

The disinhibiting effects of drugs were perceived to facilitate good times and laughter with friends or partners which might not have occurred if drugs had not been consumed.

Some drug takers also discussed how they felt more confident approaching strangers after taking drugs during nights out in clubs, pubs or bars. Lindsay particularly derived pleasure from having a laugh or banter with strangers. In her narrative, she described many instances involving poking fun at others. During her latest 'big session' taking cocaine, she met a celebrity in her local club whom she relentlessly reminded had failed to achieve success with his recent song in the music charts. She recalled:

> ... it was one of the best nights ever because we just ripped him from the minute we saw him till the minute we left. He was like talking about his clothes and we'd just take the piss out of him!
>
> (interview at age 28)

It was clear from the interviewees' accounts that pleasure arose not only from the effects of drugs, but the situations in which they were taken and the people they took them with. In many cases, these resulted in fun, bonding and memorable experiences with friends or strangers which informed their future decision making. As Pilkington (2007) argues, having fun or the 'group vibe' provides a motive for drug taking.

Profound, meaningful and 'fucked up' conversations

A further way bonds were established with friends or strangers was through sharing points of view or past experiences when taking drugs together. Duff (2008) describes this as opening up to another person. Drug takers particularly discussed this in relation to ecstasy, a drug known for its empathogenic effects, or amphetamines. In-depth and meaningful conversations with others were facilitated after taking these drugs. These conversations could occur whilst clubbing, or in other settings where drugs were taken, and often at post-clubbing parties. The following narrative from Natasha paints a vivid picture of this pleasurable bonding experience:

Straight, non-drug-taking people, people who've never had a pill and experienced what that is actually like, to have a fucked up conversation when you're on whizz. To have a conversation, and you'll know what I mean, the 'When I was two conversation', when you tell the whole person what happened in your life from your first memory to your last. And you fit it in and they do not move. They go to the toilet and you follow them and sit on the other side of the door ' ... and this happened and that happened ... ' and you can't shut up. Everyone's done it and everyone's been on the receiving end of it and you've loved every minute of it! And it's just, people can't understand that and that's a shame because I think you find out more about humanity.
[...]
People really don't get it and it's a shame because I think it makes you more in touch with who you are because you're given the opportunity to be honest with yourself in an environment like that. 'Cos you're actually being honest with another person and you're saying things that you think, 'Oh, I didn't know that about myself, I actually would do that'. And you're kind of like having this self-realizing thing, probably because your inhibitions are like way down here, so you're allowing yourself what it would be like to do this or that and you find out so much about yourself.
[...]
And we've found out so much about each other, after all these years he [her partner, Rick] makes me piss when he's on pills and on ketamine.
Yeah.
It's so funny, I'm finding out new things about him all the time. We sit and have a conversation and it's like, 'Oh really would you do? Mmm'. And it's wonderful to be able to have that freedom to express your deepest, darkest secrets or say something completely off the wall and other people just go, 'That's funny!'.

(interview at age 28)

Natasha's and other interviewees' accounts emphasize the pleasure gained from social interactions during a drug taking episode. Opening up to another person about experiences, attitudes and beliefs facilitated connecting with others and was presented as an enjoyable element of drug taking. Some drug takers established intimate relationships with other drug takers, and as Natasha's narrative highlights, taking drugs together can strengthen bonds (see Rhodes and Quirk, 1998). Even if social interactions after taking drugs are not always meaningful, interviewees discussed how pleasure is associated with 'fucked up' or messy conversations which lose their thread or have no profound message. Conversations after taking drugs can, as Malbon (1999) argues, permit drug takers to experience others in ways they would not in everyday life. Duff (2008), however, notes that pleasure is related not only in connecting with friends or strangers through social interactions, but with the self. Natasha's narrative provides evidence for this when she describes how taking drugs can allow drug takers to instigate an assessment of alternative perspectives which, in turn, can lead to a greater understanding of the self. In this regard, it can be said drug takers are learning about the world through drugs (Jackson, 2004).

Taking drugs and the profound, meaningful or 'fucked up' conversations which may take place during a drug taking episode can provoke an enjoyable voyage of self discovery: one in which drug takers consider different viewpoints. Meaningful or 'fucked up' conversations which were perceived to occur because of the disinhibiting effects of drugs, when taken in particular settings, facilitate deep connections with friends or strangers which provide motivations for future drug taking.

Flirting and sexual encounters

Bonding was facilitated further by the lowering of sexual inhibitions, usually after taking stimulant drugs. The connection between drug taking, clubbing, sexuality and sexual desire, and how ecstasy, in particular, can lower sexual inhibitions, has been documented (see Henderson, 1996; Hutton, 2006; Jackson, 2004; Saunders, 1997). A common refrain from ecstasy takers is they feel 'loved up', 'huggy' or tactile after taking it. The drug takers in this study often described flirting or sexual encounters in various settings as pleasurable experiences associated with their stimulant drug taking. Many talked of flirting with others during nights clubbing whilst dancing close to other clubbers; others recounted light-hearted flirty conversations with fellow drug takers. In these instances, drug takers felt they were connecting and bonding with others and the drug taking experience was generally enhanced by this behaviour.[3] Interviewees also described pleasurable sexual encounters after taking drugs. In this respect, some discussed how taking drugs facilitated sexual exploration which resulted in pleasurable experiences.

Natasha's narrative provides an illustration of how the effects of drugs and the settings in which they are taken can facilitate flirting and sexual encounters. In her early twenties, she started to explore alternative facets of her sexuality. In an 'open' relationship with her husband, she began to seek sex encounters with other women, some she met on the clubbing scene:

> ... I met Beth and I groomed Beth.
> [...]
> Pretty girl, but I thought, 'Ok, I'm a reasonably attractive woman when I go out so if I try and show I'm interested, I'm pretty much going to get in there'. So we were snogging a bit and blah, blah, it took me two and a half months to actually sort her out. So we ended up chilling out back here [on Sunday morning]. That was that night that we carried on [taking drugs] until Monday. Everyone went to bed, Rick went to bed, and me and Beth sat up all night and chatted.
> **Yeah.**

And it kind of like got to the stage like we were kissing a bit and then we were waiting for Rick to go to work. Then we went upstairs and [had sex] all day Monday, eight hours, Oh My God, eight hours!
Wow!
It was unbelievable, it was very good!

(interview at age 28)

Going out clubbing and taking drugs provided drug takers, like Natasha, with opportunities to meet others for sexual encounters, if they desired. This was further assisted by feeling less inhibited after taking drugs and, in turn, confident in approaching or becoming intimate with others. Some particularly referred to the 'loved up' effects they experienced after taking ecstasy as essential for making sexual connections with others. Nevertheless, although pleasure was associated with flirting or sexual encounters after taking stimulant drugs in various settings, few identified it as providing a motive for future drug taking. Those who did, discussed how they occasionally chose to take drugs to enrich sexual experiences. They described how the sensations experienced during sex are heightened after taking drugs like ecstasy or amphetamines: 'Sex was fantastic that night, it always is when you're on whizz [amphetamines], fantastic!' (Natasha, interview at age 22).

Group membership

The narratives presented so far have demonstrated how drug takers described enjoyable social or sexual encounters which occurred with others after taking drugs and facilitated bonding. Bonding or connecting with others also appeared to have another function: feeling part of a group, a sense of belonging or identity. It has been argued one of the pleasures derived from clubbing and taking drugs is being part of the crowd (Hutton, 2006; Jackson, 2004; Malbon, 1999). For Malbon (1999: 182) clubbing has 'more to do with belongings and the establishment of identifications' than distinctions. Similarly, Becker (1963) observed how the subcultural setting generated a sense of identity akin to others in the group. As a consequence of the settings in which drugs were taken and, for instance, having a laugh, striking up conversations or flirting with others, drug takers in this study sometimes formed new friendship groups with strong ties. For some, these new friendship groups or drug takers present in a collective sense, for example in clubs, provided a sense of belonging, group membership and ultimately identity.

Natasha described the sense of unity amongst drug takers, even with strangers, she experiences in a club setting:

It's like a club that you're all members and because you're a member it doesn't matter whether you're a stranger or not, I know you're a member so you've got to be all right. And so you can meet randoms [new people] and have conversations and feel safe ...

(interview at age 28)

It has been noted how the clubbing scene embodies feelings of togetherness or unity (Hinchliff, 2001; Malbon, 1999). Interviewees who had taken drugs and frequented clubs described a similar sense of community. As Natasha's account highlights, many perceived themselves and other clubbers as alike which perhaps reaffirmed their sense of identity in this context. Consequently, because of this belief and the disinhibiting effects of drugs, they may have been more willing to interact with strangers and, in turn, perceived pleasurable outcomes, for example, enjoying dancing or chatting with others. As Malbon (1999) suggests, the practice of clubbing involves affiliation with others.

For others, being part of a group of drug takers, whether or not they are connected to the clubbing scene, generated a sense of belonging:

> For me, as well, I mean, particularly when I went to uni, not so much now, I was really shy. And it was a kind of, not being accepted, but if, if you were kind of like, 'No, I would never take drugs' you were kind of seen as a bit judgemental and it would be like, 'Oh God don't invite her again!'. *Yeah.*
> Whereas, if you were more willing, not to say that you would try every-thing, but if you kind of were seen to be well ... you don't mind if someone, if people do things in front of you, or whatever, you were accepted into the different groups that there were.
>
> (Vicky, interview at age 28)

Similarly, Jan recalled how smoking cannabis in the past made her feel as if she belonged to a group:

> I didn't enjoy it [smoking cannabis] when I was in school, when I was just trying it. But, at uni I sort of found it very relaxing and, you know, sort of joining in this little group who would all like smoke and it was quite nice and civilized.
>
> (interview at age 28)

Being part of a drug taking group, whether it is a group of friends, or a larger collective and anonymous group like clubbers, can be viewed as a source of identity, providing drug takers with a sense of belonging, acceptance and being like others which further influences their ongoing decisions about drug taking.

The significance of the practice of pleasure for drug taking decisions

So far, some of the contextual pleasures associated with the practice of taking drugs have been outlined. Pleasure is derived not only from the effects of drugs, but the behaviour which transpires during a drug taking episode, the people who are present and the setting in which drug taking occurs. Appreciating this points to the significance of setting when making decisions about drugs (see Hunt et al., 2007; Moore and Measham, 2008; Shewan et al., 2000;

Zinberg, 1984). For example, the drug takers frequently chose to take ecstasy in an appropriate dance club with friends, which they perceived to maximize pleasure and minimize harm. The fun and enjoyable events or situations in settings like these provide further reasons for continuing drug taking and are key elements of the decision making process. The positive effects and pleasures associated with the practice of drug taking often outweighed any perceived negative effects. Nevertheless, as Jackson (2004) has argued, in many circumstances, drugs heighten pleasure, but in others they may ultimately quash it. A consideration of the ways in which the positive effects, already discussed in this chapter, can also be perceived as negative in certain settings, and lead to decisions to change patterns of drug taking, will now be sketched out.

What were described as enjoyable effects leading to pleasurable experiences in specific settings by some interviewees, were by others, in the cold light of day, defined as negative and became reasons for not taking individual drugs or considering reducing the frequency of drug taking. Risk was, therefore, also connected to the situations in which drugs were taken, the behaviour which transpired and the negative reaction of others to it. The following two accounts further highlight the ways in which people within a setting, and the behaviour which occurs after taking drugs, influence future decision making.

Dean discussed how after taking ecstasy he had oral sex with a male friend:

I remember you said that you weren't going to try pills.
No, no, I did and they were all right.
(Laughter)
I took too many, I started doing some strange things with the same sex.
[…]
It [ecstasy] give me a euphoric feeling and homosexual feelings as well.
Yeah?
Mmm, definitely.
And did you act on them?
Yeah, I didn't actually have full sex with anyone, but I had oral sex and snogging and stuff with one of me mates and that's it. I don't think I would have done that if I weren't taking ecstasy.
Yeah.
'Cos you all feel loved up and everything's quite nice and you're getting quite close aren't you? That's what it was!
(Laughter)
Yeah.
So I've not done any of that since.
(Laughter)
And how were you and your mate after?
Oh no problems.
Yeah.
Just laughed about it, innit?
Yeah.

Just a laugh. Nothing too serious, I think we both know that we're not gays. It's just something to do, very funny!

(interview at age 28)

As noted earlier, feeling 'loved up', affectionate and tactile are effects many drug takers experience after taking ecstasy and are often described as positive. However, as Dean's narrative suggests, effects like these can lead to an unintended sexual encounter or, as the following account from Stacey illustrates, inappropriate flirting.

A few weeks prior to her latest interview at age 28, Stacey made sexual advances towards an ex-boyfriend after taking ecstasy:

No, it's [ecstasy] made me feel very regretful and I've said things to people that I shouldn't have said things to people. And I met one of my very first boyfriends who was 16 and I was 16 and now we're both grown up and I just embarrassed myself, off my head in front of him
[...]
But, it was drugs. I thought I loved him, I'd not even kissed him, but I thought I loved him.
(Laughter)
I went, 'I love you!', he went, 'What?!'. But, I wasn't saying it in a loving way, I was just saying, 'Ah, I love you' 'cos you just love everyone don't you? And he thinks I love him, love him, and he's gone and told half of the people that I love him.
Yeah.
(Laughter)
Oh God! I've embarrassed myself.

(interview at age 28)

For Dean and Stacey it is the behaviour described in their accounts which occurs after taking ecstasy which they regret. The effects they perceived after taking it were identified by them as fundamental to their subsequent actions. Whilst, in the moment, they may have enjoyed what was happening, it seems that the potential or actual reaction of others led them to question it later. Dean was in a long-term, straight relationship and it appeared he did not want to pursue a sexual relationship with his friend. His rejection of the idea that he might be 'gay' confirms this. Whilst he dismissed the event as 'nothing too serious', significantly, he had not taken ecstasy since. Stacey appeared to be embarrassed because her ex-boyfriend had rejected her advances and also told her friends what she had said. For this reason, she was considering whether she wanted to continue clubbing and taking ecstasy. These narratives again illustrate how drug takers perceive risk and pleasure differently. Moreover, positive effects can be interpreted as negative when the setting or people they are taken with are considered. In certain settings or situations, the same pleasurable effects of drugs that for some were influential in continuing drug taking journeys, were perceived by others to lead to negative encounters and informed future decisions to moderate drug taking or completely desist.

The role of social relationships for decisions about drugs

The first part of this chapter has largely explored how pleasure is practised in and derived from the settings in which drugs are taken. This section returns to examine the other side of the coin: risk. Following Douglas, the argument presented here suggests that interpersonal relationships form the cultural context in which the pleasures and harms we perceive are shaped and are, therefore, important locations for knowledge and decisions about risk. It has been noted how social relationships can both facilitate and constrain decisions about drugs (Abbott-Chapman and Denholm, 2001; Knowlton et al., 1998; Miller and Neaigus, 2001; Pilkington, 2007; Rhodes and Quirk, 1998). Appreciating the significance of social relationships when making decisions about drug taking highlights the importance of the behaviour and attitudes of others when learning about risk (see Tulloch and Lupton, 2003). As we will see, the drug status and attitudes of individuals involved in these relationships are pertinent (see Aldridge et al., 2011; Williams, 2007). Furthermore, it is argued that social relationships are not only a source of understandings about risk, they also subject or expose individuals to risk (Pilkington, 2007; Rhodes and Quirk, 1998). It is, therefore, important to understand how particular relationships provide opportunities to engage with risk, or drug taking, and, in turn, influence risk, or drug taking, behaviour. Whilst social relationships may expose us to risk, Rhodes and Quirk (1998) also suggest that drug taking subjects social relationships to risk. Both aspects of risk will be explored in this section of the chapter. The social relationships which will be examined focus on the family, friends and intimate partners. This section begins by outlining how these interpersonal relationships can either restrict or provide opportunities for drug taking. It goes on to explore the social meanings interviewees attach to the behaviour and attitudes of those around them when making decisions about drugs, and in the case of drug takers, their initial drug taking decisions. Finally, the role of social relationships for ongoing drug journeys is considered.

Exposure to risk or drug taking

Exploring the cultural context which influences understandings of risk, or drug taking, the narratives of drug abstainers in this study indicate they were less likely to be exposed to pro-drug attitudes and drug taking behaviour compared to drug takers because of the nature of their relationships. Fundamental to exposure to drug taking are relationships with other drug takers. It has been argued that drug abstainers are more likely to have friends who do not take drugs (Kandel, 1985). Although drug abstainers in this study did know people who took drugs, their main friendship groups, the people they predominantly spent their leisure time with, were drug abstinent.[4] Helen described her friends at age 22: 'Normally most of the people that I hang around with just aren't interested in drugs.' Similarly, none of the drug abstainers had established an intimate relationship with a drug taker and only one divulged that close family members were drug takers.[5]

In contrast, drug takers are more likely to be exposed to pro-drug attitudes and drug taking behaviour via their social relationships (Abbott-Chapman and Denholm, 2001; Aldridge et al., 2011; Knowlton et al., 1998; Parker et al., 2002; Pilkington, 2007; Rhodes and Quirk, 1998). The friendship group, for example, is a primary source of supply and contact with drugs (Aldridge et al., 2011; Measham et al., 2001; Pilkington, 2007). A common refrain from the current drug takers throughout the study was that all or many of their friends took drugs. In addition, drug takers reported they had siblings or parents who were drug experienced and many had also established intimate relationships with drug takers. An appreciation of how different cultural groups generated by social relationships form an essential foundation for the creation of understandings and meanings of risk and pleasure and, therefore, influence the decision making process, follows.

The meanings attached to the attitudes and behaviours of significant others when making decisions about drug taking

Being exposed to different attitudes and behaviours towards drug taking can partially explain decisions about drug taking; what is significant, however, is how such attitudes and behaviours are interpreted and incorporated into the decision making process. Rhodes and Quirk (1998) suggest that analysing social relationships permits us to understand how risk is socially organized through the meanings attached to the behaviours witnessed in this context. In this section, the ways in which the attitudes and behaviours of significant others inform the decision making process will be outlined. As we shall see, they can either facilitate or constrain decisions about drug taking.

As noted already, the three main social relationships which featured in the lives of drug abstainers rarely provided them with contact with drug takers. Furthermore, many discussed how their friends, partners or family members held anti-drugs attitudes which influenced their decisions not to take drugs. Family relationships were particularly important in this respect, not only for drug abstainers, but some drug takers too. Indeed, the family has been identified as a key reference point when making decisions about drugs (Abbott-Chapman and Denholm, 2001) and parental attitudes can constrain drug taking behaviour (Knowlton et al., 1998). Claire, a drug abstainer, exemplifies this here when she confirms: 'My whole family are against it [drugs]' (interview at age 22). She presented her mother as unambiguous in her disapproval of drug taking and recalled how her attitude had a lasting impact upon her decision not to try drugs:

Me Mum had us petrified [...] it was just, 'If you take drugs I will take you to the police station and you will be arrested and locked up for the rest of your life'. Too scared to ever think about taking drugs and that's just carried on.

(interview at age 28)

Other drug abstainers were also aware of their parents' disapproval of drug taking although, in some cases, their beliefs were less pronounced. Similarly, some drug takers' decision making was constrained by parental anti-drugs attitudes. Aware their parents disapproved of drug taking, some decided not to try specific drugs, like ecstasy, because of concerns about the risk of death associated with it and the media reporting of drug related deaths which might upset family members further.

Emotional and physical proximity to parents affected decisions about drug taking. Interviewees justified their decisions not to take drugs, or particular drugs, because they were emotionally 'close' to their parents. As Helen, a drug abstainer, explains, they were concerned about how choosing to take drugs might upset parents:

... just through chatting and that, you know, you get to know your parents' opinions and stuff. And I know they'd have been heartbroken, they'd have been absolutely devastated if they, you know, if anything happened to me or my brother or sister, for instance, because we'd taken drugs or say they knew we were taking them, you know, they'd be gutted. And I just, you know, I think because of that and because I'm close to my parents then it does have a big influence on you, definitely.

(interview at age 28)

For some drug takers, physical proximity to parents became significant when they returned to live in the family home after graduating from university. Concerns that parents, who did not approve of drug taking, might discover they took drugs became an issue. Vicky returned to live with her parents after completing her degree and started to take cocaine with her friends at weekends. She recalls here how frequently she would arrive home at dawn and sleep until the afternoon:

I just felt like really, well not ashamed, well yeah, ashamed I suppose.
Yeah.
'Cos you just think 'I don't want to tell them what I'm doing' and then you just think, 'If I don't want to tell them what I'm doing then it's obviously not right is it, if you feel embarrassed'. It's not like saying, 'Oh God, I went out and had too much to drink!' and they go, 'Oh, don't do it next week' or something, it's just quite bad.

(interview at age 28)

The narratives of the interviewees suggest they were plainly worried about upsetting significant others and they perceived negative consequences would occur to their relationships not only with family, but friends or partners, if they decided to take drugs. Carl, a drug abstainer, described how he believed his friend would be troubled and respond negatively if he started to take drugs: '... my mate would probably kill me' (Carl, interview at age 28). Fears about worrying or distressing significant others formed a key part of some interviewees' assessment of drug taking and their reasons not to take any or individual drugs. The risk of disappointing friends, partners or family members was, at times, too great.

Whilst fears about upsetting significant others clearly played a role in the decision making process, shame may also have operated as a powerful tool of social control (see Braithwaite, 1989). The problem, as Braithwaite (1993) has argued, is the proliferation of multiple identities in contemporary life which makes us susceptible to shame. In this regard, shame is generated by concern about a conflict between a drug taking identity and the 'good' image interviewees believe parents, friends or partners have of them. Appreciating the importance of shame helps us to understand why drug abstainers choose not to take drugs and some drug takers, as Vicky's narrative above highlights, decide, when living at home with parents, to stop taking drugs or to considerably reduce how often they take them. Examining social relationships in this way powerfully illustrates how individuals hold each other, implicitly or explicitly, emotionally, mutually and culturally accountable (see Douglas, 1992; Pilkington, 2007) and, in doing so, banish the threat of drug taking, and all its perceived negative consequences, from their lives.

In contrast to the narratives of drug abstainers, drug takers generally described how they were frequently exposed to pro-drug attitudes and behaviours in the context of their social relationships. As noted earlier, many of their friends and intimate partners were drug takers. Some also had family members who were drug experienced and parents' attitudes towards drugs were often described as liberal.[6] These pro-drug attitudes and behaviours facilitated the decision making process and initial decisions to take drugs or try different drugs. In the context of some social relationships, drug taking appeared to be normalized or socially accommodated (see Aldridge et al., 2011; Williams, 2007). Many noted how within their friendship groups, for instance, drug taking seemed to be 'normal', as Vicky explained: 'I went to uni and then everyone, it was quite normal to be smoking it [cannabis] a lot' (interview at age 28). Crawshaw (2004) argues that when drug taking is normalized within a particular social group, decisions to take drugs make sense. Normalization of drug taking within social relationships or exposure to pro-drug attitudes and behaviour only partly explains why decisions to take drugs are made. The accounts from the drug takers emphasize the significance of witnessing the behaviour of drug takers and how trust and reassurance are also important for making decisions about drug taking in this context.

Tulloch and Lupton (2003) contend understandings of risk are formulated upon observation of the behaviour of others around us. Drug normalization within many social relationships provided potential drug takers with the opportunity to witness or hear stories about drug taking which, in turn, influenced their own attitudes and decision making. Vicky decided to try cannabis for the first time with her boyfriend who had been smoking it regularly for some time in her company. She explained: 'I think I kind of saw that [cannabis], as it's not as bad' (interview at age 28). Dean, who was aware his father smoked cannabis daily, discussed how it influenced his perception of it: 'I've known me Dad has always smoked it and he seemed all right. […] I didn't think there was any major danger' (interview at age 22). Witnessing or knowing about the drug taking behaviour of others influenced potential drug takers' own opinions. Perceiving drug takers as 'all right' featured in other interviewees' narratives:

> … you think, 'Well, they're all right so I'll try it', you know.
> […]
> And the more you were accepted and trusting people about, and actually saying, 'Oh, they're all right', then, I suppose it's a bit stupid really, but you think, 'Oh, I'll be all right, I'll have a go'.
> […]
> As I say, you think, 'Well this isn't dangerous', or 'I can be a bit more adventurous in what you're trying'.
>
> (Vicky, interview at age 28)

Assessing other drug takers as 'all right', or one might say their behaviour as 'low risk', was significant for the decision making of interviewees who were considering trying a drug for the first time. Because no major negative effects from drug taking were observed in those they were close to, drug taking was viewed as an acceptable activity which does not cause considerable harm, or certain drugs were no longer perceived as harmful, and, therefore, they could contemplate trying them.

As well as observing drug taking behaviour, as Vicky's account refers to above, trust in the context of social relationships was also an important element of the decision making process. The significance of trust for decisions about drugs has been acknowledged (see Hunt et al., 2007; Murnane et al., 2000; Pilkington, 2007; Shewan et al., 2000). Drug takers recounted that when they initially tried drugs, they did so with others they trusted: 'I thought about it first and did it with people I trusted' (Natasha, interview at age 22). In this way, social relationships provide a secure and trusting environment in which to take drugs (see Pilkington, 2007). As Becker (1963) observed in relation to a drug taking subculture, members of the group provided advice and reassurance about drugs. Similarly, friends and partners who were drug experienced were also described as important and trusted sources of information about the effects of drugs, how to take them and how much to take, and often reassured drug takers about their decision making. For example, in Chapter Three, Kate described how she decided to stop taking amphetamines daily when she experienced severe effects to her health and well-being. However, despite this, she decided to try them again a few years later. This decision was not taken lightly and she recalled she was concerned she may become 'addicted' again. She discussed how her long-term intimate partner, Justin, appeased her fears:

> ... because it was such a relaxed thing, it wasn't pushed on me or pressured, 'Oh you've got to have this because I'm having it'. I think it was put across in a way, 'Would you like to have a bit? You know, if you don't want to, that's fine. You know, if you don't feel comfortable, that's okay. You know, but if you would like to, you know, we'll get some in'. So I was sort of like, 'Oh, I don't know really, I'm a bit worried because, you know, if I do take it, will I want some more? And, you know, will I end up going down that same road?' And he was like, 'No, no you won't, don't be silly, because it's only a bit and, you know, it's not on the same par as what you were doing before'.
>
> (interview at age 28)

After deciding to try amphetamines again with Justin, Kate continued to take them a few times a year.

Whilst some drug takers discussed how they sought detailed advice and reassurance from friends or partners before trying drugs, for others this was not always the case. In these circumstances, when unexpected opportunities to try new drugs arose, decision making did not appear to entail a process in which detailed information about drugs was gathered and reflexively assessed. Rather, an on-the-spot decision was made. Another extract from Kate's narrative further illustrates this decision making process. She first tried cocaine, with friends, as a teenager:

> I'd never done coke before. I said, 'Well, what's that?', and she said, 'Oh, it's coke'. And I went, 'Ooh, God, heavy. No I can't have none of that'. And they were like, 'Oh, it's all right, it's only coke, you know'. I said, 'Oh, all right then, ok, I'll have a go and see'. And I snorted it and I had a really good night ...
>
> (interview at age 28)

Accounts like these point to the significance of trust when making decisions to take drugs. The two extracts from Kate's narrative illustrate how the extent of information and advice which drug takers obtain from their drug experienced friends or partners can vary. The only information which Kate received from her friends about cocaine, a drug she viewed as 'heavy', was that 'it's all right, it's only coke'. Such accounts suggest trust, which is the foundation of and infuses most social relationships, extends to decisions to take drugs in the absence of detailed advice from friends or intimate partners (see also Pilkington, 2007).

It can be argued then, at times, decisions to take drugs do not involve a reflexive assessment of the costs and benefits based on information gained from socially situated sources or in combination with official sources of advice. It also appears decisions to try some drugs were sometimes inevitable when drug taking was socially accommodated and practised by family, friends or partners. Dean described when he first tried cannabis: '... my mate came round one night and he smoked it before me and I ended up doing it' (interview at age 22). What may also underpin decisions like these is a perception that taking drugs with others is an act of being sociable. Pilkington (2007) describes this as 'companionship' within the friendship group. Some interviewees' narratives did allude to this feature of their decision making: '... if it's seen to be more sociable and acceptable in the group that you were with I was supposedly more easily led into either trying it or having some' (Vicky, interview at age 28).

The narratives presented from the interviewees effectively illustrate the significance of social relationships for the decision making process and how emotional, cultural and mutual accountability operates to facilitate or constrain it. The drug status of significant others and trust which imbues interpersonal relationships are important in this regard. These themes re-occur in the following section. Having considered how social relationships influence initial decisions to take drugs, an assessment of their influence upon ongoing drug journeys follows.

The social and cultural influences upon drug journeys

In this section, the ways in which social relationships influence patterns of drug taking will be examined. In this respect, the different drugs interviewees take, how often they take them and how much they take will be compared to the drug taking behaviour of significant others. Rhodes and Quirk (1998: 157) argue: 'Risk behaviour is not simply the outcome of individuals' knowledge, beliefs and behaviours, but is influenced by interpersonal interactions with others which take place in the context of ongoing social relationships.' It is, therefore, also crucial to assess how changing social relationships impact upon the decision making process. Furthermore, the ways in which social relationships place individuals *at* risk of drug taking, and also subject *to* risks from drug taking, will be explored.

Deciding which drugs to try and to continue to take, for many interviewees, was largely influenced by the behaviour and attitudes of friends or partners. Some reported they had very similar drug taking repertoires. Symmetry was not, however, always the norm. Stacey, for instance, spent time with friends who smoked cannabis after clubbing and taking ecstasy, but she did not smoke it herself. Lindsay's friends took ecstasy and ketamine, but she refused to try them. In these circumstances, an individualized, cognitive health and well-being cost-benefit assessment was employed in which negative effects were perceived to outweigh potential pleasure. This suggests decisions about drugs are not solely intersubjective or based upon socially situated gained knowledge. The drug takers also have their own limits and lines they will not cross, typically informed by 'expert' or official sources of knowledge.

Some drug takers also discussed how they took drugs as frequently, or as many drugs, as friends or partners. It is likely this involved some matching of patterns of drug taking. In their study of the sexual relationships of heroin users, Rhodes and Quirk (1998) argue relationships between two heroin users result in patterns of drug taking becoming equal: generally, one partner increases their consumption to match another's. There was some evidence to support this contention, particularly from the narratives of female drug takers. Stacey stopped taking stimulant drugs when she was aged 21 and pregnant with her daughter, Chloe. Some time after the birth of Chloe, she started to occasionally take stimulant drugs again. When Chloe was three years old, Stacey recommenced her relationship with Jon, Chloe's father, and she began taking cocaine with him. On reflection, she felt she was taking it more often than she wanted to:

> I think Chloe was about three and a half, I was taking it quite, quite often. But, not 'cos I wanted to take it, it was because he had it and he'd come in on a Monday after the weekend, after he'd been hammering it all weekend, and he'd come in on a Monday and say, 'I need ...' and it wasn't just a thin line, it was big thick chunks ...

> (interview at age 28)

Other female drug takers also discussed how the frequency and quantities of their drug taking increased during the course of an intimate relationship with a drug taker. The drug status of a partner, and the frequency and quantities of their consumption, were important in this regard. Emotional, cultural and mutual accountability can also begin to offer an explanation for this: female drug takers may have felt an obligation to their partners to take drugs with them. Moreover, decisions about drugs can be understood as potentially threatening the stability or continuity of sexual relationships (see Rhodes and Quirk, 1998). As we saw earlier, drug abstainers and some drug takers were concerned that decisions to take drugs would upset others with whom they had valued interpersonal relationships. Conversely, female drug takers, whose consumption began to match their intimate partners, may have perceived that refusing to take drugs placed the continuity of their intimate relationship at risk. Rhodes and Quirk caution there may be difficulty in reducing or stopping drug taking when it is perceived to jeopardize the foundation of sexual relationships.

Whilst there appeared to be matching in patterns of drug taking for some interviewees in the context of their social relationships, others discussed how some social relationships with drug takers led them to moderate the frequency of their consumption. This occurred when friends or partners began to reduce how often they took drugs. Although Dean suggested in Chapter Three that he decided to decrease how frequently he smoked cannabis because he perceived he was suffering from paranoia when he smoked it, he also discussed how some of his friends, at the same time, were reducing how often they smoked it: 'We've all kind of just stopped smoking as much' (interview at age 28). Others also noted how decreases in their friends' drug taking influenced their own drug journeys: ' ... other friends are changing at the same time, where we're just all going, "Oh, I couldn't be arsed"' (Lindsay, interview at age 28). Vicky offered an explanation for why her friends were moderating their drug taking in their mid-twenties:

> ... they were slowing down as well.
> **Yeah.**
> I think one of them had, 'cos they were a bit older than us, one of them had a baby and then a couple got married, it was just a gradual, you know, everyone moved on with their life.[7]
>
> (interview at age 28)

The 'slowing down' of drug taking in the context of social relationships may provoke reflexivity for some drug takers and lead them to question their own behaviour. The drug status of friends or partners is significant again. As it changes, and friends or partners begin to take drugs less frequently, opportunities for drug taking become limited and it might be perceived as no longer socially accommodated.

We have seen how various social relationships with drug takers influence decisions about drugs and it is clear they are significant for the decision making process. Earlier, it was noted how drug takers are more likely to have contact with drug takers via their social relationships, compared with drug abstainers. Nevertheless, it was apparent that as friendships and intimate relationships changed, because, for example, of changes in location or an intimate relationship had run its course, so did opportunities for drug taking, or, to put it another way, exposure to 'risk'. This, in turn, affected interviewees' decisions to take drugs and the course of their drug journeys. Access to or opportunities to take drugs became greater from adolescence into the early twenties when drug takers reported knowing more drug takers. In addition, intimate partners became an important source for drugs in adulthood, particularly for female drug takers (Aldridge et al., 2011; Williams, 2007). Despite greater access, interviewees also noted it was sometimes sporadic and had become limited by their late twenties. The following account from Lindsay provides an illustration of the intermittent nature of drugs availability and, for this reason, how drug journeys can start, stop and start again throughout the life course. As we will see, at times, decisions to stop or start taking drugs occur by chance rather than a purposeful decision based upon an assessment of risk.[8]

Lindsay suggested her decisions and opportunities to take cocaine were influenced by the friends she spent time with and also her intimate partners:

> Yeah it's who you're with, who I'm with at the time or what the person's like, you know, some people can go 'Oh shall we get a bag [of cocaine]?', 'Yeah why not?' So I think it does depend on who you're with.
>
> (interview at age 28)

At age 18, she tried cocaine for the first time with a partner who was taking it regularly. A year later, she began a four year relationship with Graham with whom she had a son called Lloyd. During this period, she did not take drugs, as she recalled: 'He's [Graham's] never seen drugs or, he doesn't know what they do, he's very naïve about drugs' (interview at age 22). Once this relationship ended and Lindsay subsequently began another relationship with someone who took cocaine, she started taking it again:

> ... after I left Lloyd's Dad ... oh that was it, I started seeing, briefly seeing some guy who was kind of like, you know, 'Here you are, we'll have a line'. And then the next thing, you know, it was like, 'Oh, we're staying in and having a couple of lines' and things like that. So it slowly got me back into it.
>
> (interview at age 28)

Lindsay stopped taking cocaine when this relationship ended and she began a relationship with a non-drug taker. Her next relationship was with another cocaine user and she started taking it regularly again:

> And like I started going out with a guy who was, this guy was snorting, he used to snort coke to go to work in the morning. So that's when, you know, it was kind of like every night we'd sit there, I'd put Lloyd to bed and we'd all get off our faces and then take Lloyd to nursery the next day and it went on like that for quite a few months.
>
> (interview at age 28)

At the time of her latest interview, when she was age 28, Lindsay was again living with a partner who was a non-drug taker, but she also took cocaine a couple of times per year with friends.

Narratives like Lindsay's demonstrate how opportunities to take drugs can change throughout the life course. Changes in social relationships and who interviewees spend their time with led, in some cases, to decisions to take drugs influenced, as we have seen, by the drug status and behaviour of significant others, and, in other cases, limited their access to drugs. Rhodes and Quirk (1998) argue re-initiation into drug taking is a risk associated with sexual relationships in which a drug taking partner influences a non-drug taking partner to recommence drug taking or try different drugs. Lindsay's narrative, as did other female interviewees, provided evidence for re-initiation in this context and some also discussed how they tried a drug for the first time with an intimate partner. Importantly, in respect of re-initiation, drug takers did not purposefully seek out relationships with other drug takers in order to continue their drug journeys; rather, these relationships occurred by chance. However, intimate relationships with drug takers were no doubt sustained and cultivated by similar attitudes towards drug taking. In respect of temporary drug desistance, when a social relationship with a drug taker ended, the decision to continue drug journeys for many was taken out of their hands because they no longer had easy access to drugs. Decisions, in these circumstances, did not involve a reflexive risk assessment in which negative effects outweighed positive effects. Instead, desistance, like re-initiation, was contingent upon chance. The significance of chance chimes with the work of Biernacki (1986) who argues, in relation to heroin addiction, that desistance does not always occur because of a person's resolve. Rather, as they no longer have access to a social world involving drugs, because, for example, a partner is imprisoned or dies, they begin to associate with others who do not take drugs.

As Biernacki suggests, new relationships for drug takers with non-drug takers, particularly intimate partners, often influenced drug desistance. They constrained the decision making process further and reinforced desistance or moderation of drug taking, albeit in many cases, for the duration of a relationship. Again, Lindsay's narrative illuminates this process. By age 28, she was taking cocaine occasionally. She discussed how her current partner, Paul, a former stimulant drug taker, did not approve of her taking it. Because some of her friends took cocaine, it was still accessible to her and she continued to take it on special occasions. On one occasion, when Lindsay and Paul were out together, she was offered some by a friend. She stated: 'He went mad, you know, "We've changed. You shouldn't be, you shouldn't be!"' (interview at age 28). Negative attitudes expressed by an intimate partner, or sometimes close friends, again highlight the significance of emotional, mutual and cultural accountability for decisions about drug taking. Some drug takers perceived continuing to take drugs might threaten the stability of their intimate relationship and confessed they did not tell their non-drug taking partner when they occasionally took drugs with friends. Strategies such as non-disclosure serve to prioritize and protect the intimate relationship (Rhodes and Quirk, 1998). Perceptions of how continued drug taking might place these social relationships at risk were not unfounded. Drug abstainers, and some less experienced drug takers, reported they had terminated relationships because of the drug taking behaviour of intimate partners or friends. Accounts like these challenge the significance placed upon peer relationships in adolescence by early subcultural explanations (see, for example, Cloward and Ohlin, 1960) and highlight the role of intimate relationships for decision making in young adulthood.

Summary

The role of social and cultural influences upon the decision making process has been articulated in this chapter. Drawing on Douglas' cultural approach to understanding risk, the subjective meaning of risk which began to be described in Chapter Three and the lived experience of it have been appreciated within their cultural context. Rather than perceiving drug taking as a risky activity, we have seen how the effects experienced after taking drugs are enhanced or intensified in specific settings, or social or cultural groups, and the experience becomes even more pleasurable. Adopting a cultural perspective provides a different standpoint to agential or structural accounts. It also challenges a decontextualized risk assessment or cost-benefit approach which focuses only upon perceived physiological or psychological sensations when explaining decisions about drug taking. Recognizing the pleasurable practices which drug taking can facilitate permits us to understand the rewards and transformative effects associated with drugs or why some risks are worth taking (see Duff, 2008; Jackson, 2004; Mythen, 2004). As we have seen, the bonding experience facilitated by taking drugs generally enriched the lives of drug takers and was, therefore, an important consideration when making decisions to take drugs.

Embracing a cultural approach to understand risk also emphasizes how risk knowledge is situated and intersubjective knowledge and not wholly individualized. The social meaning of risk, or drug taking, is shaped by interactions with significant others. In this regard, the drug status of family, friends and partners is significant. Drug abstainers' decisions not to take drugs were influenced by friends, family or partners who were not drug experienced and held anti-drugs attitudes. In contrast, drug takers drew upon the experiences, and their observations, of their drug taking friends or partners when making decisions to take drugs. These sources of knowledge were perceived as trustworthy and reliable and these social relationships provided a safe environment in which to take drugs (see Pilkington, 2007; Rhodes and Quirk, 1998). The relationship between the decision making process and intersubjectivity can be further understood through what Douglas describes as emotional, mutual and cultural accountability. Both decisions to take drugs and decisions not to take them can be viewed as made from a sense of responsibility to significant others and prioritizing social relationships in the decision making process. In some ways, this could suggest that decisions to take drugs are a consequence of peer pressure. However, it is argued, as Pilkington (2007) suggests, decision making involves consensus, negotiation and disagreement. Indeed, the different patterns of drug taking within social and cultural groups indicate decisions to take drugs are not solely an intersubjective process or the result of peer pressure. Finally, the agency and rationality present in the risk assessor portrayed by Beck and Giddens and also associated with the cost-benefit approach is challenged by the accounts presented in this chapter. At times, unanticipated occasions to try new drugs presented themselves and an opportunity for a fully informed reflexive assessment of risk was not apparent. In these circumstances, trust and reassurance were highly significant.

The narratives of the interviewees also highlight how social relationships are not only sources of information and locations for the assessment of risk, they may also expose individuals to risk (see Pilkington, 2007; Rhodes and Quirk, 1998). Again, the drug status of individuals within interpersonal relationships is important. In some circumstances, female drug takers, in particular, were at risk of re-initiation into drug taking, taking drugs more frequently or more drugs than usual because they had established an intimate relationship with a drug taker. Emotional, mutual and cultural accountability again offers an explanation for their decision making. They may have felt obliged to take drugs with their partners or, as Rhodes and Quirk (1998) put it, choosing not to take drugs may have been perceived as placing their relationship at risk. Thinking about risk in this way, we can see how drug takers' social relationships with other drug takers, and those with non-drug takers, may be 'at risk' from drug taking. In this context, decision making is compelled by the very nature of these relationships. Whilst this suggests reflexivity is provoked by some social relationships, changing social relationships demonstrated how decision making does not always involve a reflexive assessment. Access to drugs and opportunities for drug taking changed during the life course. Decisions to take drugs or to desist from taking drugs were, at times, facilitated by chance and desistance was not always the outcome of individual resolve (see Biernacki, 1986) or reflexivity.

Through exploring the social and cultural influences upon decisions about drug taking, a different understanding of risk and how it is assessed is produced. The narratives from the interviewees emphasize the role of cultural settings or the context in which drug taking occurs when making decisions about drugs. Likewise, the importance of social relationships is apparent and in this respect challenges solely agential explanations. Whilst decision making, at times, undoubtedly involves an individualized assessment, it is also made by reference to significant others. In the following chapter, the theoretical framework is developed further by appreciating the role of agency, structure and changing situations when making drug taking decisions.

5 The journey to adulthood

I just think once you start working, you know, your body is a lot more tired, you've got a lot more responsibilities and you can't drink [or take drugs] to the same level. Nor do you want to because you've got to get up really early the next day. Whereas, when you're younger, at uni or, you know, you've not got the same pressures, have you, in life? So, you know, it's a lot easier. I think those changes sort of begin when you start working, and again when you get your own house.

(Helen, drug abstainer, interview at age 28)

With me job, I couldn't take a load of drugs over the weekend and then go working with [young people] during the week, it wouldn't be fair to them or me. So, I mean, I've got to think sort of, you've got to sort of be an adult about it all, haven't you really? I think 'No, don't be silly, for goodness sake!'

(Kate, current drug taker, interview at age 28)

Introduction

In the previous two chapters, the theoretical framework for exploring the decision making process in relation to drug taking outlined how it is a purposeful, meaningful and often pleasurable activity. Drug taking decisions, in one sense, involve an agential or individualistic cost-benefit approach, weighing up the perceived positive effects against the perceived negative effects. This, however, is only part of the story. When we appreciate the social or cultural situations in which drug taking occurs, various effects can lead to pleasurable encounters which are also important for decision making. Furthermore, the social or cultural groups in which interviewees are located also influence decisions about drug taking and opportunities to take them. In this respect, Chapter Four outlined how the attitudes and behaviours of friends, family and intimate partners are significant. The aim of this chapter is to develop the theoretical framework further by exploring the ways in which the transition to adulthood also shapes decision making.

Laub and Sampson (2003) argue structural turning points, such as full-time employment and marriage which can lead to parenthood, trigger desistance from crime. Accordingly, bonds are created with others which exert control over criminal behaviour, daily routines change, leaving less time to associate with criminal peers, a new way of life becomes a possibility and invested in, and agency or will is employed to resist future opportunities to commit crime and to continue in this new way of life. Desistance for Laub and Sampson is, in part, explained as occurring by chance rather than the outcome of an initial purposeful decision or action. The men in their study took advantage of structural turning points without primarily thinking about how they might impact upon their criminal careers.[1] In creating an explanatory framework for decision making, structural turning points like these are viewed as highly significant for influencing decisions about drug taking. Drawing on British youth transitions research (Coles, 1995; Furlong and Cartmel, 1997, 2007; MacDonald et al., 2001; Roberts, 1995), it is argued here that the three main transitions to adulthood, from school to work (or education to employment),[2] from dependent living to independent living and from family of origin to family of destination, interact with drug journeys and act as structural turning points (see Aldridge et al., 2011; Williams, 2007).[3] We should, however, be cautious not to overstate or simplify the impact of structural turning points or adult transitions. Delayed transitions to adulthood may facilitate drug taking (Williams and Parker, 2001) and we, therefore, might expect, as adult transitions are accomplished, recent drug taking to decline (see Shiner, 2009). Investment or attachment to the people, situations or circumstances which accompany adult transitions is, however, crucial. Hence, desistance is contingent upon the nature and quality of attachments (Rutter, 1996; West, 1982). Giordano et al. (2002) prudently advise that structural turning points act as 'hooks for change': they make change *possible*, but not *certain*. This important distinction demands that we pay sufficient attention to the complex relationship between agency and structure and the situations associated with them. Continuing to focus on how decision making may be structured, the significance of gender for drug taking decisions and transitions to adulthood will also be analysed in this chapter (see also Measham et al., 2011).

One final point to consider in relation to desistance is the construction of a new identity (see Laub and Sampson, 2003; Maruna, 2001). Although Laub and Sampson place less emphasis upon this and more upon structural turning points, with regard to drug taking, Biernacki (1986) argues that creating a new identity as a non-drug taker is essential and social settings and roles provide the material to achieve this. Contemplating how some drug takers control their consumption, Decorte (2001) emphasizes engagement with and a stake in different adult roles, and the identities they produce. Identity or multiple identities are, therefore, an important additional element to take into account when explaining decisions about drug taking.

Drugs researchers have explored the ways in which various adult roles impact upon rates of drug taking for some time (see Bachman and Johnston, 1978; Bachman et al., 1997; Johnston, 1974). It is argued, drug taking decreases as other aspects of a person's life demand more attention (see

Kandel, 1980; Vervaeke and Korf, 2006). Shiner (2009) has undertaken the most comprehensive recent assessment of the three main adult transitions and their effect upon rates of drug taking. Nevertheless, the quantitative approach he and many other researchers in this area employ can only take us so far in understanding the decision making process.[4] For example, Shiner demonstrates how drug desistance increases with the domestic transition (marriage and parenthood) and housing transition. However, the familiar problem with quantitative data is that it cannot tell us why, or how, desistance occurs or, to put it another way, what it is about the nature of transitions which are important for drug taking decisions.

The qualitative data presented in this chapter provides an illuminating account of how the interviewees negotiated their drug journeys in relation to their adult transitions.[5] In the remainder of this chapter the accounts from drug abstainers and drug takers, which explain why and how they made decisions about drug taking across the early part of the life course in relation to key transitions, are analysed. It begins with the three main adult transitions and outlines risk perceptions in relation to these and how drug taking is facilitated when adult transitions are not accomplished, and constrained when they are. Following on from this, the ways in which identity influences decisions about drug taking is considered. The final section offers a contrasting insight to deterministic structural explanations by highlighting how, despite accomplishing transitions to adulthood, some drug takers continue on their drug journeys.

The transition from education to employment

The transition from education to full-time employment was, for some interviewees, their first adult transition. For many, however, this did not occur until they completed further education courses or graduated from university, when they had already made the transition to independent living. By age 27, almost three-quarters (73.7 per cent) had made the transition to full-time employment (see Chapter One). Before outlining how this important adult transition influenced drug journeys, this section begins with a discussion of the ways in which drug taking was perceived as a risk to accomplishing it and, subsequently, outlines some of the risk management strategies adopted by drug takers.

Drug taking was identified as a risk to career progression and success by drug abstainers and some less experienced drug desisters. This was particularly a feature of the narratives of male interviewees which may reflect how some men construct their identity in relation to work (see Connell, 1987; Messerschmidt, 1993). These views were presented as a reason not to take drugs.[6] For some, the frequency of drug taking was significant. Gareth, a drug desister, who had tried ecstasy once and smoked cannabis occasionally, perceived daily drug taking as detrimental to a flourishing and thriving career:

I don't think there's major repercussions against smoking a joint unless you do it every single day.
Yeah.
If you do, you're not going to get much of a job and you're not going to have much of a life. It's something you do as a past-time, once a week or every so often, then so be it.

(interview at age 28)

These views about the frequency of drug taking and its effect on careers were also expressed by a few drug takers. In addition, the effects of some drugs, for example, feeling unmotivated after smoking cannabis, were identified as problematic in the context of employment and developing careers by drug takers. Some discussed how they may have been more successful in their careers if they had not taken certain drugs or not taken them as frequently (see Chapter Six); as Kate explains: 'I think if I'd gone through life not smoking as much weed [cannabis] or taking as many drugs, I think I probably would have been a lot further in my career' (interview at age 28). Kate went on to outline how her daily consumption of heroin and amphetamines had affected not only her employment transition, but her transition to living independently. Initially, before she started taking drugs frequently, she had successfully negotiated these transitions. However, when she had taken drugs daily for some years, the certainty of these transitions became vulnerable:

It had a massive impact on my life, completely, where I lost me job. I ended up losing me flat, well I left me flat anyway and went back home. I'd gone from being an accomplished [designer], having me own independence, do you know what I mean? Me own place, doing me own thing, to back to taking, well taking drugs really was a crash point in me life, and I think that just did not help at all. I ended up getting myself in such a horrible mess.

(interview at age 28)

Opinions about how drug taking had affected the development of careers for drug takers were often expressed retrospectively. Until a crisis point was reached, for instance losing a job, as Kate's narrative indicates, it did not form part of the decision making process which led to drug desistance. In contrast to these experiences, some drug takers continued to take various drugs frequently and were successful in their careers. For example, Natasha had smoked cannabis daily since her late teens and took stimulant drugs on average once a month throughout most of her twenties. She had also studied, whilst working full-time, and become qualified within her chosen profession.

Whilst the concern many drug abstainers and some other interviewees had related to how drug taking might affect the transition to employment and career development, the primary negative effect discussed by drug takers was how it sometimes affected their ability to function at work. Poor concentration or performance has been identified as a risk associated with drug taking in the context of employment (Measham et al., 2001; Topp et al., 1999; Vervaeke and Korf, 2006). The drug takers discussed how their ability to function at work was largely affected by the come down they experienced during the days after taking stimulant drugs. In this regard, risk management strategies were employed. Vervaeke and Korf (2006) identify some risk management techniques which drug takers adopt in relation to employment. For example, they may choose an occupation with flexible working hours or plan their drug taking around their workload and moderate it when they are busy at work. Drug takers in this study discussed a range of similar risk management strategies. Natasha explained why she decided on some occasions not to take stimulant drugs at the weekend:

> I've already got a big day on Monday at work which is why we're not going out this weekend. I'm on a conference for the next four days and it's very intense and my participation is absolutely necessary. And I'm just thinking, not that it's a come down, but having to deal with that, when my head's just like, 'I can't be arsed'. I can sit down and do it on a computer on me own, but when I'm interacting in groups and theorizing on projects and stuff, I'm just like, I'm not performing at my job and I don't like that because I like, I like to perform. [...] I need to perform next week and that's more important than going out [and taking drugs], so I'm not going out.
>
> (interview at age 28)

Narratives like Natasha's illustrate how, at times, drug takers plan their drug taking around their workload and, in turn, exert control over it (see Decorte, 2001). Moreover, the process of reflexivity in the context of employment is revealed in the risk management strategies they adopt. Others, however, were prepared to take the risk of not being able to function fully at work and chose instead to take drugs with friends or partners in their leisure time. As we shall see, the nature of employment can be critical to decisions like these. This again highlights what Beck and Giddens neglect to consider, the acceptable risks we are willing to take in everyday life (see Mythen, 2004). The remainder of this section now turns to consider how the transition to full-time employment constrained the decision making process.

Full-time employment has been identified as a key structural turning point from crime (Laub and Sampson, 2003). Shiner (2009) argues its effect on drug taking is less pronounced. In full-time education, many drug takers in this study described how they could take drugs as often as they desired. They also described how when they did not work full-time, they had more time to take drugs or recover from the effects of drug taking. Dean, who experienced a long period of unemployment, noted how it facilitated his decision to take drugs: ' ... sometimes, if I wasn't working or I was on the dole, I was signing on, I'd be smoking [cannabis] all day, all night' (interview at age 28). Stacey compared her current full-time employment situation with when she worked part-time and took drugs more frequently:

> … since I've had the [business] it can't affect it because I've got to be there every day. […] Last time I was [interviewed] […] I was working half nine to half two so if you're thinking to yourself, 'Ohs you've only got until half two and you can come home and go to sleep', then it didn't really affect it.
>
> (interview at age 28)

Accounts like these highlight the significance of time and daily routines upon decisions about drug taking. However, when daily routines changed, as drug takers gained full-time employment, they had less time for taking drugs. This transition restricted their decision making and became a key turning point in many drug journeys: ' … when I went full-time then it was just like a cut off point then, because I'd work, I'd be tired, and I'd come home, and that was it, didn't want to go out [and take drugs]' (Tony, interview at age 28). Some interviewees, like Tony, identified full-time employment as the primary reason for discontinuing their drug journeys or moderating the frequency of drug taking.

Because of changes in daily routines, arising from working full-time, long hours at weekends or night shifts, drug takers discussed how they no longer had much spare time for drug taking with friends or partners and they were also, as Tony notes above, fatigued after a full day's work. Consequently, the time taken to recover from a stimulant drug taking episode became an important element of the decision making process:

> I'm not really too fussed [about taking stimulant drugs] any more. It takes me about three or four days to recover from it as well. (Laughs) You just get, I just get absolutely knackered by it now. So I think, I get to the point now where I think, 'Well is it really worth it for one day of running around like a dickhead? Is it worth it being shattered for like the next week?'
>
> (Kate, interview at age 28)

For this reason, some drug takers had reduced the frequency of their stimulant drug taking or were questioning whether to take stimulant drugs at all.

Whilst the transition to full-time employment constrained decision making, work role and how occupations fit with career plans were also significant when making decisions about drug taking. When Dean was 22, he worked in a warehouse and went clubbing every weekend. At the time, he took stimulant drugs occasionally and smoked cannabis daily. Since then, he had retrained and gained employment in a caring profession. He discussed how his role at work in his previous employment facilitated his decisions to take drugs and how his current employment restricted them:

I was smoking [cannabis] every day, I smoked every day and still went in work there [at the warehouse].
Yeah.
It was just perfect and, you know, regimented. I'd know what I had to do and everything was in place so I could do that there. If I wanted to, I could go out drinking every night and still do that job.
Yeah.
But, I couldn't do that with this job, no way in a million years.
Yeah.
'Cos working in [a warehouse] I didn't really have to communicate with people, I was just in the back out of the way.
[...]
So I could go in there just, I could go in there under the influence of anything and still work.
Yeah.
But here, the job where I'm working now, it's in your face, you're communicating with staff, you're communicating with social workers, school headmasters, the police, everything.
[...]
It's too much communication involved in that job so I couldn't take drugs or, you know, whatever and actually expect to last very long in that kind of work.
Yeah.
There's no way, so I don't.

(interview at age 28)

We can see here in this type of narrative how decisions about taking drugs changed as roles at work became more demanding when drug takers progressed in their careers or moved from one type of occupation to another. In Dean's case, he reduced the frequency he smoked cannabis from daily to no more than once a week. He also continued to take stimulant drugs a few times per year, but chose to take them when he was not working a shift during the days after.

For many of the interviewees, their initial transition to full-time employment involved temporary employment positions, often in occupations drug takers did not intend to follow as a career. Shiner (2009) argues that the transition to full-time employment does not significantly affect drug taking behaviour. Whilst this may primarily have been the case for interviewees when they first started working full-time in their early to mid-twenties, it was clear that as they developed a career, transitions *within* employment became important for decisions about drug taking. By their late twenties, many of the interviewees reported they were now following their chosen career path and for this reason had stopped taking drugs or significantly reduced the frequency they consumed them:

... when I got me job down here, I saw it as me first like proper job.
[...]

I'd only done like officey work and stuff [before] and I thought there's no way I can do that [taking drugs] ...
Yeah.
... and have a proper job.

(Vicky, interview at age 28)

Narratives like these, and Dean's earlier, illustrate what life course criminologists (see Giordano et al., 2002) remind us about the significance of commitment or the quality of attachment to a role, and investment in a new way of life (Laub and Sampson, 2003) for desistance or, in this case, changes in drug journeys. Indeed, as Decorte (2001) argues, investment in meaningful roles controls drug taking. When drug takers in this study were pursuing a chosen career path, many decided to desist from drug taking or to considerably reduce the frequency of it. An assessment of the ways in which the transition from dependent to independent living impacted upon drug journeys and the decision making process, follows.

The transition from dependent to independent living

The transition from living with parents to living independently was accomplished by many interviewees around the age of 18. Typically, they left home to go to university or to live with friends or partners. This transition was not always in one direction or permanent; many subsequently returned home to live with their parents during vacations, after completing a degree or when an intimate relationship ended, and they subsequently left again. Over four-fifths (84.3 per cent) were no longer living in the parental home by age 27 (see Chapter One). In contrast to the employment transition, interviewees did not discuss any risks they perceived drug taking presented for the accomplishment of this transition. Instead, drug takers described how it both facilitated and, in time, constrained their decision making.

In respect of the housing transition, Shiner (2009) observes how drug taking is associated with living in rented accommodation or living with parents. When drug takers in this study first left home, they often moved to rented accommodation. This transition, and more generally the transition to living independently, facilitated their decisions to take drugs. Initially, the period of independent living was described as 'carefree'. Drug takers, and other interviewees, were able to go out socializing when, where and as often as they wanted. Stacey recalled how her opportunities to take drugs and subsequent decision making changed when she left her family home in her late teens:

> ... I lived with a girl, just me and a girl, in her house which she'd bought, and I could do what I wanted and no-one was looking over me shoulder. Like when I was with me Mum and Dad, I wouldn't have dreamt of doing anything in their house. I wouldn't ever even attempted to do it because I would have got leathered [hit]. But, in Lucy's, it was a different

matter, I used to have stuff [drugs] in me drawer and everything. I was free, I was like completely … no-one was looking over me shoulder.

(interview at age 22)

The freedom that drug takers perceived when they left home facilitated decisions to take drugs. Leaving the family home, their risk perceptions changed: they were less concerned about parents discovering their drug taking than when they were living with them. In contrast, some male drug takers were more likely to remain living in the parental home during their teens and twenties. They reported that their parents permitted them to smoke cannabis in their bedrooms. Perhaps, this partly explains their decision to continue to live with parents compared to females.

Shiner also identifies how drug desistance increases with home ownership. Similarly, as drug takers in this study became older and bought their own homes, or even set up home with an intimate partner, their decisions about drug taking became constrained. Living in their own homes, or with a partner, placed demands on their time that had not previously arisen or concerned them. Daily routines, in relation to household maintenance and chores, changed and were less likely to be a shared responsibility with a number of housemates. Because many were working full-time, these tasks were to be undertaken at weekends. The effects of drug taking, for example experiencing a come down after taking stimulant drugs or feeling unmotivated after smoking cannabis, were identified as problematic in this context. Natasha described how the effects associated with stimulant drugs and taking them frequently impacts on her ability to maintain her home: ' … it's hard to keep a house, as well, if you go out every weekend 'cos you can't be arsed ever doing anything … ' (interview at age 28).

Concerns about time for housework were expressed solely by female drug takers which may reflect a traditional division of labour and women's identity in relation to the home (see, for example, Oakley, 1974). They not only emphasized the tasks which needed to be completed, but the costs of running a home. Whilst employment on the one hand can facilitate decisions to take drugs by providing income to buy them, when costs of living began to increase, as drug takers made transitions from renting to owning a property or moved location to a more expensive area, they discussed how their decisions about drug taking were further constrained: 'It seems like, as well, moving away down here [the South], it's different to uni, you've got to pay your rent, you've got to pay your bills and you can't afford to, you know, buy other things like [cocaine]' (Vicky, interview at age 28). Vicky stopped taking cocaine when she moved from one region to another partly because her costs of living increased. By age 28, female drug takers discussed how the demands and costs of looking after their homes became a reason to stop taking drugs or reduce the frequency of drug taking.

As well as making the transition to independent living, drug takers discussed how a change in location, generated by this or other adult transitions, also led to changes in decisions about drug taking. Some described how they moved to a different area for work purposes or to live with an intimate partner. In new locales, sometimes new social relationships were formed which provided opportunities for drug taking. Others discussed how a change in location led to a decrease in the frequency of drug taking or to drug desistance. Vicky, who moved to a different region for employment purposes, explained how her drug desistance occurred:

> … me friends were moving down for their jobs and I got a job down here, and I thought 'Well, I'll just use this as a kind of break to stop taking it [cocaine]'. And me friends that I moved with, they didn't use it or anything so I haven't taken it since.
>
> (interview at age 28)

Again, the significance of the social and cultural groups in which drug takers are embedded are highlighted here. A change in location can instigate changes in friendship networks which, in turn, influence drug taking behaviour. If we explore Vicky's narrative further, it provides support for many of the stages of criminal desistance outlined by Laub and Sampson (2003). Her housing transition led to her spending less time with drug taking friends and more time with non-drug taking friends. This change in her social networks and situations served to constrain and control her own behaviour. Consequently, she is likely to have become invested in a new way of life with her non-drug taking friends. In her narrative, for instance, she described how she started to spend time in pubs and going to music events with these friends, drinking alcohol rather than taking drugs, which had not been a major feature of her social life before. Vicky did not discuss whether she had to resist opportunities for drug taking in her new location, but what her account highlights is how transitions can initiate and strengthen will or resolve. She perceived her change in location as an opportunity to stop taking drugs and was resolved to capitalize on this.

As we have seen, the transition to living independently both facilitated and constrained drug taking. Similar to the transition to employment, transitions *within* the context of housing were important. Over time, as drug takers progressed in relation to this transition and moved from rented accommodation to owning a property or setting up a home with an intimate partner, decisions to take drugs became more complex. The significance of marriage and parenthood for decisions about drug taking will now be explored.

The transition from family of origin to family of destination: marriage and parenthood

Chapter Four, which focused on the cultural dimensions of risk assessment, outlined the ways in which intimate relationships facilitated and constrained decisions about drug taking. Fundamental to this process is the drug taking status of an intimate partner. Intimate relationships with a drug taker often facilitated drug taking decisions by providing opportunities to take drug and partners were perceived as trustworthy sources of knowledge about drugs. In this section, the significance of marriage and parenthood as a structural turning point for drug desistance is considered.

Laub and Sampson (2003) and Shiner (2009) emphasize that it is the strong bonds and commitment which accompany marriage, compared to other intimate relationships, which are significant for desistance.[7] The importance of marriage for drug desistance has been noted (see Bachman et al., 1997; Joe and Hudiberg, 1978). More recently, Shiner (2009) argues marriage is associated with drug abstinence or lower rates of recent drug taking, compared to other intimate relationship status groups. By their late twenties, the majority of interviewees in this study had been or were currently in long-term relationships and a third (36.8 per cent) were married (see Chapter One). In support of Shiner's assertion, drug abstainers and drug desisters were more likely to be married compared to current drug takers. What appears to be significant again for drug taking decision making is the drug status, behaviour and attitudes of an intimate partner. Drug abstainers and drug desisters were married to non-drug takers. In addition, all drug desisters who were married stopped taking drugs before commencing relationships with their partners. Relationships between two non-drug takers are likely to reinforce drug desistance: taking drugs may pose a risk to the relationship and continuing not to take them can demonstrate commitment.

Although Laub and Sampson (2003) contend that strong marital attachments prevail and will overcome criminal behaviour, irrespective of the criminal activity of both partners within a marriage, the experiences of the current drug takers who were married suggest otherwise for drug desistance. Granted there are only a small number to consider here, however, they provide some food for thought. Three current drug takers were married, all to partners who were also current drug takers when they began their relationships. One was married in her early twenties, the other two around their mid-twenties. All continued their drug journeys with their partners, however, as we will see in Chapter Six, Gaby's journey has changed and slowed down during the course of her relationship. This is partly because of the drug taking status of her partner, who was an occasional drug taker, and partly because of her perception of the meaning of marriage or, as Laub and Sampson would argue, her commitment to the institution of marriage. Whilst investment in a marriage may reinforce decisions not to take drugs for drug abstainers and drug desisters, it does not appear to be the case for some current drug takers. This is not to suggest they are less committed to their relationships; in fact, continuing to take drugs may demonstrate investment and commitment to a drug taking partner and be a risk management strategy. As we saw in Chapter Four, choosing not to take drugs may be perceived to threaten an intimate relationship with another drug taker (see Rhodes and Quirk, 1998). The narratives of current drug takers indicated how structural turning points or domestic transitions like marriage suggest social attachments exist, but the nature and character of those attachments are important for explaining desistance. In these circumstances, marriage between drug takers does not always lead to drug desistance and, therefore, the significance placed upon this structural turning point for desistance by Laub and Sampson, and Shiner, is debatable.

Some interviewees had made a further domestic transition during their twenties and became parents: almost half (46.6 per cent) were parents by age 27 (see Chapter One). Taking drugs in parenthood was perceived by drug abstainers and some less experienced drug takers as presenting a risk to their children and was provided as a reason not to take them. They were largely concerned that children might find and take a parent's drugs: a risk which has been associated with dependent drug takers who are parents (see Barnard and McKeganey, 2004). Many drug takers, in their accounts, stressed that they were responsible parents: they rarely took or kept drugs at home, and if they did, they ensured they were safely out of their children's reach.[8]

This adult transition has also been identified as significant for desistance from crime or drug taking (Laub and Sampson, 2003; Shiner, 2009). Similarly, a major turning point, at least initially, for the interviewees' drug journeys was becoming a parent, particularly for female drug takers. In contrast, only one male interviewee became a father when he was a drug taker. A drug desister and parent by his interview at age 28, Tony did not discuss fatherhood influencing his drug journey in the same way as female interviewees did for motherhood. Drug takers who became mothers emphasized how time and social networks were important for their future decisions about drugs.[9] These narratives again illuminate how changing situations may lead to investment in a new way of life which, in turn, influences decision making.

Drug takers who became mothers during the course of the research stopped taking drugs when they discovered they were pregnant. With the arrival of children in their lives, routines changed and many described how they had less time to socialize with friends or intimate partners and to take drugs. Lack of time was also discussed in relation to the after effects of drugs and not having time to recover from a come down when they had to look after young children the following day. Available support networks to look after children when taking drugs was also presented as problematic, especially when their children were very young.

It was also apparent that motherhood instigated investment in a new way of life. Natasha, who was considering becoming a mother in the near future, discussed how she intended to stop taking drugs:

> ... if I'm going to have a child I want to put everything into that and it wouldn't be giving up drugs, it would be a sacrifice, no it wouldn't even be a sacrifice, it would be a conscious decision that that is what I want to do. I would do it willingly as opposed to feeling, resenting it and I need to get to the stage where I wouldn't resent a child for giving up a part of my life.
> (interview at age 28)

As Lindsay explained, priorities change:

> When I was 18, you know, I was loving life, it was great. You know, I was working hard, plenty of money and I was just having an absolute scream. Where now, you see, my life, like ten years on isn't it? My life now is about providing, I provide a home now, I'm looking after, you know, I'm looking after my son. Because my priorities have changed, see. And the way that I have fun now is different to what it would be ten years ago. I mean ten years ago I wouldn't have gone and like spent a freezing cold Sunday in a bloody park on a seesaw, and this Sunday, you know, chasing squirrels round a park.
>
> (interview at age 28)

Interviewees who were new mothers initially discontinued their drug journeys. Jackson (2004) notes how after the initial honeymoon period of drug taking a reassessment occurs. Reassessment is also provoked by adult transitions, like becoming a parent, owning a home or pursuing a career. As Lindsay's account above illustrates, with a change in priorities, a new perspective on life emerges which can lead to decisions to stop taking drugs or to significantly reduce the frequency of drug taking. Others discussed how it was important to strike a 'balance' between drug taking and the demands of adulthood (see Chapter Six):

> ... balance again I suppose. 'Cos you think it's got to have its place it can't create its place, you know what I mean? You've got to assign it its space and have control over when you have it ...
> **Yeah.**
> ... and the total amount of time or stuff it's going to take out of you, you've got to accept that, you can't have it take hold of you.
>
> (Natasha, interview at age 28)

For some, as we shall see, they were willing to continue to accommodate drug taking into their lives alongside the demands of adulthood.

Initially, parenthood prompted drug desistance for female drug takers, however, this was only short-term. When drug takers who had recently become mothers in their early twenties were interviewed again at age 28, they discussed how they decided to recommence their drug journeys. Typically, this occurred when their children were a few years old. Their decisions to start taking drugs again were partly influenced by changes in their personal situations, for example, they began intimate relationships with drug takers which provided them with opportunities to take drugs. In addition, a change in available social networks occurred. As their children became older, they found parents, family and friends were more willing to look after them which provided more opportunities for leisure time. When Lindsay returned to her family home for a short period after separating from her son's father, her parents were able to babysit for her regularly:

[I] went back to my parents and then it was while I was at my parents [that I started taking cocaine again]. You see, they used to go, 'You know, Linds, you go out lovie', Lloyd would be in bed for half past six, 'You go out'.

(interview at age 28)

Similarly, Kate noted how, once her children were older, their grandparents were happy to look after them over night at their house. Stacey also discussed how her partner looked after their daughter when she went out clubbing and taking drugs. With opportunities to take drugs and trusted support networks who could look after their children the day after a drug taking episode, drug takers who were mothers resumed their drug journeys. Although their drug taking journeys were at a slower pace than before they were parents, they were still willing to accommodate drug taking into their lives because they had the opportunities to do so and enjoyed its effects.

These narratives further demonstrate how transitions to adulthood can provoke changes in decision making, however, such changes may not be permanent, especially when situations or circumstances alter and drug taking is still perceived as pleasurable. Furthermore, these accounts attest to a notable benefit of longitudinal research. If the study had not continued, these young mothers would have appeared as though they had completely stopped taking drugs in their early twenties and would have been categorized as drug desisters or ex-drug users. Cross-sectional research may have reached the conclusion that parenthood was a key factor for permanent desistance. However, by continuing studies like the NWELS, we can observe changes in behaviour, which were not possible to predict previously, and explore the reasons for this. A longitudinal methodology permits us to see how drug statuses change over time and drug journeys are non-linear or unidirectional.

Constructing new identities

Beck (1992) and Giddens (1991) emphasize how the connected processes of reflexivity and individualization or the project of the self are important for the construction of identities or personal biographies. In a compelling explanation for how recovery from addiction to opiates can occur spontaneously without treatment intervention, Biernacki (1986) argues the formation of a new identity is crucial. Accordingly, this is contingent upon the extent to which social relationships and identities in 'ordinary' social worlds are not 'ruined' or 'spoiled' by a drug taking identity, and the availability of identity materials, for example, via employment. It should be noted this research was carried out with dependent drug takers who were largely socially excluded from society. Nevertheless, insights from this study can be applied to the experiences of recreational drug takers who may not suffer from the problems associated with social exclusion.

During the journey to adulthood new materials for identity construction became available. Interviewees discussed how new identities as employees, parents or older adults emerged which influenced the decision making process. For many, they appeared to conflict with a drug taking identity and were presented as a reason to moderate or discontinue their drug journeys. This conflict of identities was more salient as different social worlds collided and drug takers became concerned about the reaction of non-drug takers to their behaviour. In this regard, the following accounts also reflect the concept of societal reaction outlined by Becker (1963). It has been argued that embracing a new identity is dependent upon a commitment to a new way of life (see Laub and Sampson, 2003). For example, as we shall see, becoming a parent was a key new identity welcomed and accepted by interviewees in their twenties. The ways in which new identities conflicted with a drug taking identity and influenced decisions about drug taking will be outlined in relation to parenthood and age. However, firstly, a brief appreciation of the function of a drug taking identity follows.

From a cultural studies perspective, Malbon (1999) has discussed how taking drugs, in a clubbing context, can provide a temporary escape from identity. Similarly, Duff (2008) argues drug taking can transform the self. When Stacey talked about her past stimulant drug taking, she also explained it in terms of providing a form of escape from her everyday self:

> My escape, my escape from everything, from everyone around me. That was it really, I was just sick of me being me for a bit, I wanted to be somebody else. I had been me for like 20 odd years, I didn't want to be me anymore, I wanted to be another person, 'cos it got a bit boring. I even dyed me hair blond, went peroxide! (Laughs) So that was probably, yeah, that's when I went a bit mad.
>
> (interview at age 22)

In this sense, drug taking, and the identity which it endows, can be seen to be embraced and even desired by drug takers. Its purpose is to provide an alternative identity to that expressed in 'ordinary' social worlds and on a daily basis. However, as transitions to adulthood were accomplished, some interviewees discussed how an identity as a drug taker was at odds with their newly acquired identities.

Earlier in this chapter, it was noted how parenthood changed perspectives on lives. Becoming a parent brought with it new responsibilities. Lindsay was adamant that she would not take drugs when she was interviewed shortly after the birth of her son, Lloyd: 'It [taking drugs] was good. I did enjoy it, but I wouldn't do it now, even with being single or whatever, 'cos I've got Lloyd and I think it's totally irresponsible when they're [mothers are] out like that' (interview at age 22). As Lindsay's views here demonstrate, the responsibilities of motherhood and an identity as a mother appeared to be significant for the decision making of female drug takers. Likewise, when Stacey was a new mother, with a daughter a few months old, she emphasized the importance of her new role and the disjunction between motherhood and drug taking: 'She's my priority now and I'm glad to say it, it would never bother me if I never took anything again [...] I wouldn't be a very good Mum I don't think ... ' (interview at age 22). These perceptions are in line with previous research that has noted how mothers who are drug takers feel constrained by their role as a mother and aspire to be perceived as 'good' and 'responsible' mothers (Banwell and Bammer, 2006; Green, 2004; Mitchell, 2004). A similar process in which different identities conflict is evident in these narratives. As new mothers, Lindsay and Stacey both state they will not take drugs, therefore rejecting a drug taking identity. They seek to fit with notions of 'good' and 'responsible' mothers: Stacey declared she wanted to be a 'good Mum' and Lindsay stated drug taking is 'irresponsible' for a mother. Their identities as mothers, and how they believed they would be perceived by others as mothers and drug takers, are likely to have influenced their decisions at the time to discontinue their drug journeys. However, as we have seen, Lindsay and Stacey decided to recommence drug taking when their children were older and there was a change in their social networks whereby intimate partners, friends or relatives were more willing to look after their children. Leaving children with trustworthy babysitters, as Mitchell (2004) has found, may have enabled them to conform to an image of responsible mothering and, in turn, facilitated their drug taking decisions. Furthermore, with the passing of time, being a mother was no longer a new identity and they may have felt more confident in their role and their ability to parent appropriately as a drug taker.

Being perceived as a 'good' parent or role model by children was also significant for drug taking decisions. Martin, a drug desister, who stopped smoking cannabis before he became a parent, explained why he had not wanted to smoke it since:

> ... like I say, you know, with the kids and that, I mean I don't want to set a bad example for them and I wouldn't want anyone round here who was on drugs. I mean I don't even like people smoking round here near the kids. So it's just something I just don't tolerate for the kids really.
>
> (interview at age 28)

It is evident Martin is committed to his role as a parent. His identity in this respect, and the significance he attaches to this role, act to constrain any decisions to take drugs.

As parents, the importance of being a role model for children was also discussed by current drug takers. Stacey was anxious her daughter may find out about her drug taking in the future: ' ... when she gets to eight, she'll remember something that has happened and then before you know it she'll think, "God, my Mum's a druggie" [...] And how can you preach to your children [then] ... ' (interview at age 28). Stacey's fear was that her daughter may, in the future, connect her current lifestyle, spending weekends with friends clubbing, with drug taking. Again, it is apparent from these accounts how different social worlds and the identities connected to them may collide. Although Stacey expressed concerns about her daughter discovering her drug taking identity, she still continued with her drugs journey. However, for some interviewees, drug taking was perceived to conflict with an image of a parent and a positive role model for children, and was presented as one of a number of reasons not to take drugs.

Parenthood was not the only identity that juxtaposed with a drug taking identity as the sample reached their late twenties; age was further emphasized by interviewees as important for the decision making process. It has been argued that drug taking is 'quintessentially a youthful form of behaviour' (Shiner, 2009: 146). As young people grow older, Shiner notes, recent drug taking declines. Whilst he foregrounds the cumulative effects of age and domestic transitions in his explanation for this, it is unclear how he interprets the effect of age. It is likely age is analysed as a signifier of advancing years and, perhaps, an indicator of physical decline. In this respect, it could be argued as drug takers mature they find it takes longer to recover after taking drugs and cannot cope so easily with the after effects. Whilst this explanation may have resonance for some, the narratives of the drug takers also suggest that age, as a form of social identity, influenced their decisions about drug taking. As interviewees matured, they began to question the appropriateness of drug taking in their mid to late twenties. Similarly, Laub and Sampson (2003) argue certain behaviours may no longer be perceived as age appropriate in later adulthood, particularly as transitions to marriage and parenthood are made.

Natalie, who had stopped taking drugs by her mid-twenties, was critical of others who chose to do so: 'I just think, "How old are you?", you know, "You've really got nothing better to do with your time than sit around and snort a few lines [of cocaine]?" It's sad, I think it's really sad' (interview at age 28). Similar sentiments were expressed by other drug desisters. Vicky described how she felt when she discovered her ex-boyfriend, who was older than her, was still taking drugs:

> And he was saying, 'Oh yeah, I still go out, I still do drugs and that'. I thought, 'My God, you're nearly thirty, that's really sad!'
> [...]
> I just think it's not what I want to be doing any more.
> **Yeah, yeah.**
> And I felt quite self-righteous to say, 'Oh, you still do that. Oh, I don't do it any more.'
> (Laughter)
> I felt quite good.
>
> (interview at age 28)

Many drug desisters clearly held the view that continuing to take drugs was not fitting at a certain age.

In contrast, current drug takers distinguished between different types of drugs which they perceived as age appropriate at different stages of the life course. For instance, when they were in their teens, cocaine was viewed as a drug for older drug takers. Instead, they were more likely to take amphetamines or LSD. However, in young adulthood their perception of these drugs changed and they were perceived by some as drugs more appropriate for younger drug takers. As Stacey noted, in relation to amphetamines: 'nobody does whizz now at our age' (interview at age 28). Similarly, others associated ecstasy with young drug takers, as Lindsay explains: 'I've got one friend and she takes pills and she said to me the other day, she said "I'm gonna give you a pill and we're going to go to a club". And I went "Don't bother, I'm not 15!"' (interview at age 28). These perceptions of different drugs and how they are predominantly associated with teenagers influenced decision making in young adulthood. Certain drugs were retrospectively described as 'kiddie' drugs and the identity this communicated constrained some drug takers' decision making.[10]

The discourse of age appropriate behaviour was further present in the narratives of current drug takers. Similar to the accounts of drug desisters, some current drug takers, by age 28, were also beginning to doubt the appropriateness of their lifestyle choices. Stacey suggested she was too old to go clubbing and taking drugs with friends most weekends:

We're out every weekend, yeah, and we've got the bug!
Yeah.
We keep saying to each other, 'We're going to have to calm down now. We're nearly thirty and we're raving!'
(Laughter)
[...]
I'm at that stage in my life now where I'm too old for it. I just feel like I shouldn't be doing it really.

(interview at age 28)

Accounts like Stacey's emphasize the normative view of drug taking as a young person's past-time. The final sentence in the extract above is revealing; she states: 'I just feel like I shouldn't be doing it really'. Statements like this suggest some drug takers were aware that taking drugs in their late twenties might not be considered acceptable by others beyond their immediate drug taking culture. Nevertheless, concerns like these were not identified as a reason to stop taking drugs. However, they were significant for drug desisters in reinforcing and maintaining their drug desistance.

As we have seen, many drug desisters believed people who choose to take drugs in their late twenties are 'sad'. Jan, who had stopped taking drugs when she left university, connected age appropriate behaviour with the identity being a drug taker conveyed in her late twenties:

... I also want to be portrayed as someone that, you know, is quite clean generally and good (Laughs), as well. You know, I don't want to, you know, some people think that having this like bad image is good. But, you know, not really when you get up to my age, our age. You know, I think that being good is a better really (Laughs) image to portray. And I think in the end you'll be, you'll come out better for it ...

(interview at age 28)

Jan, and other drug desisters, associated drug taking with an essentially negative image which was perceived as inappropriate in their late twenties. Opinions like these reaffirmed and crystallized their decisions to stop taking drugs which were often based on other reasons or risk perceptions outlined in this and previous chapters.

The narratives presented in this section offer some support for Biernacki's (1986) concept of spoiled identities. He suggests desistance from addiction to opiates occurs if identities in 'ordinary' worlds are not spoiled by a drug taking identity. Emphasis is placed upon a drug taker being able to establish a new and different identity. However, in this study with recreational drug takers, because they did not endure the effects of social exclusion, the interviewees had identity materials available to them generated by their adult transitions. As they acquired their new identities in this regard, they began to question or become concerned about the appropriateness of a drug taking identity. Essentially, they were worried about how a drug taking identity might spoil their already acquired new identities. In turn, this collision of different social worlds and the identities they produce clearly further influenced their drug taking decision making.

The continuing function of drug taking in the context of transitions to adulthood

So far, the emphasis placed on transitions to adulthood has been in relation to the ways in which they generally constrain drug taking journeys in young adulthood. For many, decisions to stop taking drugs or to moderate the frequency of drug taking were explained by reference to achieving particular adult transitions or a combination of some or all of them. Nevertheless, it was apparent that others continued on their drug journeys after accomplishing adult transitions. For some, they were able to accommodate drug taking into their lives without making significant changes to it; others continued their drug journeys at a slower pace. Their decisions to continue to take drugs highlight the place and meaning of intoxication in contemporary times. When explaining their decision making, many of the positive effects outlined in Chapter Three were identified as important for continued drug taking. Ongoing drug journeys in young adulthood were, for some, a source of pleasure and an activity many chose to fit into their lives purely for the pursuit of pleasure. However, for some drug takers, their decision making was made in relation to structural and personal circumstances. In Chapter Four, the significance of the positive effects of drug taking for the decision making process were explored in their cultural settings. In this section, the journey to adulthood, with all its responsibilities and difficulties, provides the backcloth to which the positive effects of drug taking are assessed and have meaning. The following accounts highlight the complex relationship between structure and agency and how structural positions at different stages of the life course again influence decision making. The ways in which the effects of drugs function in particular structural situations and how drug taking can generally act as a form of escapism or self-medication will be explored (see also Hebdige, 1976; Taylor, 1999; Young, 1971).

In Chapter Four, interviewees described how stimulant drugs and their energizing effects facilitated nights out clubbing. These effects were also discussed in relation to adult transitions. Because work, family or homes placed increasing demands on drug takers, they described how they sometimes felt too tired to go out socializing with friends or partners. However, if stimulant drugs were available, then they could choose to go out, as Stacey explained:

> ... I went round to my friend's house and I was knackered, I could not work, I could not do any more work and I couldn't go out [clubbing] and I said, 'I'm too tired, I can't go out'. And she went, 'Have half of that [an ecstasy pill]' and then the next thing I was like, 'We're going out, we're going out!'. I took half and I was really, really up there.
>
> (interview at age 28)

Similarly, because of the demands placed on interviewees after accomplishing specific adult transitions, some drugs were taken because of their relaxing effects. In Chapter Six, Gaby and Nigel describe how their decisions to smoke cannabis were often made in relation to a demanding day at work or home.

More generally, taking drugs was perceived by many as a form of escapism. It has been argued drug taking can provide an escape from everyday life and time out to forget about current concerns (Hebdige, 1976; Hinchliff, 2001; Measham et al., 2001; Taylor, 1999; Williams and Parker, 2001; Young, 1971). Drug takers who identified this function of their drug taking did so in the context of structural positions or personal situations and circumstances which were often an outcome of their adult transitions. They emphasized how the pleasure associated with drug taking could, at least temporarily, help them forget about their current situations or concerns:

> ... having good times on drugs, yeah I've had, you know, quite a few good times on drugs. This one time at Christmas I just lied there for about three days taking [ecstasy] pills. You know, the outside world didn't seem to exist. You know, we were inside of this flat, had everything there, [ecstasy] pills, weed [cannabis], poppers [amyl nitrite], alcohol and lots of good music. Didn't have to leave the house for three days.

Was that with mates?
Yeah, just sat inside with the curtains shut, music blasting. Brilliant!

(Dean, interview at age 28)

For many drug takers, taking drugs provided a pleasurable retreat from the reality of everyday life or the 'outside world'. When they discussed the reality from which they wanted respite, it was apparent that the responsibilities associated with adulthood were significant. Natasha explained why she chose to take stimulant drugs and smoke cannabis:

> ... time out, to have a break from life. Sometimes I feel so responsible for my age, a responsible job, married, a mortgage. I don't have a lot of free time so I want to be with Rick and me mates and have fun ...

(interview at age 22)

For other drug takers, there were specific personal situations or circumstances that they required a reprieve from. One interviewee discussed how smoking cannabis daily for a period of six months functioned as a form of pain relief whilst she was receiving treatment for a medical condition. Tony recalled how his drugs consumption, either taking ecstasy or smoking cannabis, helped him, for a while, to stop worrying about his son's developmental problems:

> ... I used to blank it [out], I just carried on doing what I was doing [taking drugs]. And I've actually sat down and questioned it, I just thought, 'That's strange.' But, then my mind's just taken away from it partying, just doing stupid things really.

(interview at age 28)

These narratives emphasize how drug taking can block out physical pain or emotional concerns.

In the previous section, Stacey's account highlighted how taking drugs provided an escape from her everyday life and identity. She explained her current drug taking in similar terms: 'things just get boring' (interview at age 28). Elaborating on what she found 'boring', she discussed how she was unhappy with her current intimate relationship. When she was interviewed at age 28, she had recently returned to the clubbing scene and started taking ecstasy most weekends. Stacey described how feeling 'low' because of her current personal circumstances influenced her decision to start clubbing and taking drugs again with friends:

> ... my friends have come along and usually they'd come along and I'd go 'Oh I'm not going out, I'm not in the mood'.
> *Yeah.*
> But, for some reason I'm at a low ebb and I've said 'Oh, I'll come out' and I've gone out. The first couple of times it's not addictive or I'm not

like, 'Oh, I want to go out the next week after or the week after'. But, after the first few times, and after taking that many [ecstasy pills], I want to go out. And I do, I want to go out now, I'm ready to go.
(Laughter)
I'm ready!

(interview at age 28)

Like Dean's and Natasha's accounts earlier, the significance of pleasure is highlighted here when making decisions to take drugs in the context of difficult personal circumstances. Taking drugs with friends provided some drug takers with fun and excitement which temporarily conquered other concerns. The narratives presented underscore how structural positions may not always become turning points towards desistance. The pressures and strains, as a consequence of achieving the desired goals of adulthood, for instance, home ownership, parenthood, a successful career, provide the motivation for drug taking. These narratives offer a qualitatively different account of structural strain than that outlined by previous theories of drug taking (see Cloward and Ohlin, 1960; Hebdige, 1976; Merton, 1938) which emphasized how drug subcultures were a solution to structural positions in which failure to accomplish certain goals was highlighted.

Summary

The relationship between agency, structure and changing situations has been explored in this chapter. In doing so, an alternative perspective to the over-agential accounts of risk assessment is provided. Drawing on, and extending, the work of Laub and Sampson (2003) and Shiner (2009), the narratives presented from drug takers have provided an explanation of how transitions to adulthood can act as structural turning points prompting reflexivity and moderating drug taking or, in some cases, leading to desistance. In respect of drug abstainers' decisions not to take drugs, they were informed by the risks they perceived drug taking posed to the accomplishment of many adult transitions. Prior to beginning to negotiate adult transitions, drug takers perceived their decisions to take drugs were facilitated by a lack of adult responsibilities. As adult transitions were accomplished, their daily routines changed. They had more demands placed on their time and deciding to continue to take drugs sometimes became difficult or complex. Indeed, a balance was sought between drug taking and the demands of everyday life and risk management strategies were often employed in these circumstances. It was also apparent that new identities materialized which could conflict with a drug taking identity. For drug desisters, new identities acquired in young adulthood cemented their decisions to stop taking drugs and further constrained the decision making process as a drug taking identity was perceived to spoil other adult identities. Whilst adult transitions provoked reflexivity, they were not purposefully sought or attained to curtail drug journeys. Rather, as Laub and Sampson

(2003) contend in relation to crime, and Biernacki (1986) argues in respect of dependent drug taking, desistance was partly contingent on chance. For instance, the housing transition which could lead to a change in location, and, consequently, fewer opportunities for drug taking, was not part of a reflexive or determined decision to reduce the frequency of drug taking or to completely desist. Rather, a change in behaviour initially occurred by chance, however, for some, the transition provided an opportunity to commit to drug desistance.

There was, nevertheless, evidence to suggest that accomplishing an adult transition per se was only the beginning of the story and not the end of drug journeys. Indeed structural turning points like these can be understood as 'hooks for change' (Giordano et al., 2002) and desistance was not always guaranteed or certain. Initially, for some, gaining employment full-time did not significantly affect their drug journeys (see also Shiner, 2009). Rather, the nature of the transition and its future progression were critical. For example, how an occupation fitted with career plans or making the transition from rented accommodation to owning a property were important for moderating drug taking or drug desistance. Essentially, further transitions occur, after the initial transition to 'adulthood', which increase demands on time and are important for drug taking decisions. The journey to adulthood then can be viewed as one involving continuing transitions or, to put it another way, transitions within adult transitions. Likewise, it was apparent as situations changed in adulthood, initial desistance became vulnerable. Female drug takers who were parents, for instance, decided to recommence their drug journeys when they had available and reliable support networks to look after their children. Others, despite negotiating adult transitions, decided to continue to accommodate drug taking into their lives because they perceived it as a pleasurable activity. For some, drug taking functioned in the context of the responsibilities associated with adulthood. It provided an escape from the reality of everyday life and, as we saw in Chapter Three, the risks they perceived were manageable or acceptable.

It was also evident that different structures affected decision making simultaneously. This will be illustrated further using case studies in the following chapter. The narratives presented in this chapter, however, begin to demonstrate how different adult transitions intersect with drug journeys and gender. In effect, there was a layering or confluence of structures which impacted upon the decision making process. For instance, drug taking decisions, for female drug takers, were bound within the context of their different adult transitions and gender. Their drug journeys were often constrained after the accomplishment of several adult transitions and by the full weight of responsibilities which accompany being a mother, maintaining a home and working full-time.

By exploring how structures, in the form of adult transitions and gender, and the situations they produce, influence the decision making process and drug journeys, a more nuanced account emerges. Narratives like these presented in this chapter embody the tension between structure and agency which is characteristic of contemporary life. The agential process of decision making is framed by structural positions and the circumstances they produce. The theoretical framework created in Chapter Two has now been fully articulated and empirically illustrated in this and the previous two chapters. It has been argued that decisions about drug taking can be understood as an outcome of agential decision making situated within cultural and structural circumstances or settings. In the following chapter, a case study approach is used to further illuminate the theoretical framework at the level of the individual.

6 At the crossroads
Life journeys and drug journeys

I do strongly believe that you can partake in the odd social drug and still remain on track ...

> (Gaby, current drug taker, interview at age 28)

I'll sort it out [my life] next year, I think. I say that every year ...

> (Nigel, current drug taker, interview at age 28)

... when I was at school, like I would never have, I would never have imagined that I would have tried the drugs I have done. And, but I've thought back on it, and I think I'm sort of glad that I did, but in a way I wish that I hadn't.

> (Danielle, drug desister, interview at age 28)

I'm still very self-minded about, you know, what I want to achieve in life and, you know, outside influences like drugs and smoking and drinking, things like that, I've not really changed my views ...

> (Stuart, drug abstainer, interview at age 28)

Introduction

The analysis of the data presented in the previous three chapters has applied the explanatory framework created and argued for in Chapter Two. So far the data has largely been analysed using a cross-sectional approach with a longitudinal element. Broad emergent themes were identified from the interviewees' transcripts and it has been noted in the previous chapters how generally their decision making in relation to these themes changed over time. The problem, however, with this analytical approach is that the rich detail and narrative of interviews is lost by cutting, chunking and categorizing the data (Charmaz, 2003; Coffey and Atkinson, 1996; Reissman, 1990). The longitudinal nature of this study produced an abundance of data. Some of the interviewees were interviewed on three occasions. As they became more familiar with the research process, and as the nature of the project changed, interviews were more in-depth. Consequently, for some interviewees there are reams of rich qualitative data exposing the twists and turns, or, as Laub and Sampson (2003) put it, the 'zigzagging', of their life and drug journeys. The approach to data analysis adopted in the preceding three chapters was one way to try and make sense of the wealth of qualitative data and identify similarities and differences between interviewees. In this chapter, a case study approach is adopted to illuminate at the level of the individual the theoretical framework outlined and applied in the previous four chapters.

The qualitative longitudinal method employed in this study captures the interviewees' journey through life and how key life events, in the form of transitions to adulthood, as well as changes in interpersonal relationships, influence their decisions about drug taking. As we saw in the previous chapter, these key life events are what are often described, in biographical research terms, as revealing critical moments or turning points (see Coles, 1995; Hodkinson and Sparkes, 1997; Thomson et al., 2002). The purpose of longitudinal research is to theorize change over time (Farrington, 2003; Miller, 2000). Examining key life events, intimate relationships and the pleasures and risks associated with drug taking helps us to understand how drug journeys begin, continue, change and stop.

The aim then of this chapter is to present the qualitative longitudinal data in the form of four case studies. These case studies provide a flavour of the themes and issues which have arisen in the previous empirical chapters. The objective is to initially allow the interview data to speak for itself, free of academic analysis and interpretation. Of course, there will always be some level of analysis and interpretation: quotes have been selected from interviews and the data has been summarized and organized in such a way as to tell the interviewees' story coherently. In the final section of this chapter, an analysis of the case studies and how they relate to the explanatory framework is provided.

The case studies illustrate the diverse experiences of the sample at the level of the individual. The narratives presented are not representative of the whole sample nor do they cover all the themes discussed in the previous chapters: each life is unique, but not necessarily atypical. The four case studies which are presented in this chapter have been selected for particular reasons which are largely pragmatic. To represent all types of interviewee, one drug abstainer, one drug desister and two current drug takers have been selected. Current drug taker, Nigel, and drug abstainer, Stuart, have been chosen because they were interviewed at all three stages of the study when interviews were undertaken at age 17, 22 and 28. Current drug taker, Gaby, and drug desister, Danielle, were interviewed at age 22 and 28. The current drug takers and drug desister have also been selected because they have quite similar drugs profiles (see Appendix) to the overall sample. They have tried, or taken regularly, cannabis, amphetamines, ecstasy and cocaine. Some have taken these drugs less frequently, however, all three have been daily cannabis smokers at some point during their lives. Danielle was also chosen from the drug desisters since she was fairly drug experienced compared to other interviewees from this category who had only smoked cannabis occasionally. Although the drug takers have similar drug taking profiles, interestingly they have quite different drug and life journeys, and, therefore, different outcomes. Each interviewee's account of their experiences and views concerning drug taking, beginning with current drug taker, Gaby, follow.

Gaby, a current drug taker

When Gaby was aged 13, she began a relationship with Nathan who was three years older. He DJ-ed, went clubbing and took stimulant drugs most weekends. It was with her own friendship group, however, that she first tried cannabis when she was 16 and initially smoked it occasionally, thereafter. Gaby's decision to try stimulant drugs for the first time was made in the context of her long-term relationship with Nathan. At first, she was too young to join him clubbing. However, when she was 17, they started clubbing with his friends and she tried amphetamines for the first time. Gaby acknowledged Nathan's influence upon her decision to try stimulant drugs: '... he sort of introduced me to that whole drugs scene really. I kinda worshipped the ground that he walked on ...' (interview at age 28). Subsequently, she started clubbing regularly and would often take a gram of amphetamines. Not long after trying amphetamines, she tried ecstasy for the first time, also with Nathan and his friends. At the same time, she noted she began to smoke cannabis more frequently, particularly during the come down phase after taking stimulant drugs. Around the age of 18, Gaby tried cocaine, but she recalled she preferred ecstasy which she sometimes took concurrently with amphetamines or on its own.

In making decisions to try and continue to take specific drugs, Gaby asserted: 'I've always said I'll try anything once. You don't know whether you like something until you try it. So I've got my parameters in which I'll work within' (interview at age 28). Despite declaring she would try anything once, the parameters within which Gaby's decision making was bound meant she refused to try LSD as she perceived it would make her feel out of control:

> *So are there any drugs that you'll never take then?*
> Trip, LSD, I never would.
> *Just cos of what you were saying before, being out of control sort of thing?*
> Yeah, the whole, that's the whole ... I'd just question it too much I'd be like, 'Why is that doing that?' and 'Well, what's going on?' I'd lose it, I'd send my own head right up my arse.
>
> (interview at age 22)

Once she had tried cocaine, she stated she preferred not to take it because she perceived the physiological sensations she experienced were less intense or pleasurable compared to ecstasy: '... when you're taking [ecstasy] pills and it hits you and you know that it's hit you, but with coke it's very subtle ...'

(interview at age 22). In addition to these constraints upon her decision making, Gaby usually confined her stimulant drug taking to the weekend. After first trying stimulant drugs, she continued to take them most weekends for a period of at least a year prior to leaving her home town to go to university.

When she explained why she decided to take certain drugs again after initially trying them, Gaby also identified specific functions and pleasures she associated with them. Although she was not keen on the after-effects of amphetamines, she noted they provided her with energy to dance all night in clubs. Ecstasy also had the same function. In addition, she perceived it produced enjoyable physiological sensations: '... it's just a bit of a buzz innit? And [...] The feelings that you have' (interview at age 22). At age 28, when Gaby had not taken ecstasy for many years, she still recalled the pleasure she experienced when she took it:

> ... the anticipation of waiting to feel that rush, you know, waiting for it to hit you. And there's no doubt when it has, and it's great. I mean it probably used to make me sick actually, but even that was an enjoyable part of it somehow. And just, I don't know, it was a really sort of 'feel the love' sort of drug wasn't it? You know, it sort of epitomized the whole old skool, happy house, rave scene. Yeah, they were good times, good times.
>
> (interview at age 28)

Gaby also described the clubbing scene as a unifying place which she found pleasurable and which provided her with a sense of belonging:

> **And you had that period of, like you say, you called yourself 'a bit of a raver', you'd go to Roxy's.**
> ... you can hear a tune and just think, 'Oh yeah, I remember when 10,000 people were all going like this [puts her arms in the air], you know, all together' and it's just amazing!
>
> (interview at age 28)

During Gaby's late teens, around the age of 17, her relationship with Nathan ended and she started a relationship with Liam who also took stimulant drugs. They spent weekends clubbing and drug taking. At the time of this relationship, her mother found a letter Gaby had written to a friend about taking ecstasy and smoking cannabis. Rather than admonishing her, Gaby recalled her mother was curious and hoped her drug taking was just an adolescent phase: 'I think she knows that putting pressure on me will probably just make it worse, with the kind of person that I am, so she'll just hope that I'll grow out of it, which I did ...' (interview at age 22).

Gaby left home to study at university when she was aged 18. At first she came home at weekends and continued to go clubbing, taking stimulant drugs with Liam and friends. However, when her relationship ended with Liam, she stopped returning at weekends and spent her time with her new friends at university. Drug taking, with the exception of occasional cannabis smoking, did not feature within her new friendship group at university. Instead, her social life revolved around the pub scene. Gaby did continue to take stimulant drugs occasionally for the next few years when she returned home during university vacations and went out with old friends. However, she recalled, over time, how her friends from home began to moderate their stimulant drug taking: 'the people that I know, friends don't do it as much as they used to do …' (interview at age 22). When Gaby returned to live with her parents to complete her final year of her degree, she began to spend more time with her friends from home. Although they had reduced the frequency of their stimulant drug taking, her friends regularly smoked cannabis and so did Gaby. At age 22, she was smoking it daily and noted that all her friends were regular smokers. During her interview at age 22, which took place in the day time, she disclosed she had already smoked a joint that day.

The pleasure Gaby derived from smoking cannabis with her friends was clear from her narrative at age 22. She described a specific occasion after smoking it when they could not stop laughing: '… we were just battered, we were like that [giggling] walking into a bar, we couldn't even order a drink 'cos we were just laughing so much' (interview at age 22). In addition, smoking cannabis helped her to feel relaxed: 'I just like the feeling, I just like feeling chilled out' (interview at age 22). For Gaby, smoking cannabis was multifunctional: it helped her to relax with friends, to have a laugh and lose her inhibitions:

> **But what are the effects that you particularly like about it, and in what situations do you prefer to take it?**
> Just sat round with my mates having a laugh, tunes on, reminiscing or discussing what's gonna go on, whatever, I mean it's just kind of normal. […]
> … I just like feeling chilled out and I think you do get a heightened sense of awareness, you just chat shit, sometimes it's funny …
>
> (interview at age 22)

During her interview at age 22, although Gaby identified pleasures and functions associated with smoking cannabis, she also recognized there might be a time in the future when she could no longer smoke it:

> … at the moment, I perhaps do have a selfish outlook on life which is why I don't want a regular boyfriend so I can just go off and do what I wanna do. But, I feel very strongly about when you have kids then, you know, your kids are carrying your life and you can't do things without them and you have to, in every aspect, going on holiday, everything, they play such a big part. So that's why I'm happy having a good time now, you spend enough time with someone and doing what you're supposed to do, so why not?
>
> (interview at age 22)

As well as smoking cannabis with friends, at this stage of her life Gaby also smoked it on her own. When she was re-interviewed at age 28, she reflected at the time: 'I was as addicted to weed as you could get'. She described how she distinguished her 'addiction':

> ... when it's not there [cannabis], you feel better without it, but when it is there it's almost like, you know, My Precious on Lord of the Rings? And it's kind of, there's something about it that, I mean they say it's not addictive, but I don't believe that. There's something in it that causes you to, when you're running out, and you think, 'Oh my God, I'm gonna run out tomorrow, when I get in from work, I'm not gonna have a spliff'. But, the thought of it not being there is worse than actually getting ... you know, 'Right, well I'll do the washing and I'll do this and I'll do that'. And then, before you know it, you've sort of, your evening's gone and you're like, 'Oh I've not had anything to smoke all night'. So, so there is, I don't know, there is, whether it's just me, I don't know, but there is something that, sort of almost the fear of not having it there, but actually when it's not there it's fine.
>
> (interview at age 28)

Gaby admitted that there were times when she felt she would rather stay in and smoke cannabis than go out with her friends:

> ... you can feel yourself sometimes, you know, cancelling a night out, when you just wanna go and have a spliff, and that's no way to live your life, is it? You only get one chance, so it's like you've gotta make the most of the time that you've got, I think, and that's just not, not a valuable use of your time.
>
> (interview at age 28)

Around the time of her interview at age 28, she had recently reduced how often she smoked cannabis and she had periods of time when she did not smoke it. One of her reasons for doing so was to give her body time to recover from the effects of smoking it. She also described how she was 'bored' with smoking it:

> ... I do want to get to the point where I have no desire to smoke weed, and it's gradually coming, you know, I'm just gradually getting bored with it, and just think it's boring really, just to make you lazy when your time is so precious in the evenings.
>
> (interview at age 28)

In addition to reducing her consumption of cannabis over time, the frequency that Gaby took stimulant drugs also changed. Once she completed her degree, she started working for a temporary employment agency and applied for various jobs. She presented the new millennium as a key turning point in her stimulant drugs journey. To celebrate, she met friends and they drank alcohol and took a variety of stimulant drugs:

> ... it was just such an overwhelming night and it was like everyone in [the city] was just united and whether that was 'cos we were all fucked and loving each other anyway, but ...
> **Yeah.**
> It was just a fantastic night, so I think it was different, it was a great way to say, 'Right, well I had such a top night that I'm not gonna risk having another pill'. Well, I just remember that is the last time that I really took [stimulant] drugs. It were good.

> (interview at age 22)

In addition to the millennium celebrations, Gaby's career was also a key turning point in her drugs journey. She left her home town and moved to a different area to pursue her career. She explained why, at this time in her life, she decided to stop taking stimulant drugs:

> ... with me moving down to [the South] as well, it was the real, it was the start of my career then. You know, I'd got my degree, I'd done what I wanted to do and, you know, let's crack on. So I didn't want those distractions really.

> (interview at age 28)

The 'distractions' Gaby wanted to avoid were stimulant drugs. During her interview at age 22, she described how she thought her stimulant drug taking would impact upon her career:

> Well, with pills I could take them forever.
> **But why would you not take them again then?**
> 'Cos it's not doing me any good, I'm very career minded, I want to do well.
> **Don't you think that taking the odd E is ... ?**
> Yeah, but I know what I'm like, if I get the odd E then I'll want to do it again, but at the same time, the next day I'll think, 'Oh, I just can't function'.

> (interview at age 22)

For Gaby, the come down she perceived after taking stimulant drugs became a justification for her to stop taking them once she started her career. She recalled, at age 22, how the come down after taking amphetamines was a 'proper downer'. At age 28, she expressed in more detail how she believed an ecstasy come down would make her feel:

... I can't face the Tuesday after you've been out at the weekend, that's your real day that you feel so, 'Ugh, God!'. Because it's just you can feel like that on a normal day when you've been at work, you know, you can feel so miserable and stressed out, that what's the point in making it worse by putting chemicals into your body? And, you know, sort of that's very much how I feel about it now. I've got no desire to go out and get fucked any more.

(interview at age 28)

Within a year of moving from her home town and starting her career, Gaby met James whom she married a few years later. Although James had some drug experience (in the past cocaine was his preferred drug), when he met Gaby he rarely took stimulant drugs and he occasionally smoked cannabis. Since meeting him, Gaby had taken stimulant drugs on a few occasions. On one occasion with James, they took cocaine at a friend's party, and a couple of times she has taken ecstasy with a friend at an annual event. At age 28, Gaby recounted further reasons for no longer taking ecstasy:

I kind of joked, 'This is it, next year I'm gonna be a married woman, so I'm not gonna carry on doing this', you know, I really am an adult now, sort of thing. You know, sort of in jest more than anything. But, yeah, probably deep down that's sort of how I do feel, I think. I'm growing up, I'm on a new road, a road that I very much want to be on, with the person that I want to be with.

(interview at age 28)

Gaby's commitment to a new way of life with James is apparent here. When they met, she still smoked cannabis daily. However, since starting a relationship with James, she began to reduce the frequency with which she smoked it. She noted James' influence upon her decision:

... I still carried on [smoking it] when I came to [the South]. And then James did smoke [cannabis], but not very much. So that sort of started to make me think, 'Well, do we need to do it all the time?'. So we did used to, then we introduced sort of breaks and would not have it for a week or two weeks or whatever, and then we'd get some more.

(interview at age 28)

In addition to James' influence upon her decision to moderate her cannabis consumption, Gaby noted how her transitions to employment and independent living were significant too.

... when you're getting in from work anywhere between, well half six on a good night or you know, anything up to eight, nine o'clock really, if we're busy at work.

[…]
But, you know, you've got the washing to do, your phone calls to make, tidying up, you know, you have all these things to do. And actually, when you've had a spliff it just makes you not wanna do anything.

(interview at age 28)

By age 28, Gaby was smoking cannabis occasionally. She described how she decided with James when to smoke it:

… he's quite good actually. He's the one that says, 'No, no, no'. But, when he says, 'No', I'm like, 'You can't say no. You can't tell me I can't!', you know. But, if he says, 'Yes' then I'm like, 'All right, let's get some!'

(interview at age 28)

She recalled what might prompt them to buy cannabis:

If you've got the prospects of say a whole weekend at home doing DIY and you just think, 'Oh do you know what? Let's just get some to help pass away the time'. Or if we've come back from [the North West] …
[…]
… you literally just turn off [the motorway] to [our dealers] and say, 'Oh let's just get a bit, you know, we've just done a four hour journey, we deserve it'.

(interview at age 28)

By age 28, Gaby noted how achieving 'balance' between drug taking and other priorities was now important to her:

But, now it's all about the balance, which is the big shift in … I think, probably with everything, it's all about balance. A little bit of what you like does you good, so both in terms of booze and weed.

(interview at age 28)

She could not, at this age, confirm when she would completely stop smoking cannabis, but she foresaw a future where she would probably still smoke it occasionally, opportunistically and as a treat:

It is gradually coming round, as I say, to getting a bit boring now, so doing it less and less. So in the end it will stop. But, it won't be a, 'Right, I'm never going to smoke weed again' stop, it's a, sort of moved on from it.
[…]
… if it was there and someone was like, 'Here you are', 'Yeah, why not?', you know.

(interview at age 28)

When Gaby reflected upon her drugs journey at age 28, she was positive about her experiences:

> [I'm] living proof really, that you can go out there, you can have a good time, you can try lots of different drugs and so on, and you can still come out the end of it without being a smackhead [heroin user]. You know, you can have a career, you can get married, you can live a completely normal life, but still have had a bloody good time. Yeah, yeah it's been a good journey, long may it continue.
>
> (interview at age 28)

Whilst Gaby presented a largely optimistic account of her drugs journey, the narrative which follows from Nigel is in stark contrast to Gaby's and highlights some of the negative aspects of drugs journeys discussed by interviewees.

Nigel, a current drug taker

Nigel started smoking cannabis when he was aged 14. He initially tried it with an older friend whom he met at school. During his teens, he became a regular cannabis smoker and by age 18 he was smoking it daily. Nigel first tried amphetamines when he was aged 15 and ecstasy when he was 16, with friends. He began to take them occasionally at weekends when he went to raves. Nigel also tried LSD, when he was aged 15, and took it most weekends during the summer with friends. He stopped taking it because he thought he was experiencing 'flashbacks' when the effects of LSD had worn off. When the opportunity arose again, at age 17, he did try it but he has not taken it since.

When he was a teenager, Nigel noted all his friends took drugs. He described how he made his drug taking decisions:

> *What have been the main things which helped you make up your own mind about whether to have drugs or not?*
> Mostly just mates deciding to, but I have before I took things asked people if I'll be all right.
> *So you tended to take advice from other people?*
> Yeah. Not all the time, but mostly I'll ask them, but I'll decide in my own head whether to do it or not.
> *Any other factors which have brought you round to a state of mind where you think, 'Yeah I'll take drugs'?*
> I've not been pressured into taking it, but I have thought because everyone else is doing it, I'll try it just to see.
>
> (interview at age 17)

By the age of 17, Nigel presented himself as drugwise: 'I feel like I know what's what. I know what drugs I would take and what I wouldn't, the amounts of drugs I would take and so on'. He was still making similar assertions at age 22.

In his late teens, Nigel was unsure how his parents would react if they knew he had taken drugs:

> If I came out and told them I don't know what their response would be. But, I think they've got a fairly good idea.
> **Do they have a fairly good idea about all the drugs you take or would they think there is only a certain amount you would use?**
> I think they definitely know I smoke weed. I think they must know I take something to go out raving.
>
> (interview at age 17)

At this stage of his life, cannabis was Nigel's preferred drug, followed by amphetamines when he went to raves. He described the functional effects of cannabis: 'I forget all my worries' (interview at age 17) and he remarked it also helped him to relax. He also described smoking it as pleasurable: 'The positive side is that we just had a laugh and that's really good' (interview at age 17). When Nigel was interviewed at age 17, the only negative effect he identified in relation to his drug taking was how it impacted upon his attitude to work and study. This became a recurring theme in his interviews.

In his account of his drugs journey, Nigel discussed how taking drugs expanded his social networks:

> 'Cos like in a way, like when I was sort of 15, 14, 15 taking drugs was what sort of brought me out of my shell. Like I said, I spent a lot of time on my own as a kid and like from high school I was just like pretty quiet up until like I was associating with these cool guys, you know, as well, 'cos I was smoking pot with them as well.
> **Yeah.**
> So I suppose it introduced me in different circles as well like.
>
> (interview at age 28)

Around the age of 20, Nigel began spending more time with friends who smoked cannabis rather than with his friends who went to raves. Through work, he also established a new friendship group and they began to spend their leisure time at their local pub. Previously, he had been an occasional drinker preferring instead to smoke cannabis or take stimulant drugs, but from this age onwards, Nigel's alcohol consumption began to increase. It was with this new friendship group that he first tried cocaine when he was aged 21. He began to take it occasionally when it was offered to him. He commented how when he took cocaine he 'felt good'. However, he perceived the after effects the following day as negative: 'But with, sort of chemical drugs, it's the come down afterwards, afterwards, always afterwards. That's why I'm not keen on them anymore, drugs that, that let, you know, give you an effect the day after' (interview at age 22). Despite identifying this risk to his health and well-being he carried on taking take cocaine when it was offered to him.

In his early twenties, Nigel continued to smoke cannabis daily. At age 22, he was smoking three joints per night. He described its function as still helping him to relax and escape from life. Having a laugh with friends was no longer present in his narrative. At times, he purposefully smoked cannabis: '... when I want to blank something out so I'll just smoke weed, don't think about it' (interview at age 22). He also noted how after smoking cannabis, he often felt unmotivated:

> ... smoking weed, like you just can't be arsed doing anything, it just totally messes your life up really, I must admit it.
> **But you do it every day?**
> I must admit it right, it's totally, you don't do any, get nothing done, you're a complete waster and that's that.
>
> (interview at age 22)

In his early twenties, Nigel was stopped and searched by the police who found a small amount of cannabis in his possession. He received a caution for possession. Since being cautioned, he commented he conceals his cannabis more carefully when he takes it out with him.

Although Nigel perceived various negative effects and risks as a consequence of taking drugs, he still continued to take cocaine occasionally and smoke cannabis daily during his early twenties. He did, however, express a desire to stop taking drugs in the future:

> I'd love to stop.
> **Everything?**
> Everything, everything.
> **What do you think realistically you would, you know ...**
> Give up? Ecstasy, coke, stuff like that.
>
> (interview at age 22)

Since Nigel was 22, he has had two long-term intimate relationships. His first relationship was with a drug taker whom he smoked cannabis with, but they never took stimulant drugs together. During his second long-term relationship, he largely stopped taking stimulant drugs. He explained that his partner did not approve:

> **And what about your ex-girlfriend, the one that you were with for like two years, did she do coke?**
> No drugs.

No drugs?

Smoked a little bit of pot with me and that was it. She didn't take any drugs, she didn't agree with it either.

Yeah.

She wasn't bothered about me smoking pot, but anything else [sharp intake of breath] that would've been a killer if she'd have known.

Yeah.

I don't think I took anything during that time, like I said, I didn't take any pills during that time and besides the New Year's Eve, the one just gone, she wouldn't have known I was on coke.

(interview at age 28)

As soon as this relationship ended, he began spending more time with his friends and started taking cocaine again:

... late January it was I split up with her and the next night went to the pub to watch the [football] match

[...]

and by this time a lot of like younger lads had started going in the pub. I say younger, but I'm talking like only about two, three years maximum younger than us.

Yeah.

A lot of them I didn't know and that night we all went out on the piss, I had a good laugh. And then I started hanging around the pub again for months.

Yeah.

Getting really pissed, doing outrageous shit, sniffing a lot of coke with them lot, like especially the young lads.

[...]

So you've got all these groups together, all really like getting into it like, sniffing, and it's terrible, it's terrible, it's worse than Columbia that pub!

(interview at age 28)

Nigel's narrative highlighted the opportunistic nature of his stimulant drug taking:

They're [ecstasy pills] just not around. I'm sure we could go and get some right now if we needed to like, but no, I think that's the only reason we took it in the pub was like someone said, 'Yeah, we've got these Es'.

Yeah.

'Right, let's have one'. I think I even said, 'Oh I don't want some', 'No, no you just have this half', 'I don't want it', I was like, 'All right'.

Yeah.

That was what it was. Like I say, I think if it was just down to me I probably wouldn't take hardly any drugs. It's just people saying, 'Just have that, just have that' and I'm like, if I have a few drinks, I'll be like, 'Yeah'.

(interview at age 28)

In his twenties, Nigel stated he rarely initiated buying stimulant drugs and often did not have to pay when his friends offered them to him.

As Nigel noted above, he started to take cocaine again after an intimate relationship ended. One of the functions he associated with taking it was that it helped him to sober up when he had consumed too much alcohol, but it also permitted him to drink more alcohol:

> ... we all went out Thursday night, and Friday morning this lad rang me up 11 o'clock, 'Come to the pub'. Went to the pub, stayed in the pub all day, went into town in the day time, all afternoon drinking. Then I was fucking out of my face, I couldn't even see by 5 o'clock.
> **Yeah.**
> So we all got loads of coke to bring us back round.
> **Yeah.**
> Sniffed a load of coke that night. I stayed out till four again that night and then like the next day I think I just needed therapy.
>
> (interview at age 28)

At the time of his interview, at age 28, he was taking cocaine with his friends approximately once a month. Despite discussing how his cocaine consumption was functional, he also discussed how he perceived he felt paranoid the day after he had taken it:

> That's the problem you see now with sniffing the coke, it is giving me the bad paranoia to the point like if I have a night out, the next day I spend all next day ringing people saying, 'I'm sorry about that. Did I do this? What did I do? Did I do that?' That's no good, you go out to have a good time, not to like wake up the next day and think, 'What did I do wrong?' all the time.
>
> (interview at age 28)

Two weeks prior to his interview at age 28, Nigel took amphetamines for the first time since he was aged 21. A friend offered it to him when they had been drinking alcohol. The day after, he recalled he suffered another bout of paranoia:

> And like the next day, I was so paranoid it's untrue. 'Cos like my leg was twitching while I was sleeping.
> **Yeah.**
> And then we went to this pool tournament on the Sunday. I was feeling like shit then, paranoid to death already. I'd been losing it me, I'd just

been losing it since Thursday. We went to this pub and it was like the roughest pub you've ever seen in your life.
(Laughter)
I didn't know it was that bad. I got barged by this big lesbian, out of the way and stuff. That was just for being there!
Yeah.
And I'm not joking, I was just there like, it was very miserable, and they played *Paranoid* by Black Sabbath, *The Drugs Don't Work* by The Verve, all one after each other, right!
(Laughter)
All these guys staring at me. I was just like losing it me.

(interview at age 28)

Nigel remarked how he generally suffered from paranoia in his daily life. At age 22, he was asked if he ever had any problems related to drugs and his health. He replied: 'Not health, mental health may be. [...] Just paranoia, very paranoid.' He continued to make the connection between his drug taking and levels of paranoia which he experienced in his late twenties. He recalled he had suffered from paranoia for some time, but he was unsure if it was always drug related. These episodes of paranoia often made him feel emotional. When he felt paranoid at the pool tournament he described above, he recounted how it reduced him to tears:

I was that paranoid, I'm not joking, I got out of there and I got me mate, me mate's Dad was there and I felt tears come into me eyes in the car. I'm just like that, 'I'm going to actually cry in front of me mate's Dad in a minute'. I can't believe it, that's how bad it was. And I'd texted some girl I know from [town] and I think she just thought I was joking around with her, but I was like, 'No, I'm serious I think I'm going to fucking cry in a minute' and that was like, 'Fucking hell, you are losing it here!'

(interview at age 28)

Despite these negative effects he associated with taking stimulant drugs, Nigel still continued to take them. In his late twenties, he described all his friends as drug takers, who frequently offered him cocaine: ' ... I don't even really buy coke, but it's there, it's always getting offered to me and stuff like that' (interview at age 28). Consequently, he found it difficult to control the frequency of his cocaine consumption. Lately, he felt he had taken more cocaine than he intended:

... coke, not even realizing like fucking hell, you know, how you used to think like coke's really bad and I'd never do a lot of it and I never have done a great deal, I'm not regular, but like I've done it where I've done more than I wanted to.

(interview at age 28)

Nigel suggested he would have to stop spending time with friends who took drugs to be able to stop taking them himself in the future.

During his latest interview, at age 28, Nigel revealed that his parents were now aware he smoked cannabis and his mother knew he had tried ecstasy. They did not, however, know about other drugs he had tried or the frequency of his drug taking. Despite his parents' knowledge of some of his drug taking, Nigel continued on his drugs journey. Occasionally, he felt 'ashamed' after taking cocaine when he thought about the way his parents had raised him:

> … sometimes you do feel ashamed at like, you know, 'Did I really have like that last night?' you know, 'Is that the way I was brought up?' You know, you were brought up [well] and you were pissing yourself and abusing people and sniffing coke and sticking shit up your nose and doing all kinds of stupid shit.
> **Yeah.**
> Like, you know, I do feel sometimes very disappointed in meself.
>
> (interview at age 28)

Throughout his twenties, Nigel's consumption of cannabis remained largely steady and consistent. At age 28, he stated he was still smoking three joints per night on his own: 'usually just to sleep, to stop my thinking' (interview at age 28). He explained how he sometimes intentionally smoked skunk, a particularly strong form of cannabis, so that he could forget about his worries, but it was only a temporary relief:

> I'd just think like, the only way I'm not going to think about this now is if I just smoke loads of skunk.
> **Yeah.**
> (Laughter)
> I don't even smoke skunk 'cos that makes me paranoid!
> […]
> … I know I won't give a shit after smoking it 'cos I won't think of much, I'll just sit there and not say a word. Yeah, I've done that loads of times, too many times.
> **Yeah.**
> But, like the problem's always there the next day, isn't it?
>
> (interview at age 28)

Nigel also discussed how he was not able to function well the morning after smoking cannabis:

> And it's horrible, do you know, I never used, when I worked at the factory we started at eight, I didn't function really until twelve. I was just like completely dead especially up till ten, your first brew, I was out of it,

'No-one talk to me'. I just had nothing to say for myself, just standing there very quiet.

(interview at age 28)

Overall, he felt that smoking cannabis regularly made him feel unmotivated:

> ... when I was saying, I've looked back on my life and it's just been one long thing of just smoking pot, and records and that, and just lazing around and basically being a slacker all your life, that is purely pot related. Definitely, it just makes you a complete no-goer.

(interview at age 28)

Like other interviewees, Nigel at age 28 had aspirations he wanted to fulfil. He longed for a full-time job that would provide him with enough income to leave home and live independently from his parents. At age 28, he had yet to make the transition from dependent to independent living. He also wanted a long-term intimate relationship and eventually to become a father. However, the reality of his situation was that he was dissatisfied with his achievements by age 28. He had left school with few qualifications. He started a course at further education college, but left before the end of his first year. After a period of unemployment, he started working in various manual occupations. By age 28, he had two part-time jobs: both manual occupations, one which he repeatedly and sarcastically described as 'glamorous', the other was working with his father. Nigel aspired to work in the cultural industries and had bought equipment to do so for which he was still paying off the loan. Occasionally, he worked in this sector. He reflected that his drug taking had impacted upon his career development:

> ... like jobs and stuff, you think, 'Oh God, if I hadn't been such a waster I could have done this', you know, stuff like that. So yeah I am quite negative towards it [drug taking] in that way, yeah.

(interview at age 28)

During his three hour interview when he was age 28, Nigel appeared depressed by his current circumstances. His lack of success in the cultural industries and his current occupation contributed to what appeared to be low levels of self esteem. He found himself trapped: wanting to change his job, but feeling too old to retrain and not having the economic resources available to do so. Without a job with a good income, he could only afford to live with his parents. When his most recent intimate relationship ended, he felt like he had been ' ... transported back and I'm like, "Shit, now what do I do like?"' (interview at age 28). He compared his achievements with his friends and noted that many had made adult transitions to which he aspired, for instance, they had bought their own homes or were parents. Nigel resolved, at the beginning of the year, that he was no longer going to be a 'knob, sort life out' (interview at age 28), a resolution he said he had also made the previous year.

Given how he felt about his life, it was no surprise that at the age of 28 Nigel again expressed a desire to moderate his drug taking in the future. At the time, he was also struggling to control his consumption of alcohol. He stated he drank four cans of lager per night. He described how he wanted to reduce his consumption of alcohol and other drugs in the future:

> … it could just be like a couple of drinks on the weekend …
>
> **Yeah.**
>
> … smoke a bit of pot maybe during the week and then a few on the weekend or whatever.
>
> **Yeah.**
>
> That's the ideal, that's how I'd like it to be like and then maybe on special occasions obviously cut loose and do some stupid shit [take cocaine] 'cos it 'can be fun occasionally.
>
> […]
>
> I think if I had a bit more responsibility in my life then I wouldn't be this, you know, I wouldn't be getting like, you know, if you're thinking like, 'Shit I've got to get up and take the kids to such and such!' and you're thinking, 'Well I'm not going to have eight cans tonight and I'm not going to go and get fucking out of my face'.
>
> **Yeah.**
>
> It's a deterrent isn't it like?
>
> **Yeah.**
>
> So like, but like, until then, it's up to like myself to sort of like, you know …
>
> **Self control?**
>
> Yeah, definitely, yeah, self control all the way.
>
> **And do you find that hard?**
>
> [Exhales breath] Yeah, the hardest thing.
>
> (interview at age 28)

Overall, Nigel was negative about his past and current drug taking: 'I think if I could go back and change things I probably wouldn't take any drugs' (interview at age 28). He did not appear to feel secure with his status as a drug taker partly because it had, as he perceived, prevented him from getting on in life, particularly in terms of his career and other transitions to adulthood. All Nigel wanted was to be 'sensible and go home' (interview at age 28) rather than consume alcohol and drugs to excess. With his thirtieth birthday on the horizon, he felt his behaviour was no longer appropriate for his age.

The following case study highlights how Danielle, a drug desister, started her drugs journey and decided a few years later to end it.

Danielle, a drug desister

Danielle's drug taking journey began at age 17 when she took a quarter of an LSD tab for the first time at a club with a friend. It did not have the effect she expected:

> ... it didn't really do anything, I didn't think. I just laughed a lot. But, it didn't, like loads of people had said about it and like you'd see things and stuff, but (Laughs) I didn't see nothing. (Laughs) Pointless.
>
> (interview at age 22)

Clearly, Danielle did not find her experience with LSD entirely pleasurable or unpleasurable. As she put it, she thought it was 'pointless' and, therefore, did not try it again. At age 18, she started spending more of her leisure time with friends she met at further education college. Her friends from college smoked cannabis and took amphetamines and cocaine. Danielle first tried cannabis with these friends when she was 18, after a night out drinking alcohol. She found smoking cannabis pleasurable, particularly when it made her feel 'dead giggly' and relaxed. She became a regular cannabis smoker with her friends, smoking it at least a couple of times per week when she spent time with them. However, she rarely bought it herself. Although Danielle described smoking cannabis as pleasurable, she recalled a negative experience when she once ate it in her late teens:

> The first time though I ate it, I thought I was gonna die, in fact that's the worst time I think.
> *Why 'cos you took too much?*
> Yeah, I think it's 'cos I took too much.
> [...]
> It was really bad, yeah I was shaking 'cos I ate it and like 20 minutes later I was walking back to the shop and I just felt really, really strange and I went back to my mates.
> *Did a few of you like eat it at the same time?*
> No, it was just me. But, I thought I was gonna die, I really thought I was gonna die. I was scared to wake up in case I didn't wake up, but yet I didn't want to be awake 'cos it was horrible.
> *So what happened in the end, did you just end up going to sleep?*
> Yeah, just ended up going to sleep. And I used to say ... I didn't bother eating it again, but I didn't smoke it for a bit either.
> *So it just put you off it for a bit?*
> Yeah, but not for very long though, unfortunately.
>
> (interview at age 22)

On Danielle's nineteenth birthday, she tried amphetamines for the first time when she went clubbing with friends. She continued to take amphetamines whenever she went clubbing and her friends had bought some. There was no set pattern to her consumption, and as with cannabis, she rarely paid for them herself. She noted how when she took amphetamines she had fun and a laugh with her friends. Danielle described the first time she took them: '... we'd been out, we'd been to town and I don't know it was just a really good night, a good laugh and that' (interview at age 22). Subsequently, Danielle stopped taking them because she perceived risks to her well-being. The last time she took them with friends, they were ill: '... like all the other times I'd had it I was all right, apart from this one time. But, everyone else that had it, apart from one other person, they all threw up' (interview at age 22). Danielle and her friends thought they had a 'bad' batch of amphetamines. At this time, she also became concerned about other risks she associated with amphetamines:

> ... after the time when I threw up, I just never bothered with it. And like as well, I don't know, it just sort of, 'cos when I first had it I only had half a gram, but I was drinking as well and that was all right. I'd go to bed and I'd be able to go to sleep. And then it got to the point where like I had a gram and I didn't drink as much alcohol with it.
> [...]
> And then I didn't sleep. I could get to sleep eventually, but like it got to the point where I felt really bad the next day, you know, I felt like I had a headache and everything, whereas the first few times when I had it I didn't get that. I think probably that's another reason why I just never bothered with it again.
>
> (interview at age 22)

Danielle took amphetamines for the last time a year before her interview at age 22.

When Danielle was around 21 years old, she tried cocaine for the first time with her friends from college. At the time, she was still taking amphetamines when they were available to her. Again, Danielle rarely planned to take cocaine nor did she pay for it, but like amphetamines and cannabis, she took it when it was offered to her: '... just 'cos it's there and someone's said, "Oh have some"' (interview at age 22). Her access to cocaine was provided through her friend's partner:

> ... this girl who I was friends with, like her boyfriend started dealing it, I don't think he still deals it now, but at one point he started dealing it. So like he just had it, so we just had it.
>
> (interview at age 22)

Danielle only took cocaine on a few occasions. Despite easy access to most stimulant drugs, Danielle refused to try ecstasy. She believed her mother would be 'disappointed' if she knew she took it. Similarly, she noted her parents would disapprove if they knew she smoked cannabis and they would have thought she was a 'druggie' if they were aware she had taken cocaine. Her decision not to try ecstasy, however, was also influenced by the risk of death she associated with it: 'I'll probably be the person that dies!' (interview at age 22). By age 28, she still perceived death as a potential risk: '... 'cos people just die don't they (Laughs), with taking ecstasy. Like seemingly they just take one and then they're dead and I thought that would be me (Laughs), I would die' (interview at age 28). Because she believed her mother would be upset if she tried ecstasy and also because she connected the risk of death with it, Danielle never tried it.

When Danielle decided to stop taking amphetamines and cocaine she also stopped spending time with friends who provided her with access to them. One of her closest friends within this friendship group moved to a different area and so did Danielle. Consequently, she lost touch with her friends. During this stage of her life, she noted how her consumption of alcohol increased. When she went back to college to study, she met a new friend who she felt had a significant impact upon her drugs journey:

> ... like me friend from college, the one that I did the [course] with, 'cos she's really good, she doesn't take any drugs.
> *So do you think that's had any influence on you?*
> Yeah, yeah I think it has. Yeah, I think it has. Because possibly, if she'd taken drugs as well I'd still be taking them ...
>
> (interview at age 28)

By age 22, Danielle had not seen her former college friends for a year. Stimulant drugs were, therefore, no longer easily accessible to her:

> ... never really had anyone come up to me and say, 'Oh, do you want to take some whizz [amphetamines]?' or whatever, so I've just not bothered. Probably if someone came up to me and said, you know, I'd probably just say, 'Oh, go on then'.
>
> (interview at age 22)

Although she suggested she may take stimulant drugs again in the future if they were offered to her, she could not conceive she would take them regularly or in the long-term:

> ... I think what it is, is like really I'm just a piss head! (Laughter) But, on occasion I just like end up taking drugs, like I don't think I'll, apart from weed, I don't think I'll ever end up taking drugs as a long-term thing.
>
> (interview at age 22)

A further key factor in the slowing down of Danielle's drugs journey was the nature of her employment. When she was 18, Danielle went out most nights either to friends' houses, to pubs or to clubs. By age 22, she was working weekend shifts in retail and could no longer go out as often as she had previously and take stimulant drugs.

Approximately a month before her interview, when she was aged 22, Danielle met her partner Ian whom she was still with at age 28. They started cohabiting not long after they met. He smoked cannabis daily and Danielle also began to do so. She predicted, at age 22, that she would continue to smoke it daily out of 'habit' and because Ian was a daily smoker. However, at this stage of her life, she was beginning to question why she smoked it: 'Something to do, I should do something different' (interview at age 22). She had previously tried to stop smoking it for two weeks, but found she craved it: '... there was once I didn't smoke it for about two weeks, and I just really, really felt like smoking it 'cos I hadn't. I sort of missed it' (interview at age 22). Although Danielle was beginning to re-assess the benefits of smoking cannabis at this stage of her life, she continued to smoke it daily with Ian and their friends. She remarked her friendship group comprised cannabis smokers: '... I know lots of people who smoke weed regularly' (interview at age 22). However, she was still not paying for it herself.

Danielle did eventually stop smoking cannabis. After her interview at age 22, she continued to smoke it daily with Ian and their friends. However, when she was aged 25, she decided she wanted to stop smoking it completely and for Ian to do so too. At the time, Danielle was smoking approximately two joints per night. Her decision to stop smoking it was prompted by what she acknowledged as unusual circumstances:

> ... this is gonna sound really stupid, but it was only really the fact that I'd got me [dog], and I didn't, I don't know why, but I didn't want to sit smoking weed around the [dog]. And plus I spent a lot of time with the [dog] and it kind of, it was something else instead of ... so I just kind of thought ... and just stopped.
> [...]
> I think it's 'cos I've found something better to do with me time.
>
> (interview at age 28)

Danielle believed smoking cannabis made her feel unmotivated which she thought impacted on her ability to care for her dog. In addition, she discussed how she perceived smoking cannabis as 'pointless', as she similarly had assessed LSD:

> **And why do you think it was pointless?**
> (Laughs) 'Cos it just, 'cos you just like sit at someone's house and smoke it, don't you? Instead of like going out anywhere or doing anything. I don't know, it seems kind of, I don't know, I just think it's kind of pointless.
>
> (interview at age 28)

At age 28, Danielle believed Ian had not stopped smoking cannabis. Although he was not allowed to smoke it at home, she thought he continued to smoke it elsewhere with friends. Since she stopped smoking it, Danielle began spending more time with her new friend from college, who did not take drugs, and less time with her friends who smoked cannabis. An unintended consequence of Danielle's decision was that she no longer spent much time with Ian: '... it [smoking cannabis] was something that we did together. (Laughs) And now (Laughs) it isn't 'cos we don't do it any more' (interview at age 28).

When Danielle was age 22 and had recently stopped taking stimulant drugs, she identified long-term risks to her health and well-being which she associated with them and provided as a reason for no longer taking them: '... what effects it's gonna have if I like do it long-term sort of thing ...' (interview at age 22). When she was 28, and had not taken any drugs for four years, long-term risks to her health and well-being from prolonged drug taking were still a feature of her narrative and were presented as a reason for not taking drugs again in the future. She explained why she was relieved she no longer took drugs:

> ... taking drugs isn't necessarily, for everybody, a bad thing. It's just I'm glad I don't because when you, like ... It's like with smoking, like when you think about it, and if I am going to live till I'm about 70, if I smoked and took drugs my quality of life when I'm 70 is going to be more crap than if I didn't and my body's healthy. Do you know what I mean?
> [...]
> 'Cos I want to be like, 'cos I've never thought about living very long before until recently. And then I've thought, 'Well if I do, you know, if I am going to live that long, I want to carry on being as healthy as I can for as long as I can'. Do you know what I mean?
> *Yeah, yeah and so that ...*
> So that makes a difference and I think probably if I took drugs for many years it's going to deteriorate, well me body's going to deteriorate because of it. Whereas if I don't, I think it's got a better chance of being fitter and healthier.
>
> (interview at age 28)

At the beginning of this chapter, Danielle expressed her surprise that she had taken different drugs in the past and she went on to explain that she had mixed feelings about this:

> *Why would you wish that you hadn't [taken drugs]?*
> 'Cos you really don't need them. 'Cos you don't, like they make you feel good at the time, but there's things that you can do in your life that can make you feel good anyway.
> *Mmm, so in a way, are you saying that you wish you'd had other things, that you'd found other ways to make you feel good?*

Yeah, yeah. But, then I can, it's like an experience isn't it? So in that way, I don't really regret it because it's like an experience that I've been through in my life.

[...]

... 'cos I've done it, and I don't feel I need to do it again.

(interview at age 28)

Whilst Danielle had begun to perceive long-term risks to her health and well-being that reinforced her drug desistance, Stuart's narrative, which follows, illustrates some of the more serious risks perceived by drug abstainers which informed their decisions not to take drugs.

Stuart, a drug abstainer

Unlike some interviewees, Stuart never commenced a drugs journey. Throughout all his interviews, he described drug taking as a risky activity. He believed taking drugs would place his life and health at risk. During his first interview, he declared: 'I feel strongly about not taking drugs because they're probably lethal and dangerous to your health' (interview at age 17). His message to drug takers, when he was younger, was: 'Just say, "No". Really, drugs can be fatal, your lives can be at risk ...' (interview at age 17). In later interviews, he still discussed how he perceived the risk of death associated with drug taking. Stuart, however, did create a hierarchy of risk in which he perceived cannabis as less harmful than all other illegal drugs. This view led him to the opinion that it should be available strictly for medicinal purposes.

When Stuart was 16, he went to further education college. Whilst at college, he took part in a variety of sporting activities from tennis to running to outdoor pursuits. When he was interviewed at age 17, he explained that taking drugs did not fit with his active lifestyle: 'I'm quite a sporty person [...] so it [taking drugs] doesn't appeal to me' (interview at age 17). Throughout his twenties, he continued to partake in different sports. He could still not perceive any advantages in taking drugs and again referred to his healthy life-style: 'I'm quite a sporty person and I can't see the benefit at all [in taking drugs]. I don't know why people do it' (interview at age 22). When he was last interviewed, at age 28, he was a member of a gym and keen runner and he was still making similar statements about not taking drugs.

A further reason for not taking drugs, which Stuart discussed, was the fear they may cause him to lose control. This risk perception was partly informed by observing drug takers in clubs:

... you go out to a club and you see people smashed out of their brain, and you think, 'What's the point of doing that?', you know, they can't stand up, they just look out of it, it's just a joke.

(interview at age 17)

Being out of control was not a feature of Stuart's social life; he rarely drank alcohol to excess. As he recalled, at age 28, he had never wanted to feel out of control:

> Thinking back, I never really got into a state where I was really not in control. I think one of the things that I always used to worry about was not being in control of my, you know, my, my ability to know what I was doing.
> **Yeah.**
> And I've always had that really. I've never liked not knowing that I was doing something I couldn't control and it was the same when I was 18, and it's the same now really.
>
> (interview at age 28)

In addition to these negative effects and potential risks, Stuart's decision not to take drugs was also made by reference to his family life. He was concerned, at age 17, that if he was caught with drugs it would have a negative impact upon his family's business. Furthermore, he stated his parents held strong anti-drugs attitudes. Although he was aware of their opinions, he could not recall a specific conversation with them about drugs. He was conscious, however, they had 'strong views' about drinking alcohol or getting into trouble; therefore, he believed taking drugs would also not be acceptable:

> ... it was always like the consequences are ... I remember back speaking to my Dad and my Mum and I remember them saying, 'Oh, if you ever come home drunk or, you know, you've ever been in some sort of a fight, or anything like that, this is what'll happen' and I can only relate it to that really. Yeah, I think it [not taking drugs] was to do with some strong views from my parents really.
>
> (interview at age 28)

Despite his family attitudes towards drug taking, since his interview at age 22, Stuart became aware his two younger brothers had smoked cannabis in the past. One began to smoke it regularly. Although Stuart presented himself as someone who did not mind if people took drugs, he was 'disappointed' when it was a member of his own family:

> A bit resentful, in a way, disappointed. Feel sorry for him, in a way, that he's had to use that type of relaxation, stress relief, whatever you call it, to get away from the issues that our family has faced really. Things like my Mum dying, you know, I personally believe that's got quite a bit to do with why he's gone down that route really, just smoking cannabis.
> [...]

... he's got a different way of dealing with issues than I have and I just wish sometimes that he'd follow my route and be a bit stubborn, a bit self-minded and follow my route.

(interview at age 28)

Stuart was one of a few interviewees who discussed drugs education and how it had influenced their attitudes towards drugs. At school, he watched a video about the risks associated with taking heroin and cocaine which he felt had a lasting impact upon him:

... there was like an awareness created of the dangers of taking drugs and I was, you know, quite switched on to that really. I don't know about the rest of the people in the class, don't know how switched on they were, but for me it was like something was triggered really. As though it was, you know, some sort of safety mechanism was switched on to say, 'Whatever happens, don't go down that route'.

(interview at age 28)

When Stuart was interviewed at age 17, he reported that a few of his friends had occasionally smoked cannabis and tried amphetamines. His friendship group at this stage in his life, and previously during secondary school, consisted largely of non-drug takers. However, when he was in his mid-teens, he was presented with a situation where he felt pressured by a friend to take drugs:

A couple of years ago I went to [the South] with the school. My friend, I've known my friend for about five or six years, and you could tell by his appearance he was into drugs, into cannabis anyway. I got offered it when I was in my hotel room. I just refused and that was when the friendship fell apart ... We were really good friends and over a period of about two months his attitude changed and you could tell by his personality. He just got really heavy and tried to push me into things that I didn't want to do. [...]
Well, he was trying to push me into smoking, and he had, I think it was speed [amphetamines] ... trying to get me to take one of those. I was in the same hotel room, so there was even more pressure. He just wouldn't take no for an answer, so I just walked out and stayed in someone else's room. I haven't seen him since then.

(interview at age 17)

On reflection, Stuart felt upset that his friend had pressurized him when he was aware of his attitudes towards drugs:

... I didn't really speak to that individual again because I felt resentful that he'd put me in that situation, even though he knew I was anti-drugs.

Because he knew that I was into my sport, he knew I didn't smoke and he knew that I'd probably feel quite uncomfortable if someone tried to do that. And I resented him for that, for doing that, and that's why I didn't really speak to him again after that really.

(interview at age 28)

Evidently, Stuart was disappointed his friend had made him feel uncomfortable. Secure in his views about taking drugs, Stuart did not succumb to what he described as peer pressure: '... some people do get involved with it [taking drugs] and maybe it's because they don't know how to say no or they're afraid of being seen as an outsider and I'm not afraid of that' (interview at age 28).

Throughout his interviews, Stuart expressed the opinion that drug taking occurs because of peer pressure. No doubt this was partly informed by his experience on the school trip he described above. At age 28, his greatest fear was that he may find himself in a similar situation again:

I think for me it's being put in a difficult situation with it. So, you know, if I walked into a toilet and someone locked me in and said, 'Right, there you go, take a line of that or', you know, '... have a drag on this or take one of these tablets', I'd feel really uncomfortable with that. And I know I wouldn't do it, but I don't know what I would do to try and get out of that situation. So, I'd probably just try and jump out of a window or something. (Laughs) Yeah, but it's being put in that situation because I've been there before.

(interview at age 28)

Despite presenting himself as confident to assert his views about drugs and preserve his non-drug taking status, Stuart was still fearful of being subject to peer pressure and placed in an awkward situation where he was required to reject drug offers. The strength of his fear is apparent in his statement that he would be willing to 'jump out of a window'. The likelihood of being pressured to take drugs in this way is questionable, but for Stuart it appeared real and serious.

When Stuart left further education college he began working in the finance industry and has always worked for the same organization. Although he attempted to minimize contact with drug takers in his social life, he came into contact with them at work. He recalled how he sometimes overheard his team members talking about taking drugs at the weekend. He also witnessed colleagues at a Christmas party distributing ecstasy pills to friends. Stuart and other colleagues arranged for the bouncers to eject them from the venue and the following week they were dismissed from work which he felt was an appropriate response. For Stuart taking drugs posed a risk to career progression. He explained he was motivated to be successful in life, and in his career, in particular. He presented himself as goal driven, not only in relation to his work, but also in relation to other aspects of his life:

... I've always wanted to achieve something, so I've always had a goal, so I've never really thought, 'Well, you know, what am I going to do with my life?' I've always set myself milestones and I think that's helped me because anything that could affect those milestones, which drug taking could do, I've always stayed away from.

(interview at age 28)

Stuart went on to describe some of the goals he had set and some he still wanted to fulfil:

Well obviously getting a good job, buying me own house, getting married, I know I said last time about marriage, but that did happen and it's worked out all right. (Laughs) So far, touch wood! Yeah, career progression and moving forwards positively by achieving things that I want to achieve. Health, you know, I said to you before, you know, doing a marathon or something, that is something that I'd like to do because I didn't think I could do a 10K and I did do it. And that was one of the milestones that I set myself, so I've done that, you know, 'What's the next step?' And I do seem to be, my motivation is to be achieving something and to have something to achieve towards.

(interview at age 28)

Setting goals for himself was clearly important and helped maintain and justify his drug free status. Stuart discussed how he could not associate taking drugs with being successful:

... I can't link it [taking drugs] to how you can be successful and I've always thought that. Because you hear about it, and you see it, the people that take drugs, are they successful? I suppose, for me, I don't see them as being successful. But yeah, I think if I was to like do a bit of an analysis of my friends and people who took those drugs, maybe at the time they didn't have something to work towards or they couldn't see where they were going and I could ...

(interview at age 28)

Stuart's motivation to 'achieve something' and be successful was evidently significant in his discussion of both his own, and his peers', drug taking decision making.

At age 22, Stuart met Hannah whom he married a few years later. He started spending more time with her friends who were all non-drug takers. Hannah had also never taken drugs. By age 28, Stuart was quite emphatic that he did not want drug taking to be a part of his social life:

Because the past has shown that the people generally that I've been around who took drugs, I don't really stay friends with them too long because I don't want to be involved in that type of aspect of that social circle.

(interview at age 28)

He was however also keen to assert throughout his interviews that drug taking is an individual choice: '... if people want to take drugs, then they can do, as long as it doesn't directly affect me ...' (interview at age 28). Stuart appeared secure with his drug abstainer identity. He did not describe himself or his lifestyle as 'boring' during any of his interviews, as other drug abstainers did. When he reflected on the situation with his friend at school, Stuart felt that he had made the right choice at the time:

> Personally, I'm just pleased that I've not took drugs. I'm happy that I've made the right decisions along my life path. And also I'm pleased that I did have to feel that uneasiness when I was in [the South] because if I didn't, then two or three years down the line it might have been a totally different story. But, at that time it was like something switched on for me. And I'm just, you know, I'm grateful that I followed my own beliefs at that time really, because that's put me on this path that I'm on at the moment. So, you know, I'm happy, I don't feel I need to take any drugs, I don't worry about it, I don't reflect on it at all. Yeah, I think I made the right decision.

(interview at age 28)

Stuart clearly believed taking drugs would have changed the direction of his life journey and he would not have achieved what he had so far.

Summary

The case studies presented here typify many of the explanations provided by other interviewees during the course of this research for why and how decisions about drug taking are made. They emphasize the significance of agential processes, identifying and assessing the perceived positive and negative effects associated with different drugs, and the influence of cultural and structural factors upon decision making. Cultural influences were present in all accounts either in the form of pleasures in context or the significance of social relationships for decisions about drug taking. The impact of various adult transitions were also apparent in structuring the decision making process. To primarily analyse the case studies in this respect would be to go over old ground which has been covered in the previous three chapters. Instead, the analysis here focuses on a major benefit of longitudinal research explaining: onset, desistance, continuity and change and what it can tell us about drug journeys and decision making over time.

Starting with onset of drug taking, it is clear from the narratives of the drug takers that they embarked on their drug journeys at different stages of their lives. When Gaby first tried a drug she was aged 16, Nigel was aged 14 and Danielle aged 17. Not only did their drug journeys commence at different stages of the life course, but their initiation into drug taking involved different drugs. Gaby and Nigel tried cannabis first whilst Danielle tried LSD. The types of drugs they chose to try thereafter, the age at which they tried them, and the drugs which became features of their drug taking repertoires were also different. Typically, they all tried and continued to smoke cannabis and take some stimulant drugs. However, Gaby, unlike Nigel and Danielle, refused to try LSD whilst Danielle, unlike Gaby and Nigel, would not try ecstasy.

The frequency of their drug taking also progressed at a different pace. Gaby and Nigel were quite similar in this respect, for instance, during their teens they became regular stimulant drug takers. However, in his mid to late twenties Nigel also started taking cocaine regularly, whereas Gaby only took it on a few occasions. In contrast, there was no set pattern to Danielle's consumption of stimulant drugs. She took them when they were offered to her, when she went clubbing with friends. Indeed, her account was particularly illustrative of the opportunistic nature of drug taking and how some drug takers do not purposefully seek drugs, but will take them if they are on offer. Interestingly, all three became daily cannabis smokers during their drug journeys. Coincidentally, perhaps, the period of time which elapsed from onset until this occurred was similar for all three: approximately three to four years. The duration that their daily consumption lasted was similar for Gaby and Danielle, roughly three to four years, and much longer for Nigel who had been smoking cannabis daily for ten years when he was interviewed at age 28. The variation in the accounts from the three drug takers underlines the diverse nature of drug journeys.

Turning to desistance, it is apparent from the drug takers' accounts that they also decided to stop taking specific drugs at different points in time during their drugs journeys. The narrative from Danielle, a drug desister, demonstrates how desistance can be a gradual process, rather than involving a decision to stop taking *all* drugs at once. For instance, she stopped taking stimulant drugs when she was aged 21 and stopped smoking cannabis when she was 25. Likewise, we can see the slowing down of Gaby's drugs journey from her account. She was an occasional stimulant drug taker in her early twenties and by her mid-twenties she had ceased taking them. Around the same time, she also began to reduce how often she smoked cannabis from daily to occasional consumption by age 28. Nigel's account illustrates how, at times, his stimulant drugs journey also slowed down, however, by age 28, he was taking cocaine more frequently than he had done before and still smoking cannabis daily. There were no signs of imminent desistance for him. Narratives like his demonstrate how drugs journeys can slow down and become more frequent over time. Given his current consumption patterns and reasons for drug taking, it is likely he will continue to take drugs well into his thirties.

Life stories like these also highlight continuity and change in decision making. Stuart's account provides a good example of continuity. His decision not to try drugs surfaced when he was a teenager, around the age of 15. The risks he perceived were initially shaped by drugs education. He believed drugs, other than cannabis, may cause him to die and he was fearful of losing control if he took a drug. His risk perceptions have remained stable over time. They have consistently been assessed against his healthy and sporting lifestyle which he practised since he was a teenager, and his parents' attitudes, illustrating what Lupton (1999) describes as the context of a person's life which influences risk assessments. As he became older, adult transitions provided further reasons not to take drugs and served to reinforce his decision making. There was also continuity in terms of some of the risks perceived by drug takers. For example, as noted above, there were some recreational drugs they refused to try from an early age. The accounts from the drug takers, however, are more illustrative of change in assessments of drug taking during the life course. This was pertinent for both onset and desistance. For instance, initially, when all three drug takers talked about smoking cannabis, they emphasized the pleasurable aspects of it: having a laugh with friends. However, with more frequent use, they began to identify some negative effects, for example, feeling unmotivated after smoking it or needing to smoke it to feel relaxed. Changes in their evaluation of different drugs influenced decisions to take them or not and can be further understood by exploring social relationships and transitions to adulthood.

As discussed in Chapter Four, onset of drug taking is related to access to drugs via interpersonal relationships and the attitudes of significant others towards drug taking. Nigel, for example, described how his initial decisions to take drugs were made with friends who were also drug takers. Changes in social relationships and accomplishing transitions to adulthood were important for desistance. The narratives in this chapter particularly highlight how desistance is contingent upon a number of factors and the relationship between agency, structure and changing situations (see Laub and Sampson, 2003). For both Danielle and Gaby, changes in whom they spent time with occurred because of adult transitions which, in turn, impacted upon their access to drugs. Moving location, they no longer had easy access to stimulant drugs via their friendship groups or intimate partners. Furthermore, their decision to stop taking certain drugs was strengthened by other adult transitions. Danielle discussed how she no longer had time to take stimulant drugs when she started working a weekend shift and, therefore, stopped going to clubs with friends. Whilst Gaby's decision to moderate how often she smoked cannabis was made by reference to her intimate partner, she also described how the negative effect of feeling unmotivated after smoking it was assessed in the context of her employment and housing transitions. It was apparent from Danielle's and Gaby's accounts that adult transitions led to changes in current situations which prompted changes in their drug journeys. However, change was contingent upon the nature of these transitions. For instance, Gaby's initial transition to employment did not significantly affect her drugs journey. However, when she started on her chosen career path, it crystallized her decision to stop taking stimulant drugs. The narratives from Danielle and Gaby also highlight how the confluence of different adult transitions is significant for reductions in the frequency of drug taking or for drug desistance. The impact of different transitions to adulthood accumulated and made decisions to continue to take drugs more complex. Conversely, Nigel's account illustrates how he had yet to accomplish many of the transitions associated with adulthood and he also still spent time with friends who could provide him with access to drugs. He suggested because he had not taken on the full responsibilities of adulthood, he had the freedom to continue his drugs journey.

Whilst the accounts of drugs journeys provided by Gaby and Nigel were often similar, they were also in stark contrast. Of particular note was their discussion of how, at times, they felt their consumption of cannabis was out of control and the ways in which they exerted control over it. With frequent and regular use, they described 'needing' to smoke it to relax and feeling concerned if, for some reason, they could not smoke it. Interestingly, as was the case with other interviewees who described some of the features which we might associate with addiction, Gaby expressed these concerns with hindsight. Her transition to adulthood helped her to exercise control over her consumption of cannabis. Control for Nigel was less easy to achieve when he had not accomplished many adult transitions and smoking cannabis had several functions for him, for example feeling relaxed, not worrying about current concerns and aiding sleep. In this regard, his decision to continue to smoke it is a form of self medication or escapism (see Hebdige, 1976; Taylor, 1999; Young, 1971). It was apparent that Nigel's inability to control his consumption of cannabis, as well as cocaine, brought several risks with it; not only the negative effects he associated with these drugs, but also an inability to move forward in life as he wished. He aspired to leave his family home, start a long-term relationship, become a parent and retrain to work in a profession he would find fulfilling. However, his narrative powerfully illustrates the tensions between structure and agency – in this case, how his decisions to continue to take drugs limit his structural positions, but are also made by reference to his current structural circumstances. He was caught in a vicious circle which he seemed unable to break out from and for this reason regretted pursuing his drugs journey to the extent that he had. Interestingly, it chimes with Stuart's account which underscored how he believed he would not have accomplished what he had so far in life if he had taken drugs. In contrast to Nigel, Gaby was more positive about her drugs journey and emphasized the importance of balance: being able to continue to accommodate drug taking into her life, but less frequently and as a treat. Again, narratives like these demonstrate how drug taking may persist further into adulthood than has traditionally been the case.

By exploring life journeys and drugs journeys using a qualitative long-itudinal case study approach, we can see the diverse nature of both of these journeys. They illustrate why and how onset and desistance occur at different stages of the life course, and continuity and change in decision making over time. Adopting a life course perspective which emphasizes the significance of interpersonal relationships and transitions to adulthood highlights the ways in which life journeys and drug journeys intersect and impact upon decisions about drug taking at an individual level. In this regard, the push and pull factors associated with structure, changing situations and agency are revealed. In the final chapter, the theoretical framework created in this book will be evaluated and what we can learn from this study, in terms of both future research and drug policy, is discussed.

7 Drug taking and risk assessment reconsidered

Introduction

> Innit just natural that when you're a kid you're off your box and when you're a grown up, you're not? It seems totally normal to me, that.
>
> (Shaun Ryder, Manchester Evening News, 4 July 2007)

A central task of this book has been to understand and unravel the conundrum embodied in the above quote from Shaun Ryder, formerly of the Happy Mondays, when he accounted for his desistance from drug taking in his early forties. The aim has been to understand the micro level process which underpins decisions about drug taking across the early part of the life course, not only decisions to take drugs, but decisions to abstain from drug taking and decisions which lead to changing patterns of drug taking behaviour. In Chapters One and Two, a case was made for viewing drug taking decision making through the lens of risk theory and life course criminology. It was argued that by doing so, with regard to decisions to take drugs, we can explain onset, continuity, change and desistance. Furthermore, we can begin to answer the following questions: Why is drug taking often associated with youth or young adults? And why does it decline with age often around the mid-twenties? Questions like these, however, reflect the orthodox view of drug taking, yet, as we have seen, it is not always the case that drug taking desists in the mid-twenties. Whilst the proportion of current drug takers who are in their late twenties and thirties may be small, compared to younger cohorts, they are still an interesting group to analyse and understand.[1] Shaun, like others who grew up in Britain in the 1990s, continued his drugs journey beyond the conventional age for desistance. Why, then, in relation to this sample, has drug taking remained a feature of their lives into their late twenties and looks set to continue for some into their thirties and possibly beyond? It is acknowledged that theories about the impact of social change at a macro level over the past 50 years offer some answers to these questions. Undoubtedly, globalization, deindustrialization, the commercialization of leisure, the ascendance of the night-time economy and extended transitions to adulthood all have their part to play. Explaining drug taking in relation to broader societal changes which have occurred recently has much utility and provides the conditions for understanding changes in micro level behaviour. For example, as we have seen, the journey to adulthood impacts upon individual drug journeys. It is crucial, however, to further understand drug journeys, that we focus on the micro level decision making process which underpins them.

To fulfil the central task of this book – why and how decisions about drug taking are made across the early part of the life course – it was argued in Chapter One that insights from previous theories and explanations arising from the sociology of deviance and cultural studies still remain relevant today. Nevertheless, these theories can be developed through applying a conceptual framework drawing upon the social theories of risk offered by Beck and Giddens, cultural risk theory put forward by Douglas, and the life course criminology perspective of Laub and Sampson. The specific purpose here has been to employ concepts from both social and cultural theories of risk to explore how risk, or drug taking, is assessed by individuals. This endeavour not only develops a theoretical framework for explaining how decisions about drug taking are made, but also permits us to examine and evaluate how the 'big picture' theories provided by scholars on risk operate at a micro level. In doing so, we can consider how they might need to be modified and improved. In this respect, life course criminology has also been incorporated into the conceptual framework. Analysing life journeys and the impact of key life events facilitates an understanding of onset, continuity, change and desistance in behaviour over time and also responds to some of the criticisms directed at the decontextualized accounts arising from the work of Beck and Giddens. Indeed, as Lupton (1999) argues, engagement with risk should be recognized and understood within the context of a person's life. The life course, therefore, provides the backdrop against which decision making occurs. This conceptual synthesis also contributes to debates about the significance of agency, structure and culture in contemporary society, played out in many theoretical domains.

To draw the book to a close, and in light of the findings and arguments made in the previous chapters with regard to the theoretical and analytical framework, this chapter is concerned with addressing the following questions:

- How can past theorizing on drug taking be developed by applying insights from risk theory and life course criminology?
- How well do these perspectives function to explain why and how decisions about drug taking are made across the early part of the life course?
- What implications does this study have for the development of research on drug taking in the future?
- In light of the findings from this study, how appropriate are current drug policy responses and how can they be developed?

The following section re-assesses the relevance of past drug theories, risk theory and life course criminology for developing our understanding of drug taking and the decision making process in contemporary society. This is followed by a discussion of how research can progress in the future. The chapter concludes with a consideration of current British drug policy and how it can be developed in the future.

Reflections on past drug theories, risk theory and life course criminology when explaining decisions about drug taking

The theoretical framework which has been created in this book makes a case for the importance of agency, culture and structure when making decisions about drug taking. In line with the composition of this framework and the book, this section of the chapter begins by addressing the significance of agency, followed by culture and then structure. With regard to agency, the individualistic, rational assessment of risk based upon 'expert' knowledges will be evaluated. Turning to culture, the ways in which a cultural perspective from risk theory can develop insights from the sociology of deviance, as well as the theses advanced by Beck and Giddens, will be outlined. Finally, in relation to structure, the insights offered from life course criminology are assessed.

The role of agency is noticeably absent from early theories explaining drug taking. In these accounts, the significance of structure is emphasized when explaining why drug taking occurs (see Becker, 1963; Young, 1971). We only begin to see agency being considered when risk discourses, developed by Beck and Giddens, had begun to penetrate and influence different academic debates. In their accounts of how risk is assessed in contemporary life, they characterize it as an agential or individualistic process involving rational and cognitive evaluation of objective 'expert' knowledges. In contrast to the emphasis placed upon the influence of members within a subculture, cultural studies commentators (see Bennett, 2000; Miles, 2000) similarly argue that lifestyle choices are individualistic. Drugs researchers in the 1990s (Coffield and Gofton, 1994; Measham et al., 2001; Parker et al., 1998) also began to outline and advance an agential, rational cost-benefit assessment to explain how decisions about drug taking are made in contemporary society. A cost-benefit analysis clearly has value to explain drug taking decision making, for example, various positive and negative effects are assessed and a decision is made about how to act. The problem is not whether a cost-benefit assessment occurs, rather it is the rationality and individualistic or agential nature of this analysis which is debatable. Furthermore, the extent to which a cost-benefit assessment or risk assessment is based solely upon 'expert' knowledges is also questionable.

So let us begin then by evaluating the agential, rational decision maker who draws on 'expert' knowledges when making decisions about risk, portrayed in the accounts of Beck and Giddens. There appears to be some utility in this perspective, for example, the different drug taking repertoires of the interviewees in this study offer support for decision making as the product of agency. If decisions to take drugs were solely influenced by the attitudes and behaviours of other drug takers, then we would likely see corresponding frequency and patterns of drug taking within social and cultural groups. Whilst there was some matching in drug taking repertoires, there was also diversity for this sample.

There are however problems with conceptualizing decision making about risk, and in this case drug taking, as a rational process. There is a sense from risk theory and drugs research that a reflexive assessment of drug taking is applied judiciously and with the freedom to make a considered decision. Whilst this may apply to important life decisions, for example, whether to accept a job offer or whether to move location, and even decisions to abstain from drug taking across the life course, decisions to take drugs provides an altogether different scenario. The emphasis placed on rationality is somewhat erroneous (see Aldridge et al., 2011). Initial drug taking decisions may involve a considered process over time in which a person has observed other drug takers and thought about the prospect of trying drugs, however, once a drug journey has commenced, future decision making may not always be rational or measured. Decisions about drug taking rarely entail a one-off, immediate process which occurs at the beginning of a drug taking episode. Some drug takers may plan what they intend to take for a night clubbing, however, as drugs are consumed during an occasion, decision making can change and may be affected by levels of intoxication. Moreover, as we have seen, opportunities to try new drugs can present themselves unexpectedly and there is little time for a measured, reflexive analysis to occur. Decisions in these circumstances may be based on trust, companionship or going with the flow (see Pilkington, 2007).

Connected to the view that risk assessment involves a rational calculation, Beck and Giddens portray risk taking as something negative, to be avoided and as detrimental to the process of individualization or the project of the self. From this perspective, if we are to reach our full potential, risk must be prevented or minimized. The conclusion reached by Beck and Giddens is that, given the available 'expert' knowledges, risk takers, or in this case drug takers, are irrational and flawed decision makers. The narratives of the drug takers challenge such a depiction. It has already been noted in Chapter Three that drug takers do perceive risks associated with drug taking, however, they often differ from those highlighted by 'experts'. Whilst to outsiders drug takers may appear to be taking risks, they also adopt risk management strategies to ameliorate the negative effects they perceive in relation to drug taking. Adams (2003) argues drug takers are 'risk managers' in that they choose to take drugs rather than having risk imposed upon them. Moreover, the perspectives offered by Beck and Giddens fail to acknowledge risk tradeoffs (Mythen, 2004). In some cases, certain risks or negative effects, such as the whitey experienced after smoking cannabis and consuming alcohol, were perceived as acceptable and part and parcel of the drug taking experience (see also Hunt et al., 2007; Shewan et al., 2000). When risks associated with drug taking, whether or not they are serious, are weighed up against the potential pleasure or functions of drug taking, we can understand why decisions to take so-called 'risks' are made. Indeed, for many of the drug takers, drug taking was a pleasurable and functional, rather than negative activity, which had its time and place in their lives.

Turning to the sources of information and advice which inform risk assessments, objective 'expert' knowledges, as Beck and Giddens contend may have some influence. For example, the risks drug abstainers and drug desisters identified in this study tended to be more serious or long-term and reflected those which are emphasized by medical 'experts' or policymakers (see Chapter Three). Even current drug takers, when discussing their reasons for not taking specific drugs, perceived risks which mirrored those highlighted by 'experts'. Nevertheless, their risk perceptions also changed and no longer replicated 'expert' knowledges when they tried new drugs and included them into their drug taking repertoires. It was, therefore, argued in Chapter Three that risk perceptions act to justify and rationalize current behaviour (see Reith, 2004). Perceiving less serious risks, for instance, may rationalize continued drug taking. These changing risk perceptions challenge the weight Beck and Giddens give to 'expert' knowledges when making decisions about risk. Indeed, current drug takers' risk perceptions did not, on the whole, mirror 'expert' knowledges. The risks they identified were more likely to be less serious, more immediate or short-term and often manageable or acceptable. These different perceptions of risk point to its subjective meaning which has been the focus of cultural theories of risk. So far, then, the value of an agential perspective on risk for developing an understanding of drug taking decision making has been considered. An evaluation of the cultural standpoint on risk and how it can develop past theorising on drugs and the theses offered by Beck and Giddens follows.

In contrast to the prominence placed by Beck and Giddens upon objective 'expert' definitions of risk, the cultural perspective on risk advanced by Douglas highlights its subjective or 'lay' meanings. Similarly, the sociology of deviance and the cultural studies perspectives on drug taking emphasize the subjective meaning of drug taking. A different understanding of risk, or drug taking, is produced by these explanations; one which appreciates the pleasure associated with normatively defined risky activities and the hermeneutic dimensions of risk assessment or decision making. In Chapters Three and Four, the narratives of the drug takers highlighted the significance of pleasure when making decisions about drug taking. In addition, the hermeneutic dimensions of decision making were apparent in the differences in perceptions of physiological and psychological effects between drug takers. As Mythen (2004) observes, this further illustrates differential perceptions of risk. Loss of control associated with hallucinations experienced after taking drugs was, for example, identified by some drug takers as a negative effect whilst others defined it as pleasurable.

Since the groundbreaking work of Becker (1963), the significance of pleasure as a motivation for drug taking has been emphasized. In relation to risk, Douglas' approach acknowledges the role of pleasure when making risk assessments and further counters the negative portrayal of risk offered by Beck and Giddens. Douglas departs from their work by examining the meaning of risk within its cultural context. This not only develops our knowledge of the different pleasures connected to drug taking, but also further contests the decontextualized accounts of risk offered by Beck and Giddens. Recent drugs research has noted how the enjoyable effects of drugs are enhanced in the environments in which they are consumed and the people they are taken with (Duff, 2008; Jackson, 2004; Malbon, 1999). Drug takers in this study also discussed how the pleasurable effects were further improved when taking drugs with others in particular settings (see Chapter Four). These situations often led to enriching and memorable bonding experiences, for instance, having a laugh with friends. In addition, it was also apparent that risk is linked to the settings in which drugs are consumed (see also Shewan et al., 2000; Zinberg, 1984). Appreciating drug taking in its various cultural settings offers a different perspective on risk and a more nuanced understanding of the subjective meaning of drug taking and the decision making process.

The thrust of Douglas' argument is that risk perceptions are culturally determined. The similarities between this and the sociology of deviance are apparent: belonging to a particular social or cultural group influences behaviour. This perspective on risk facilitates an appreciation of how interpersonal relationships can expose individuals to 'risk' (see Rhodes and Quirk, 1998). In this regard, this is the first step of the process of decision making; without exposure to risk, or drugs, decisions whether or not to take them cannot be made. The sociology of deviance, however, privileges the subculture as a place which provides access to drugs and fails to fully consider how desistance is not always the outcome of a purposeful decision. Rather, it can occur when drugs are no longer easily accessible. In Chapter Four, interviewees in this study described how they gained access to drugs via their different interpersonal relationships. As these changed, usually for reasons not related to drug taking, so did their opportunities for drug taking and their decision making. By drawing on insights from a cultural perspective on risk, we can see how persistence and desistance is contingent upon interpersonal relationships which expose individuals to risk. Drug desistance may occur for several reasons, yet when we explore how social relationships change across the life course, it can also transpire that it is because drugs are no longer easily accessible. To avoid exposure to risk, or drugs, drug abstainers, in contrast, discussed how they purposefully fostered relationships with non-drug takers.

Turning to how the subjective meaning of drug taking is acquired and developed, early drug theories still offer some insights which remain relevant today. They emphasized the significance of the subculture as a place in which drug taking is a shared and learned cultural practice. For example, Becker (1963) observes how rationales for drug taking are provided by subcultural members and Young (1971) notes how the norms and values of others within a subculture are important. These insights chime with the conclusions reached by Douglas about the role of intersubjectivity when assessing risk. Yet, Douglas' work allows us to traverse beyond the confines of the subculture to consider other important reference points when making decisions about risk or drug taking. For Douglas, the meaning of risk is influenced by the experiences and opinions of friends, family, partners and colleagues. This perspective challenges the focus of early explanations of drug taking which privilege the peer group subculture as a place which influences attitudes and behaviour, over other social or cultural groups. The relevance of the concept of subculture in contemporary life has been disputed (see Bennett, 2000; Miles, 2000; Parker et al., 1998) on the grounds that we can choose to belong to multiple cultural groups. Whilst it may be appropriate to explain relationships in adolescence as centred around one peer group, early explanations of drug taking are less able to appreciate the significance of the different social and cultural groups to which individuals belong as they mature and the ways in which they may influence behaviour in adulthood. As control theorists and life course criminologists note, the social bond in adolescence is weakened, however, it is strengthened in adulthood (see, for example, Laub and Sampson, 2003; Matza, 1964) and different interpersonal relationships established become highly significant. The narratives in this study demonstrated how when interviewees made their transitions to adulthood they forged new friendships or intimate relationships and some became parents developing further relationships with their children (see Chapter Five). All of these social relationships in adulthood are important for making decisions about risk, or drug taking, and suggest that focusing only on the role of friendship groups within a subcultural setting is misplaced.

When Douglas emphasizes the significance of intersubjectivity for understandings of risk, she notes the importance of cultural, mutual and emotional accountability. To some extent this resonates with the concept of 'societal reaction' developed by Becker. However, where Becker considers how the negative reaction of others beyond a subculture might lead a drug taker to reassess their behaviour and desist from taking drugs, Douglas' concept of accountability allows us to understand decision making in relation to 'insiders' and 'outsiders' – those within and beyond a social or cultural group – *and* decisions to take drugs or to abstain. In this regard, the behaviour and attitudes of others towards drug taking are extremely important and illustrate what Pennay and Moore (2010) describe as the 'micro-politics of normalization'. In their study, however, they only focus upon the anti-drug attitudes of others towards drug taking. In Chapter Four, the accounts from interviewees in the present study highlight how both pro- and anti-drug attitudes and behaviours towards drug taking can influence the decision making process. In this regard, the concept of social accommodation (see Aldridge et al., 2011; Parker et al., 1998, 2002) was applied and extended to examine decision-making at a micro level. It illustrates how different levels of social accommodation within interpersonal relationships with family, friends and intimate partners impacted upon decisions about drug taking. In Chapters Four and Five, the drug status of significant others was demonstrated as important in this respect, as was emotional and physical proximity. Returning to Douglas' concept of accountability, both refusal to take drugs or deciding to take them can communicate commitment to others.

Further exploring the mechanisms of the decision making process, proponents of the sociology of deviance argued that drug taking, or as Douglas contends the assessment of risk, involves social learning. For Becker, rationales or justifications for drug taking provided within a subcultural setting facilitate this process. Drawing on Douglas, Tulloch and Lupton (2003) argue risk assessment is based upon observation of the behaviour and attitudes of others. There appears to be value in both of these assertions. In Chapter Four, drug takers discussed how they received reassurance from friends and intimate partners when making decisions about drug taking. In addition, they discussed how they witnessed their drug taking friends or intimate partners, and even parents, take drugs without experiencing harm, therefore, it became something they could also consider trying. Where the cultural perspective on risk further develops the social learning process outlined by Becker, is through the application of the concept of trust. Pilkington (2007), for example, argues the friendship group provides a safe and trusting environment in which to make decisions about drugs. To this we can also add intimate relationships. Drug takers in this study discussed how they took drugs for the first time with others they trusted and they perceived friends and intimate partners as dependable sources of information. Trust in respect of social relationships becomes even more significant when we appreciate the concept of 'ontological insecurity' developed by Giddens. He notes how we are subject to conflicting 'expert' knowledges in contemporary life, such that we often do not know what to believe. It is no surprise then that novices draw upon the knowledge and experiences of drug takers who they perceive as reliable and drugwise. Indeed, it was argued in Chapter Four that trust forms the foundation of many interpersonal relationships and, therefore, extends to decisions about drug taking.

In addition to the significance Douglas places upon social influences when assessing risk, she also emphasizes the importance of our own experiences with risk. This again is in direct contrast to the objective 'expert' knowledges which Beck and Giddens revere. Whilst it can be argued that 'expert' knowledges were dominant in informing the risks to health and well-being perceived by drug abstainers, their lack of experience with drugs was also important for their perceptions of risk (see Chapter Three). Drug abstainers acknowledged because they had never tried drugs their knowledge was limited. In contrast, drugs takers' awareness of drugs, and assessment of risk, was partly founded upon their own drug experiences (see Chapter Three). When they initially tried different drugs, the effects they experienced were evaluated in terms of how they made them feel. If they found them pleasurable or functional and the negative effects minimal, manageable or acceptable, they often became a feature of their drug journeys. Their lived experience of taking drugs, therefore, informed their ongoing decisions and, in doing so, created an alternative 'lay' knowledge about risk. Thinking about risk assessment in this way challenges

the emphasis placed upon decision making which involves weighing up perceived costs and benefits when making initial decisions to try drugs. It is
apparent that the costs and benefits associated with individual drugs are
learned through drug taking experiences and cannot be fully known before
they have been tried. This further highlights the importance of interpersonal
relationships and trust when making initial drug taking decisions since it is
the information and advice from other drug takers which must be primarily
relied upon.

How, then, does a cultural perspective on risk extend our understanding of
decisions about drug taking in contemporary life? It develops past theories of
drug taking through exploring how pleasure is connected to the settings in
which it occurs, how risk, or drug taking, is assessed and perceived in relation
to different social and cultural groups, beyond a specific drug (sub)culture to
which drug takers belong, and highlights the significance of trust and drug
takers' own experiences when making decisions about drug taking. Turning to
the theses advanced by Beck and Giddens, a cultural perspective on risk
develops these approaches by emphasizing the significance of subjective
meanings, 'lay' knowledges and intersubjective relations when assessing risk.

So far, then, how the agential and cultural perspectives on risk can develop
past theories of drug taking have been considered. In addition, the ways in
which they can also be synthesized to create a better understanding of our
relationship with risk in contemporary society have been outlined. The
importance of structure for risk assessment, or decisions about drug taking,
will now be addressed. Although Beck and Giddens have been criticized for
the over-emphasis they place on agency at the expense of structure (see Lash,
1994; Roberts et al., 1994), the significance of structure was a focus of early
theories explaining drug taking. In this regard, subcultures were viewed as a
solution to structural positions and members of a subculture were united
against the wider society. Relatively recently, we have witnessed a paradigm
shift which focuses on the role of agency to explain drug taking (see Parker et
al., 1998). However, there have since been calls to recognise the continuing
importance of structure (see Aldridge et al., 2011; MacDonald and Marsh,
2002; Measham and Shiner, 2009; Shildrick, 2002). In some of these accounts
socio-demographic variables have been privileged to explain drug taking. It
has been argued here, however, that insights from life course criminology (see
Laub and Sampson, 2003) incorporated in the theoretical framework
demonstrate how events experienced on the journey to adulthood also structure drug journeys (see also Aldridge et al., 2011; Measham and Shiner, 2009;
Williams, 2007). Moreover, the life journey provides the context against which
risk assessment is made (Lupton, 1999).

Focusing then on the role of structure when making decisions about drug
taking, it has been argued that transitions to adulthood are important (see
Chapter Five). Whilst Young (1971) observed how the freedom associated
with youth facilitated drug taking, he also alluded to the significance of the
journey to adulthood for constraining 'subterranean play' and emphasized

the role of work in this regard. As we have seen in Chapter Five, the narratives of the drug takers offer support for Young's conclusion, however, the conceptual framework employed here also considers how the various competing demands, not only from employment, but domestic circumstances, can constrain decisions about drug taking. Indeed, Vervaeke and Korf (2006) argue, control over drug taking is exerted in the context of the greater demands placed upon a person's life. We saw, for example, how drug takers decided to moderate their drug taking when they were busy at work or their family or domestic circumstances required it. In this respect, the nature of transitions to adulthood are extremely important. Shiner (2009) has noted the significance of transitions to adulthood for constraining drug taking. There was, however, evidence from the interviewees' accounts to suggest that accomplishing certain adult transitions was not necessarily the beginning of a journey on the road to desistance. The undemanding nature of some initial adult transitions facilitated the continuation of drug journeys. Nevertheless, over time, as Laub and Sampson remind us, situations change, and transitions *within* adult transitions occurred. For instance, transitions within employment careers that led to greater responsibilities at work and commitment to an occupation, in turn, made decisions to take drugs more complex and moderation or desistance more likely. From the narratives presented in this book, we also gain an insight into the ways in which different adult transitions impact concurrently upon decision making. Here, gender was also an important structural variable. It was apparent that some female drug takers had to contend with the demands of motherhood, working full-time and managing their homes when making decisions about drug taking. These individual biographies have highlighted that whilst explanations offered by, for example, Young and Shiner, have value, they somewhat fail to recognize the complexities of young adulthood.

Young and Shiner also emphasize how drug taking declines with age due to the impact of structural factors, however, there was evidence to suggest drug journeys in young adulthood may continue beyond the orthodox age associated with desistance. Drug takers in their late twenties discussed how they continued to accommodate drug taking into their lives because they enjoyed it and they felt that achieving a sense of balance or space for drug taking was important (see Chapter Five). In this respect, pleasure and drug taking were seen as a vital counterbalance to the responsibilities of adult life. The ongoing accommodation by these interviewees of drug taking offers support for drug normalization in adulthood (Aldridge et al., 2011). Theories of drug taking arising from the sociology of deviance and cultural studies point to societal changes and explain drug taking as a form of escapism from structural positions, for example, a 'dead-end' job or unemployment. Whilst drug takers in this study discussed how their drug taking functioned as a form of stress relief in relation to their structural circumstances, they also described unique personal situations which provided a motivation in this respect for continuing drug journeys.

In Chapter Five it was apparent different identities which emerged on the journey to adulthood were also significant for decisions about drug taking. Previous theories of drug taking have highlighted how the attainment of a drug taking identity is important for persistence (see Becker, 1963). More recently, cultural studies proponents have emphasized how a drug taking identity generated in cultural settings provides the motivation for drug taking. For example, it can engender a sense of belonging or group membership with other drug takers (Malbon, 1999). There was evidence from the accounts of drug takers in this study to support this contention. However, the narratives also revealed that, rather than focusing solely upon a drug taking identity, it is important to acknowledge how multiple identities impact upon decision making. By applying a life course perspective, we can see the ways in which different identities are generated as various transitions to adulthood are achieved. It was apparent that interviewees had multiple identities as employees, parents and intimate partners, which, in turn, influenced their decisions about drug taking. These identities connected them to society and were often perceived to conflict with a drug taking identity. Consequently, some drug takers decided to moderate the frequency of their drug taking. As we saw with the females in this study, their identities as new mothers led to desistance, however, this was only temporary. Focusing on the different and multiple identities, in addition to a drug taking identity, which are accomplished across the life course provides an alternative understanding of the role of identity when making decisions about drug taking. A life course perspective, therefore, provides a different understanding of how structural factors influence risk assessment or decisions about drug taking. It permits us to see how adult transitions, in addition to socio-demographic variables, are important in this respect. Yet it also appreciates the ongoing conflict between structure, agency and culture.

The overarching argument made in this book then is that risk assessment, or decisions about drug taking, involve the interplay of agency, culture and structure. All three elements shape the decision making process in various ways. To place too much emphasis upon the role of any one of these constituents would fall into the trap of determinism. Decisions about drug taking can be understood as agential, at times involving a cost-benefit analysis weighing up the various perceived positive and negative effects associated with drugs. However, this assessment must be set in context. The experiences of interviewees and the cultural settings to which they belong, and, for drug takers, in which drug taking occurs, offer further insights into how drug taking decisions are made. Likewise, individual life journeys condition responses to risk or drug taking. The journey to adulthood structures decision making, and, in doing so, can either facilitate or constrain the decision making process. When the positive and negative effects associated with drugs are appreciated in their cultural settings, and the social and cultural groups to which drug takers belong are also recognized, together with the impact of transitions to adulthood, decisions to take drugs, and to moderate drug taking or completely desist, begin to make more sense. Similarly, this theoretical framework facilitates an explanation of drug abstinence across the life course. Drug abstainers identify risks which are more serious and because they are not drug experienced, they are unable to identify the pleasurable features of drug taking to balance or offset some of the negative effects they perceive. Furthermore, their cultural and structural locations provide additional reasons or perceived risks which inform their decisions not to take drugs. The theoretical framework then explains both decisions to take drugs and not to take them as a product of agency bound within cultural and structural circumstances. Applying this framework reveals the complex nature of both risk assessment and decisions about drug taking. The following section outlines a future research agenda for the study of drug taking.

Researching drug journeys

This study has provided insights into the process which underpins decisions about drug taking during the early part of the life course, but what are the implications for future research?[2] Undoubtedly, the theoretical perspectives and methodology employed here have been, in many aspects, enlightening. Life course criminology has provided a framework and vista which sets the decision making process across the early part of the life course in context. Whilst previous research (see Young, 1971) has referred to the significance of adulthood for maturing out of drug taking, it has neglected to consider the various life events experienced in adulthood which are significant for decision making and how they facilitate or constrain it. Likewise, drawing upon a cultural perspective on risk, the context of decision making is further revealed in its social and cultural environments and groups. In this respect, we have seen how both the settings in which drugs are taken and the cultural groups to which interviewees belong are important for the decision making process. It is imperative that future research continues to collect data on the context in which drug taking decision making occurs.

Turning to the methodological approach, longitudinal studies, unlike cross-sectional studies, uncover changes at a micro (individual) rather than macro (population) level. Whilst cross-sectional studies are useful in revealing population trends in behaviour over time, longitudinal studies, as it was argued in Chapter Two, are more adept at unearthing what happens in between onset and desistance: the ways in which intensity and the frequency of drug taking change over time, or the twisting and turning nature of both life journeys and drug journeys. Longitudinal research offers a more fluid perspective compared to static cross-sectional research. Furthermore, dependent upon continued funding, longitudinal studies like the NWELS can continue to collect data from the same people beyond the typical age at which drug taking begins to decline. In doing so, as we have seen with this study, late onset for individual drugs can be revealed as well as re-initiation into drug taking. For instance, some interviewees declared when they were in their late teens that they would not try specific drugs, but went on to take them, and others were adamant in adulthood they had stopped taking drugs, but recommenced their drug journeys at a later stage. Although longitudinal research is costly, time consuming and subject to the vagaries of attrition, it still offers many valuable insights for policymakers which cannot be garnered from cross-sectional research (Measham et al., 2011).

Whilst debates about the advantages of qualitative research over quantitative research are well rehearsed and familiar, it is still worthwhile highlighting a particular problem associated with quantitative data: its inability to reveal the *meaning* which underlies certain behaviours. It was argued in Chapter Two that Shiner (2009) presented a very persuasive explanation of the significance of transitions to adulthood to explain desistance from drug taking, however, it was also noted that given the nature of his data there is a limit to the interpretations and conclusions which can be reached by a solely quantitative approach. Although it was apparent that transitions to adulthood impacted upon recent rates of drug taking, what was missing from Shiner's analysis was an understanding of what it is about the nature of adult transitions which constrains drug taking. The qualitative approach adopted in this study has revealed the meaning of adult transitions for decisions about drug taking and how they generally have a gradual rather than immediate impact upon decision making. In this respect, the significance of transitions within transitions have been identified which could not be envisaged or measured using quantitative data.

What direction then should research on drug taking take in the future? Policymakers and research funders should focus their efforts on supporting and funding more longitudinal studies and continuing to fund them for longer into adulthood beyond the traditional age at which drug taking declines. There is a group of older adult recreational drug takers, albeit small, that remain worthy of study. Currently, they continue to accommodate drug taking into their lives and they can, therefore, tell us about the meaning and place of intoxication in contemporary life. Their future is unknown, however, if we continue to collect data from them we can understand how and why drug taking might change when people reach their thirties, forties and beyond. It is just as important to continue research with drug abstainers further into adulthood. They can tell us how they maintain their drug abstinent status. It is also vital we understand the ways in which drug desistance and abstinence are sustained in adulthood and what might replace the pleasure associated with drug taking, for instance, alcohol. These are just a few research objectives we should keep in mind for the future.

In terms of specific methods, although this book has drawn on and championed the benefits of qualitative longitudinal research, the NWELS collected both quantitative and qualitative data. Some of the relevant quantitative data was presented in Chapter One, however, it was noted that there was insufficient data for the analytical focus of this book to present both quantitative and qualitative data in the empirical chapters. Whilst the qualitative data from the NWELS has demonstrated how quantitative research like that from Shiner can be extended and the conclusions reached can be developed, the way forward is to adopt a mixed methods approach which collects sufficient quantitative and qualitative data to measure the motivations for drug taking, the risks perceived and key life course events, over time. The implications this study has for British drug policy will now be outlined.

Reflecting on British drug policy

The accelerating trend in the prevalence of recreational drug taking in Britain from the 1960s until the millennium has posed a drug policy dilemma. The policy response to this new social problem has largely been enforcement and prevention led, with pockets of harm reduction practice emerging over time.[3] The Misuse of Drugs Act 1971 embodies the prohibition and enforcement ethos of British drug policy with penalties imposed for those caught in possession and/or supplying certain drugs. In recent times, we have seen a number of new drugs, which were formerly sold as legal highs, banned under this Act. Paradoxically, the increasing trend towards using prohibitive measures has occurred at the same time as drugs have become more widely available in Britain and prevalence of drug taking has sharply increased. This has led Newcombe (2007) to conclude that continued prohibition has proved to be somewhat of a failure.

With the ascendance of discourses on risk, we have also witnessed the language of risk infusing drug policy (Jones, 2004; Seddon et al., 2012) and rationalizing further enforcement and control focused approaches. The establishment of the Drugs Intervention Programme (DIP) is a prime example; it uses the criminal justice system to identify and divert adult drug takers, who pose a risk to our society, into treatment. Predominantly, its objective is to detect problematic drug takers, however, recreational drug takers, typically cocaine users, have also been caught in its net (Seddon et al., 2012).[4] The problem with current British drug policy is that initiatives like DIP are designed to address problematic drug taking which represents a small minority of drug takers (Kushlick, 2007; Pearson, 2001). When attention is turned to recreational drug taking, with the exception of using the powers of the Misuse of Drugs Act, the spotlight is on young people, typically teenagers, with prevention as paramount. Past prevention led initiatives have focused on warning about the dangers of drug taking, for example, the *Just Say No* campaign of the 1980s and *One Pill Can Kill* campaign after the death of Leah Betts in the 1990s. The current website and helpline, *Talk to Frank*, funded by the British government, provides prevention information and advice about drugs for teenagers, couched in the language of risk and risk avoidance. What we find, then, is that the lived experiences and needs of adult recreational drug takers are ignored by policymakers (Measham et al., 2011; Pearson, 2001). Such experiences, as the narratives from the drug takers in this study have shown, are at odds with one sided government messages which focus heavily on the harms that drug taking can cause and neglect to fully appreciate or acknowledge the positive, functional and pleasurable effects of drug taking. In the remainder of this section of the chapter, the trouble with formulating drug policy upon concepts of risk and the ways in which policy can develop to address the needs of adult recreational drug takers will be discussed.

It has been argued that drug policy is framed through 'expert' knowledges about risk (Duff, 2003; Jones, 2004). There are several problems with designing drug policy and official advice based upon notions of risk identified by 'experts': it often constructs drug takers as rational decision makers; homogenizes them; ignores their own experiences and 'lay' knowledges; and characterizes them as risk takers. The focus on risk in drug policy clearly links with the rational decision maker who assesses 'expert' knowledges when making decisions about risk, portrayed in the accounts of Beck and Giddens. It follows that the aim of drug policy or official advice is to make individuals fully aware of the risks associated with drug taking and, in doing so, hope that they will make a sensible and reasoned decision not to start taking drugs or to stop taking them. It was argued earlier in this chapter that an emphasis on rationality and 'expert' knowledges is, however, misplaced. Whilst 'expert' knowledges may be easily accessible, for instance, via websites like *Talk to Frank*, they are of little use and unlikely to be accessed when unanticipated new drug offers or situations present themselves and demand an immediate decision. In Chapter Four it was noted that decision making in these circumstances is likely to be influenced by interpersonal relationships and the trust which underpins them.

Drug policy and official advice also homogenizes drug takers; it treats them as one group with the same perceptions and attitudes, yet, as we have seen, their perceptions of drugs not only differ from 'expert' knowledges but also from different drug takers. Nutt (2009) argues, the problem with divergent opinions about drugs, particularly between 'experts' and drug takers, is that it can lead to ontological insecurity and mistrust of any messages governments are trying to convey (see also Duff, 2003, 2004).

Part of the problem then is that drug policy largely ignores the meaning of drug taking for different drug takers and the importance of 'lay' knowledges when making drug taking decisions. Indeed, an understanding of the meaning of pleasure and an acknowledgement of it as a motivation for drug taking is curiously absent in British drug policy (Coveney and Bunton, 2003; Kushlick, 2007). Furthermore, it can be argued the function of drug taking is also often ignored. When we appreciate the pleasures and functions associated with taking drugs, we can further see how the focus on risk in drug policy is problematic, and understand why decisions to take drugs make sense. Indeed, although some drug takers did discuss some potentially serious harmful outcomes to their health and well-being which they connected to their drug taking, it was rare that these experiences led to drug desistance. In these circumstances, desistance was either temporary or the frequency and quantities of their drug taking were reduced. Moreover, as we have seen, a focus on health and well-being risks may also be mistaken. It was apparent that these risk perceptions can act to justify current behaviour (see Reith, 2004). The road to desistance is not based solely upon specific perceived health or well-being risks. Instead, desistance is the outcome of a combination of different perceived risks either to health and well-being or adult transitions, assessed in the context of adult lives and changing social relationships.

The absence of a consideration of 'lay' knowledges in drug policy also promotes a portrayal of drug takers as risk takers. Drug policy constructs drug taking as a risky past-time, yet for many drug takers it is a low risk and acceptable activity. Nutt (2009) argues recreational drug taking often involves the consumption of low risk drugs, for example, cannabis, whilst stimulants are taken less frequently. As the drug takers in this study observed, legal drugs may be more dangerous than illegal drugs. In a comparison of the harms associated with alcohol and ecstasy, Nutt (2006) concludes that alcohol is far more harmful than ecstasy, a Class A drug under the Misuse of Drugs Act. He also remarks on the inequitable treatment of recreational drug takers by the law, who risk up to a seven-year prison sentence for possession of ecstasy, which is less harmful than a legal drug. Furthermore, when drug takers do perceive risks, they adopt strategies to manage them. Rather than being risk takers, drug takers are competent risk managers (see Adams, 2003). Over time and through their own experiences and the experiences of others they compile an extensive knowledge about drugs. Indeed, the drug takers in this study knew which drugs they could take for a specific function or pleasure, how much, how often and which to take in combination. Moreover, they managed risk in relation not only to the effects of drugs, but the responsibilities associated with their adult lives. In doing so, they exerted control over their drug journeys. Some of the drug takers in this study have taken drugs recreationally for a decade or more, yet they have also studied, worked and trained or qualified in their chosen occupation. They discussed how drug taking was rarely prioritized over other commitments to work or family life (see Decorte, 2001; Zinberg, 1984). The portrayal of drug takers as risk takers is, therefore, mistaken. Indeed, the contemporary recreational drug taker pursues 'controlled loss of control' or 'calculated hedonism' as 'time out' from work and other responsibilities without it hampering them (Measham, 2004).

Given the increasing trend in recreational drug taking towards the end of the last century and the failure of drug policy to control it, it seems incongruous that politicians and policymakers neglect to accept that drug taking is a feature of contemporary life, a reality we live with and one which can be approached in a different way. It is with despair that we have to read the following moralistic statement in the current Coalition Government's Drug Strategy 2010: 'People should not start taking drugs and those who do should stop' (HM Government, 2010: 9). It conveys a lack of understanding of the meaning of drug taking, the ways in which different drugs are assessed differently rather than homogenously as 'drugs', and a failure to fully consider how we should address drug taking. The policy response to recreational drug taking, particularly for adults, is to approach it via the criminal justice system and the Misuse of Drugs Act. There appears to be no respite in this culture of prohibition for recreational drug takers. Theresa May MP declares in the Drug Strategy 2010: 'The Government does not believe that liberalization and legalisation are the answer' (HM Government, 2010: 2). The problem with pursuing a policy of drug prohibition is that it criminalizes recreational drug takers who are often, otherwise, law abiding; it is only their behaviour, or choice to take drugs, which gets them into trouble in the eyes of the law, often because of possession or other offences connected to their lifestyles.[5] Moreover, as we have seen with the recent banning of various legal highs, drug prohibition creates an illegal market where drug purity decreases and the cost increases (Winstock et al., 2010). How then should this approach to adult recreational drug takers change? In recent times, there have been various calls for depenalization, decriminalization and legalization or regulation of drugs. Perhaps, given the declaration from Theresa May in the foreword of the latest Drug Strategy, any one of these policy options is a step too far for the present government, or indeed, any government in the near future. We must, therefore, consider how we can work with the policy we have, to improve it. It will be argued we need to develop appropriate and meaningful advice and interventions for adult recreational drug takers.

It has been noted that there is a lack of appropriate advice or support for adult recreational drug takers (see Measham et al., 2011). This is due to a policy focus in recent decades on responding to problematic drug taking which has resulted in drug services largely designed to address the needs of problematic or dependent drug takers who consume heroin and/or crack cocaine frequently, usually daily. A consequence of this is that drug services are perceived by recreational drug takers as places predominantly for these clients whom they often do not want to be associated with or spend time with. If we are to encourage adult recreational drug takers to seek appropriate advice when necessary, a change not only in the interventions on offer by drug services, but also the perception of them is required. There is also a lack of appropriate and easily accessible official advice for adults online. *Talk to Frank* specifically targets teenagers and is disparaged and viewed with contempt by adult recreational drug takers (Measham et al., 2011).[6] These major gaps in service provision and advice for adult recreational drug takers, therefore, need to be addressed.

Whilst *Talk to Frank* may not be an appropriate information source for adult recreational drug takers, there is a need for open and candid advice to be easily accessible. It was apparent that drug takers in this study relied upon and trusted the advice of their drug experienced friends and intimate partners who were often perceived as more knowledgeable than 'experts' or official sources of information about drugs (see Chapter Four). To address this problem, official advice should incorporate 'lay' knowledges. Furthermore, in order to be perceived as more credible and trustworthy, when risks are highlighted, the key question to address is how they might impact upon a person's life. For example, medical 'experts' emphasize how a risk associated with drug taking is memory loss. This has been linked in particular with the consumption of cannabis or ecstasy. However, some people will continue to function perfectly well despite experiencing memory loss. We are rarely informed by medical 'experts' how much memory loss will occur and what effect different levels of memory loss might have. If British drug policy embraced a harm reduction approach, it could be more transparent in providing detailed information about the harms associated with drug taking and, in particular, acknowledge that many of the harms identified by 'experts' are more likely to occur with frequent and excessive drugs consumption.

A focus on developing harm reduction policies based upon both 'expert' and 'lay' knowledges requires providing advice to drug takers about how to take drugs safely. Although drug policy has largely been focused on prohibition and control, there have also been some locally designed, commendable harm reduction initiatives. Interestingly, because of the implementation of DIP, we have witnessed a net widening effect which has referred an increasing number of recreational cocaine users into drug treatment via the criminal justice system (Seddon et al., 2012). In the North West of England a local drugs service devised an intervention to respond to this new client group (see Ralphs et al., unpublished). Clients were compelled[7] to attend a one-off event where they joined other recreational drug takers for an hour presentation about the effects of cocaine, for example, how it works once it has been consumed, the effects of taking it concurrently with alcohol, and information to reduce the harm associated with taking it, for instance, the spread of blood borne viruses. They were also given the opportunity to ask questions. Clients who attended these sessions were generally experienced adult recreational drug takers, yet they reported how they acquired new information about cocaine and how this knowledge subsequently changed their behaviour. Few desisted from taking it, however, many discussed how, to reduce the risk of contracting a blood borne virus, they no longer shared banknotes or straws with friends or intimate partners when inhaling or snorting cocaine. Furthermore, because of information about how cocaine depletes levels of dopamine in the brain during a drug taking episode and a 'buzz' or high is, therefore, less likely to be achieved with the greater amount of cocaine that is consumed, they had also reduced the amount they took per drug taking episode. Whilst on the whole adult recreational drug takers may be knowledgeable about drugs and largely control their consumption, brief interventions like these could be implemented nationally to help those, like Nigel (see Chapter Six), who experience problems with their drug taking.

Turning now to the legal status of drugs, as noted, the various policy options, depenalization, decriminalization and legalization or regulation, are unlikely to be implemented in the near future. However, as an alternative to decriminalization, the Advisory Council for the Misuse of Drugs has recently suggested a distinctive policy response for those caught in possession of drugs for personal use (Advisory Council for the Misuse of Drugs, 2010). It proposes they should be diverted away from the criminal justice system to educational or drug awareness courses, much like those available for people caught exceeding road traffic speed limits in their cars, or alternative sanctions could be imposed, for instance, the removal of a driving licence or passport for a specific time period. Suitable educational courses could involve, for instance, a similarly designed brief intervention to that described above. There are clear benefits in diverting those caught in possession of a drug for personal use from the criminal justice system, not least they would not have a criminal record which can be personally damaging, and they may be able to access appropriate advice which informs their future decisions about drug taking.

Some of the ways in which drug policy could be developed in the future have been outlined in this section. These suggestions have been made with the sample from this study in mind. At age 28, many of the drug takers have successfully negotiated their drug taking journeys and their transitions to adulthood. Some will continue to take drugs without major harmful outcomes as they travel through adulthood, whilst others will also make the decision to desist. The extent to which current drug policy will drive these different decisions is clearly questionable. It will be interesting to see how policy develops in the future when the recreational drug takers of the 1990s become parents of teenagers. Because of their own pleasurable and often unremarkable experiences with drugs they may be less tolerant of prohibitive legislation which continues to criminalize them and their friends (if they are still taking drugs) or their children. Whilst a significant change in the legal status of drugs is unlikely in the near future, there are signs of hope on the horizon that perhaps recreational drug takers can be diverted away from the criminal justice system. A further task to be addressed by policymakers is to offer accurate information and advice which reflects and builds upon the knowledge that drug takers possess, and to provide appropriate sources of help, if and when they are required. Until it does so, then it is unlikely that drug takers will take official sources of advice seriously or seek help from drug services. For now, they will rely upon the advice from their friends and intimate partners whom have experience of taking drugs, whom they have observed taking drugs, whom they trust and whom will reassure them that it is unlikely to be a harmful activity, but one that will often be immensely pleasurable.

Appendix

Interviewee profiles

Carl

I like more physical exercise and doing stuff like that rather than getting drunk and taking drugs and stuff.

Carl, a drug abstainer, has never taken drugs. He drinks alcohol, but over the life course his consumption has been changeable. By the age of 28, he was drinking most days of the week; usually one alcoholic drink after a sporting activity. Partaking in sports with friends and family was a central feature of Carl's leisure time. During his interview at age 22, he remarked that exercise was his drug and he still felt the same in his late twenties. When he was interviewed at age 28, he was working full-time in a management position for a company. Previously, he had studied at university, but did not complete his degree due to financial constraints. In his mid-twenties, he left his family home and since then has lived in rented accommodation with a friend. At the time of his latest interview, he had been in an intimate relationship with Laura for over a year.

Claire

I'd say [not taking drugs] it's really down to the way I've been brought up, and to know the limitations, and to know what's right from wrong.

Claire, a drug abstainer, has never tried drugs herself. She recalled, however, that some of her friends from college smoked cannabis in her presence. At age 18, her social life involved going to pubs, bars, bowling alleys or cinemas with friends. As she became older, she saw less of her friends socially because she worked night shifts. By age 28, Claire spent her leisure time with her family and the family of her husband, John. John and Claire started a relationship when she was 19 and they have two children. Over time, Claire's alcohol consumption has changed: she drank more frequently when she was younger, but rarely to excess; by age 28 she seldom drank alcohol, instead preferring to drive when she goes out. She has held a number of part-time occupations and had been working in the same position in an educational a establishment for the last five years.

Danielle

> ... when I was at school, like I would never have, I would never have imagined that I would have tried the drugs I have done. And, but I've thought back on it, and I think I'm sort of glad that I did, but in a way I wish that I hadn't.

Danielle, a drug desister, has predominantly spent her leisure time in pubs and clubs with friends. Over time, how often she went out to these venues reduced. By age 28, she was going out less than once a week. When Danielle talked about her alcohol consumption, she described how she drank most days of the week in her early twenties and would often pass out or forget events. Significant incidents which occurred after drinking alcohol to excess led her to moderate her consumption in her mid-twenties. By age 28, she was drinking alcohol two or three times per week. Danielle noted she had always known friends or work colleagues who had taken drugs. Her first drug taking experience was with LSD at age 17, however, she never took it again. Cannabis became Danielle's preferred drug together with amphetamines. She first tried cannabis when she was age 18 and continued to smoke it regularly until she was age 25. However, she never bought it herself: she smoked her friends' or intimate partner's supply. Danielle tried amphetamines for the first time when she was age 19. Subsequently, there was no set pattern to her consumption; she would take them when she went clubbing and they were available to her via her friends. She stopped taking amphetamines shortly before her interview at age 22. Danielle has also taken cocaine with friends on a few occasions since she was age 21. From age 18 onwards, she has worked full- and part-time and attended college to gain a qualification in a service industry profession. At age 28 she was working full-time in the food industry. Danielle's parents are divorced and she was living with her father and brother when she was age 22. Since then, she left home to live in rented accommodation and she was living with her current partner, Ian, in a house they bought together, when she was age 28.

Dean

> I'm open to anything. [...] I'll never say I'll never take a certain kind of drug, I can't. [...] I may take any kind of drug in the future.

Dean, a current drug taker, spent his leisure time playing sports, in pubs, at friends' houses and, in his early twenties, regularly attending clubs. By age 28, he was going to clubs occasionally. He started drinking alcohol regularly at age 18 and although he has drank to excess in the past, he has never drunk alcohol on a daily basis. He was drinking alcohol less than once a month at age 28. His drugs journey began with cannabis which he first tried when he was in his late teens. By age 22, he was smoking it most days of the week.

Since then he has reduced his consumption. At age 28, he no longer bought it himself and smoked it less than once a week. He tried amphetamines for the first time when he was aged 20 and has taken them occasionally thereafter. Since his interview at age 22, he also tried ecstasy and cocaine for the first time. He regularly took ecstasy over a period of a year with his friends and has taken cocaine less frequently, usually when it was offered to him. At age 28, he was working full-time in social care. Previously he had been employed in a number of unskilled occupations. He completed his full-time education at age 18. Since then, he had a period of unemployment and retrained to work in his current occupation. Dean was living with his mother and brother at age 28. He left home in his mid-twenties to live with his partner, Sarah, whom he has been in a relationship with for ten years. However, after a year of living together Dean moved back to live with his family.

Gaby

> I do strongly believe that you can partake in the odd social drug and still remain on track ...

Gaby, a current drug taker, described herself as a 'raver' when she was 18. She had been regularly attending clubs at the weekend with her friends since she was 16. However, when she went to university, she started spending her leisure time in pubs and bars, rather than clubs. From age 22 onwards, Gaby rarely went clubbing. At age 28, she was drinking alcohol once or twice a week; previously at university she drank most days of the week. Her alcohol consumption has gradually reduced over time. Gaby first tried cannabis at age 16 and started smoking it occasionally. When she began clubbing at age 18, she smoked it afterwards with friends. She continued to smoke cannabis occasionally even when she had stopped clubbing. Her consumption became more frequent and by age 22, she was smoking it every day and continued to do so until her mid-twenties. From this age onwards, her consumption began to decrease and by age 28, she was smoking it occasionally again. Gaby tried ecstasy and amphetamines for the first time when she was aged 17. She took amphetamines occasionally, however, ecstasy became her preferred drug when clubbing. At the time, she took up to nine ecstasy pills during a weekend. When she went to university, her consumption reduced and she has only taken it occasionally since then. At age 18, Gaby tried cocaine and also took it occasionally. When she graduated from university she was employed in various temporary occupations. Around the age of 23, she left her family home to pursue her career. At age 28, she was working full-time in the publishing industry. When she initially left her home town, she lived in rented accommodation with friends. However, within a year, she met her current partner, James, and they started living together. Subsequently, they were married and have bought a home together.

Gareth

> I always wanted to excel at whatever I did.

Gareth, a drug desister, started going to pubs regularly when he went to university at age 18. Over time, he went to pubs less often; by age 22, he usually went out once or twice a week. From this age onwards, his leisure time was spent watching sports on television at the weekend or going to a gym. If he did go out at age 28, it was with his current partner, Leanne, for a meal or to the theatre, which was usually less than once a week. They met when he was aged 22 and married two years later. At university, Gareth began to drink alcohol two or three times per week and has reduced the frequency of his consumption since then. By age 28, he was drinking alcohol on average once a week. Gareth tried cannabis for the first time with friends at university and smoked it occasionally, thereafter, when it was offered to him. After he graduated from university, his brother occasionally gave him cannabis, but he seldom smoked it and has not done so for the past three years. Gareth also tried ecstasy once, in his mid-twenties, when he was at a party with his ex-girlfriend, Dawn. Since completing his degree, he has worked for the same financial organization and been promoted to a managerial position. Initially, after graduating, Gareth lived in rented accommodation in his home town, however, he moved location for work purposes. At first, he lived in rented accommodation and then bought a house with Leanne.

Helen

> I've never hung around with anyone that really sort of was taking hard drugs […] just that the kind of people probably that I hung around with, just wouldn't …

Helen, a drug abstainer, started going to pubs and clubs in her late teens. As she became older, she stopped going to clubs and instead went to the theatre or cinema with friends. At age 28, she was going out one or two evenings per week. She has also regularly attended a gym since she was aged 18. When she was a teenager, she began drinking alcohol occasionally and her consumption has remained stable over time. In her late twenties, she was drinking alcohol less than once a month. Although she had never tried drugs herself, she thought her brother had smoked cannabis and some of her friends at university also smoked it. After finishing her undergraduate degree, she went on to complete a postgraduate degree. Since graduating, she has been employed in various full-time occupations. She left her family home to go to university and returned to live with her parents. Subsequently, she left home to buy a house with her current partner, Ben. They met when she was 20 and married four years later.

Jan

> I'm sort of disappointed in myself […] I've smoked cannabis, you know, quite a lot, you know, since being basically at university the first time. And, you know, reading that [interview transcript] you would think, you know, 'This girl would never take drugs'.

When Jan, a drug desister, was at sixth form college her social life revolved around pubs and clubs, as it did when she initially went to university. By age 28, she rarely went to pubs or clubs, partly because she spent most of her time studying for a postgraduate degree. She first started drinking alcohol with friends from school when she was aged 14 and she was drinking regularly from age 17. By age 28, she was drinking alcohol once or twice a week, usually one alcoholic drink, at home. Although Jan knew some of her friends at school had tried cannabis and amphetamines, she did not try drugs until she went to university. At university, in her early twenties, she started a relationship with Darren who smoked cannabis daily and she began to smoke it occasionally with him. After nine months, when their relationship ended, Jan stopped smoking cannabis and since then has smoked it occasionally when it has been offered to her by other boyfriends. After graduating from university, Jan gained full-time employment and has since returned to education at postgraduate level. She was living in rented accommodation at age 28, whilst studying, returning to live with her family during vacations. At the time of her latest interview, Jan had been in a relationship with Alex for the past three years.

Kate

> I could strangle people sometimes, because it really isn't worth it at all. It's like if I could do my time again, I would not even entertain it. […] I'd probably still try drugs, but not to the degree that I did.

Kate, a current drug taker, started attending clubs when she was a teenager. From age 18, she went clubbing or to raves all weekend, every weekend, starting on a Friday night and finishing on a Monday morning. By age 22, she had stopped clubbing, preferring to spend her time with her current partner, Justin, and their young son Bradley. Occasionally, they would go to a pub or a music event, but on average she was going out less than once a week after the birth of her son. When Kate was aged between 13 and 15, she drank alcohol every weekend, however, her consumption reduced once she began taking stimulant drugs regularly in her late teens. By age 28, she drank alcohol occasionally, usually one or two drinks per occasion. Kate has tried a variety of drugs including LSD, tranquillizers, GHB and cocaine, however, ecstasy, heroin, amphetamines and cannabis have featured most prominently in her drugs journey. Around the time she left school, at age 16, she was taking amphetamines and ecstasy when she went clubbing or to raves.

Amphetamines became her preferred drug and she continued to take them regularly. At age 17, Kate initially started smoking heroin at weekends and progressed to smoking it every day for 12 months. She also continued to take amphetamines, but once she stopped smoking heroin, her consumption of amphetamines increased. She began to take them daily and by age 21, she was consuming seven grams per week. When Kate was interviewed at age 22, she had reduced her consumption of drugs considerably and was occasionally taking amphetamines and ecstasy. Cannabis rarely featured in Kate's drug taking repertoire until she was in her mid to late twenties. At age 28, she had been smoking it on a daily basis for the past six months and she had just reduced this to once a week. At the time of her latest interview, she was working part-time at an educational establishment. Previously, she had been employed in various full-time occupations. She was living with her partner Justin in rented accommodation and they had been living together since Kate left her home town in her early twenties. Kate now has two children, Bradley and Phoebe, with Justin whom she married in 2001.

Lindsay

> ... taking the coke, it was kind of like just for laughs and, you know, the circle we were in at the time.

Lindsay, a current drug taker, first left home at age 18 and started to go out every weekend with her friends to clubs and all night parties. However, once she became a parent in her early twenties, she tended to socialize at friends' houses with friends who also had children. At age 28, she was still socializing with friends at home, but also going out to bars or restaurants less than once a week. She described herself as 'permanently drunk' at age 18 and continued to drink excessively when she was in a relationship, in her late teens and early twenties, with Graham. At age 28, she was drinking alcohol a few times per week. In her mid teens, Lindsay started her drugs journey. She tried LSD at age 14 and began to take it regularly between ages 15 and 16. Around the same time, she tried amphetamines but only started taking them regularly when she started clubbing at age 18. She also tried cannabis for the first time when she was aged 15 and smoked it daily with a friend until she was aged 16. Since then, she has smoked it occasionally, when it has been offered to her. At age 18, Lindsay tried cocaine for the first time and initially took it occasionally when she had access to it. During her twenties, she has taken it more regularly, at times, on a daily basis. However, by age 28, she was taking it occasionally again, typically a few times per year. Since she left college at age 18, Lindsay has worked full-time in the beauty industry. When she initially left her family home, she lived in rented accommodation with friends locally. Subsequently, she started a relationship with Graham and they began living together. They had a son, Lloyd, when she was in her early twenties. The relationship ended when Lloyd was young and Lindsay returned to live with her parents for a few years. When she left home again, she moved into rented accommodation. By age 28, she had been in a relationship with her current partner, Paul, for a year, and they were in the process of buying a house together.

Martin

> They [drugs] might make you feel good for a bit, but they're ultimately going to do you harm.

Martin, a drug desister, spent his leisure time in local pubs and pool halls during his late teens. When he went to university, he started going to pubs and clubs more regularly. By age 28, he was going out one or two evenings per week, usually to a pub or local pool hall with friends. Martin first tried alcohol at age 17. His consumption increased when he went to university, but has since reduced and he now drinks once or twice a week. At university, Martin's brief drug journey commenced: he tried cannabis a few times with friends and has not smoked it since. After graduating from university, he gained employment full-time and, by age 28, he was working in a management position in the food industry. Initially, he returned to live with his parents when he graduated from university, but soon left home to rent a flat with friends. Around his mid twenties, he met his current partner, Jodie, and they subsequently bought a house together. At the time of his latest interview, they had two daughters and were planning to get married.

Michelle

> I don't feel I've missed out on anything. [...] I'm glad I haven't taken anything really.

Michelle, a drug abstainer, spent most of her social life with her long-term boyfriend, Patrick, at each other's homes when she was 18. By age 22, when this relationship had ended, she was spending her weekends in pubs, bars and occasionally clubs. She also went to the gym in her spare time. However, at age 28, she rarely went out and, if she did, it was for a meal at a local pub with her current partner, Kevin. When Michelle was younger, she rarely drank alcohol, although her consumption increased around the age of 22 when she was spending more time with her friends in pubs or clubs. By age 28, she seldom drank alcohol. Michelle has never taken drugs herself, but was aware that Kevin was drug experienced before meeting her, and some of her friends and her brother have also tried drugs in the past, mainly cannabis. After completing her degree, she started a full-time career in the health sector and, after becoming a parent, started working part-time. Michelle lived with her family when she went to university. Shortly after her interview, at age 22, she bought her own home. Not long after this, she met Kevin and they bought a house together when she was aged 25. A year later their daughter, Charlotte, was born.

Natalie

> ... I think, yeah, probably a bad experience [with drugs] is what puts me off. But, more the fact that it's just wrong, it's just naughty (Laughs), you know, it's stupid.

Natalie, a drug desister, started going to pubs at weekends when she was aged 18. When she was at university, she went to them more frequently. In her mid-twenties, Natalie began to socialize with friends at home rather than going out to pubs. In her spare time, she also goes to a gym. Natalie began drinking alcohol at age 18. By age 28, she was drinking alcohol three or four times per week. Her drug journey started at university when she tried cannabis for the first time. She smoked it occasionally, but has not smoked it since she was aged 21. At university, when she was aged 20, she met her current partner, Dan, and they married when Natalie was in her mid twenties. After completing her degree, she returned home to live with her parents but soon left again when she bought a house. Subsequently, she also bought a house with Dan. At the time of her latest interview, Natalie was working full-time leading a team of staff.

Natasha

> ... life's too short, I'm not here for hassle, I just want to have a good time ...

Natasha, a current drug taker, has spent her leisure time mainly with Rick, her current partner, and their friends. At age 22, going to clubs or parties was a feature of their social life. By age 28, she was clubbing on average once every four to six weeks. Occasionally, Natasha drank alcohol, however, she preferred to take drugs. Her drugs journey began when she was aged 20 and tried cannabis for the first time. By age 22, she was smoking it most days of the week and she was a daily smoker at age 28. Amphetamines became Natasha's preferred stimulant drug in her early twenties, which she first tried when she was age 21 and started taking regularly when she went clubbing. Natasha tried ecstasy for the first time at age 24 and since then has taken both amphetamines and ecstasy when she goes out clubbing. In her early twenties, she tried magic mushrooms once and from her mid twenties onwards she has also tried MDMA powder and crystal, cocaine and ketamine, although she does not take these drugs as regularly as amphetamines and ecstasy. The most prolific drug consumer per drug taking episode in the interview sample, she consumed 12 ecstasy pills, a couple of grams of amphetamines and a small amount of crystal MDMA when she recently celebrated her birthday before her latest interview. At age 28, she described several other occasions when she consumed larger quantities of drugs. After leaving full-time compulsory education at age 16, Natasha gained full-time employment and subsequently studied part-time to qualify in a profession in the finance industry. She was still working full-time in the finance sector at age 28. She left her family home at age 18, when she married her current partner, Rick, whom she met at school. They subsequently bought a house together.

Nigel

I'll sort it out [my life] next year, I think. I say that every year ...

Nigel, a current drug taker, spent most weekends at dance music events at age 17. By age 22, he was spending more time in pubs rather than at clubs or raves. When he was interviewed again at age 28, his social life revolved around going to a local pub, club or to visit friends a few evenings per week. Nigel started drinking alcohol regularly when he was aged 19. At age 28, he was drinking approximately four cans of lager per night. His drugs journey started when he first tried cannabis at age 14. He began to smoke it daily when he was 18 and has done so ever since. At age 28, he was smoking two joints per night. Nigel also tried LSD, ecstasy and amphetamines in his mid teens. Ecstasy became his preferred stimulant drug during this stage of his life when he was attending raves frequently. In his twenties, he has only taken ecstasy occasionally. He stopped taking LSD when he was 16 and amphetamines when he was 18. However, he tried amphetamines again, once, in his late twenties. At age 22, Nigel tried cocaine for the first time. His consumption was sporadic at first. He rarely bought it himself, but took it with friends when they offered it to him. At the time of his latest interview, he was taking it approximately once a month. Nigel's work history has involved various manual occupations; he has also had periods of unemployment and started but not completed college courses. He had not left the family home. At age 28, he was in a long-term relationship, but he thought it was likely to end soon.

Stacey

We're out every weekend [taking ecstasy], yeah and we've got the bug.

Stacey, a current drug taker, went to pubs and clubs a couple of times per week when she was aged 17. At age 22, she had just become a parent for the first time, and was going out once or twice a month. Since then, her social life mainly revolved around her home or her friends' homes with occasional clubbing nights out, until she started going clubbing with friends most weekends at age 28. When she was aged 17, Stacey declared she did not like drinking alcohol. By age 28, she was drinking two or three times per week, but rarely to excess. Her drugs journey commenced at age 14 when she tried cannabis and LSD for the first time. She only took LSD a few times and occasionally smoked cannabis, but has not continued to do so in her twenties. Throughout her teenage years, she took amphetamines regularly when she went clubbing with friends. She tried ecstasy for the first time when she was aged 17 and continued to take it and amphetamines when she went clubbing. In her early twenties, she also tried cocaine for the first time and started taking it a few times per week. When she became pregnant with her daughter, Chloe, in her early twenties she stopped taking all drugs for a few years. By her mid-twenties, cocaine was Stacey's preferred drug and there were periods of time lasting several months when she would take it most days of the week. At age 28, she had recently returned to the clubbing scene and started taking ecstasy most weekends. Stacey left full-time compulsory education at age 16. She initially worked full-time in the travel industry, reducing her hours to part-time after her daughter was born. Since then, she has established her own business in which she works full-time. When she was 18, Stacey left her family home to live in rented accommodation, but shortly returned and remained there until not long after the birth of her daughter at age 22. She has both lived in rented accommodation and bought and sold a few houses with her current partner, Jon, the father of her daughter, since leaving her family home.

Stuart

> I'm still very self-minded about, you know, what I want to achieve in life and, you know, outside influences like drugs and smoking and drinking, things like that, I've not really changed my views …

Stuart, a drug abstainer, had a relatively active social life when he was at college. Friday nights were spent in pubs with friends and sometimes he would go on to a club. By age 22, he rarely went clubbing, preferring to meet his friends in pubs, to go out for a meal or to spend his spare time with his current partner, Hannah. At age 28, he was going out once or twice a week with Hannah, usually to a pub. Although he spent his leisure time in pubs, at age 28, he only drank one alcoholic drink per occasion. Throughout his life, he has been a keen sportsman taking part in various outdoor sports activities and more recently attending a gym regularly. Stuart has never taken drugs himself, however, at college and work he has met drug takers. Both of his brothers have also smoked cannabis in the past. After completing his A-levels, he started working full-time in the finance sector and has remained with the same organization where he was employed in a management position at age 28. Stuart lived in the family home until he was aged 22 and bought his own house where he lived with Hannah. They married when he was aged 25.

Tony

> I kept getting to a point where I was thinking, 'Right, basically I must stop dead. 'Cos I was such a late starter, I had fun on it and then I just stopped, stopped dead.

Tony, a drug desister, had not been interviewed as part of the NWELS previously. At age 16, he went to further education college and became involved in stealing cars and selling cannabis to friends. Subsequently, he was cautioned for drugs possession. However, he continued to supply cannabis to his friends and after some years he became concerned that he might be sent to prison, which prompted him to stop selling it. When he was aged 28, he drank alcohol less than once a month but, noted in the past, he drank it daily with friends. His drugs journey began when he was at college and tried cannabis for the first time with friends. He started to smoke it daily, smoking up to ten skunk joints per day. When he was aged 20, he tried ecstasy for the first time and took it fairly regularly over the next few years whenever he went clubbing with friends. In his early to mid twenties, he stopped taking all drugs, which was around the same time he stopped selling cannabis. He also started working a night shift in the catering industry to earn money to buy a house for his family. When he was interviewed at age 28, he was studying at university full-time and working a full-time night shift. He lived with his current partner, Lucy, whom he met when he was at college, and they had two children, a daughter, Katrina, and a son, Leon.

Vicky

… taking stuff that's doing you harm, it's not going to help at all, is it?

Vicky, a drug desister, had also not been interviewed as part of the NWELS. She started drinking alcohol around age 16 in her local pub with friends. When she was at further education college, she began going out to city centre bars at weekends. At university, she also started clubbing once or twice a week with friends. Vicky's drugs journey began when she tried amphetamines, cannabis and ecstasy at age 18. Amphetamines became her preferred drug at university when she went clubbing. She tried ecstasy on a few occasions and often smoked cannabis when it was offered to her. When Vicky returned home after completing her degree at age 21, she tried cocaine for the first time with friends and stopped taking all other drugs. She started taking cocaine most weekends for a period of a year. Initially, after graduating, she lived with her parents and gained various temporary employment positions. After a year, she left the family home to move for work purposes. At the time of her interview, she was employed full-time in human resources and studying for professional qualifications related to her work. When she first moved for work purposes, she lived in rented accommodation with friends and then with her current partner, Mark. She started a relationship with him when she was aged 24.

Notes

1 Understanding and researching drug taking

1 Nevertheless, some insights are drawn from this study to further our understanding of decisions about drug taking.
2 The profiles of the interviewees provided in the Appendix give a brief summary of their alcohol consumption patterns over time.
3 Details of the methods of the NWELS and the ways in which the study has been developed are presented later in this chapter.
4 The sociology of deviance is a collective term referring to the theorizing by academics which emerged around the 1950s and 1960s. Some key proponents include Howard Becker, Stan Cohen, Erving Goffman and Jock Young.
5 Young (1999) has latterly observed how, with the emergence of the night-time economy in recent decades and the decline of various industries, our society is now largely focused towards leisure rather than production.
6 Initially rave culture was known as Acid House.
7 A further problem is recanting or inconsistent reporting. Despite attempts by the research team to ensure honest and accurate reporting, the study was subject to some inconsistent reporting. Parker et al. (1998) initially attributed this to 'bravado' in the early stages of the study (see also Fendrich and Macksey-Amiti, 2000), levels of commitment to the study or a reconstruction of the past. They later argued that the main reason for such anomalies was biographical reconstruction (see also Johnston and O'Malley, 1997; Percy et al., 2005; Plant et al., 1985). The key problem longitudinal projects must grapple with is that respondents may under- or over-report their drug taking at various times throughout a study for multiple reasons (Percy et al., 2005).
8 I was responsible for managing data collection from the sample when they were aged 22, the last full sweep of the NWELS. In order to attain a good response rate and to handle the data generated, we employed a team of ten researchers. Their role was to contact and encourage respondents to return questionnaires, input the data, and interview respondents.
9 Consistent with previous practice on the project, a small incentive of a £5 high street voucher was offered to respondents for completing and returning a questionnaire.
10 A description of these drug status categories is provided below.
11 Early onset of drug taking was defined as taking any illegal drug prior to and including at age 15, average onset included drug initiation between ages 16 and 18 inclusive and late onset included drug initiation from age 19 onwards.
12 Of those who were selected, two declined as they did not have time to be interviewed due to work commitments and one was no longer contactable. Two of these

respondents were drug desisters and one was a current drug taker. Since interviewing had already commenced, and by the time it was known that three people could not take part in the research, there was a risk that there would be an over-representation of current drug takers in the interview sample if the longitudinal element of the sampling criteria was strictly imposed. Therefore, two new respondents, drug desisters Tony and Vicky, were selected. However, they had not previously been interviewed for the NWELS.

13 Again, consistent with previous practice on this project, interviewees were paid an incentive of a £10 high street voucher for taking part in an interview.

14 The interviewees' profiles have been constructed from both the quantitative and qualitative data collected.

15 In the following empirical chapters when drug takers are referred to, they include both current drug takers and drug desisters. The latter two categories are only used when it is necessary to distinguish between these types of interviewees for analytical purposes.

16 A life history is viewed as a more in-depth exploration of all aspects of a person's life (Hakim, 2000), whereas an oral history focuses on a particular aspect of a person's life pertinent to the research focus (Berg, 2001). Moreover, a life history often involves multiple interviewing of one person over several years. Shaw (1930), for example, spent six years collecting data from his informant. Conversely, an oral history permits one-off, in-depth interviewing of multiple interviewees.

17 Although many of the drug journeys described in the following chapters fit with definitions of recreational drug taking, some do cross the boundary between recreational and dependent or problematic drug taking.

2 Theorizing decisions about drug taking

1 This framework has largely been informed by the following key publications: Beck (1992) *Risk Society*; Douglas (1992) *Risk and Blame: Essays in Cultural Theory*; and Giddens (1991) *Modernity and Self-Identity: Self and Society in the Late Modern Age*.

2 The theories presented by Beck and Giddens will continue to be evaluated throughout this chapter when alternative perspectives on risk are discussed.

3 More recently, some of the main contributors to the normalization thesis have reconsidered this rational, agential account of the decision making process (see Aldridge et al., 2011) and this will be discussed further later in the chapter.

4 *Talk to Frank* is a government funded project for young people which provides information and advice about drugs online or via the telephone.

5 For Douglas (1985), the political dimensions of risk involve identifying particular groups as 'at risk' and in need of some kind of intervention. The risks which receive most attention are those that transgress moral principles and drug taking can be considered as such. Identifying drug takers as 'at risk' justifies all kinds of services, interventions and pre-emptive control measures by so-called 'experts' or policymakers. The focus, however, in this section is upon the cultural aspects of risk which are significant when making decisions about drug taking.

6 Beck (1992) did, however, allow for the impact of class when he conceded poverty attracts a profusion of risks and the wealthy may purchase safety from them.

7 Reference in this part of the chapter is largely made to Laub and Sampson's later work published in 2003 which updated and reassessed their original work.

8 Shiner (2009) does note how the domestic transition in relation to marriage can change and he provides an analysis of respondents' drug taking for those who have been divorced, separated or widowed.

3 A balancing act? Weighing up the costs and benefits to health and well-being

1 It is acknowledged that other risks, such as legal, employment or relationship risks, are also important to the decision making process and these will be discussed further in Chapters Four and Five.

2 The significance of the setting in which drugs are consumed will be discussed in more detail in Chapter Four.

3 The British teenager took an ecstasy pill and a few hours later collapsed and slipped into a coma from which she did not recover. An inquest later adjudicated that Leah's death was not a direct consequence of neurotoxicity from ecstasy, but water intoxication from excessive consumption of water during a short period of time.

4 Dean and Nigel, who both smoked cannabis daily for some years, also described how they experienced a come down the morning after smoking it. They discussed feeling 'groggy', unable to function or communicate with other people. Nigel describes this in more detail in Chapter Six.

5 It is worth noting both these interviewees admitted to feeling paranoid at times when they had not taken drugs. Nevertheless, they also attributed feelings of paranoia to specific drug taking episodes.

6 Hunt et al. (2007) also note changes in drug taking occur when drug takers feel they have gained all they can from taking drugs or they are growing out of it because of lifestyle factors. This will be addressed in Chapter Five.

7 In Chapter Five, he also discusses how his employment status influenced his decision to reduce how often he smoked cannabis.

8 In the UK, heroin is often sold in £5 or £10 bags weighing approximately 0.1g and 0.2g respectively.

9 An ounce is equivalent to 28 grams. On average Kate was taking 4 grams of amphetamines per day.

10 Noticeably, male drug desisters rarely discussed such risks. Instead they were more likely to perceive different risks related to taking drugs, for instance, to their career progression. The reasons they did not perceive these long-term health and well-being risks may be a product of their drug journeys. Only one, Tony, had taken stimulant drugs occasionally. Gareth tried ecstasy once, but did not enjoy its effects. All three male drug desisters smoked cannabis; two were occasional smokers. Generally, they were less drug experienced than the female drug desisters.

4 The meaning of pleasure and risk in a cultural context

1 Giddens (1990) does note that perceptions of risk vary in different contexts, however, the thrust of the arguments made by Beck and Giddens are that our decisions about risk are individualized.

2 Other perceived effects can be examined in this way. For instance, interviewees reported how taking some drugs made them feel relaxed. Choosing to take drugs for this purpose can be understood further by exploring interviewees' current circumstances in respect of employment, intimate relationships and so on, and will be discussed further in Chapter Five.

3 It is acknowledged that flirting or sexual attention from other drug takers may also be unwelcome.

4 Interestingly, drug abstainers in earlier sweeps of the NWELS described how they were friends with drug takers (see Parker et al., 1998, 2002). However, the small sample of drug abstainers in the present study discussed how their friendship groups were comprised of non-drug takers.

5 This interviewee discussed how his younger siblings had tried cannabis and one smoked it regularly. When he talked about their drug taking he did so in a negative way, emphasizing the detrimental effects he perceived it had upon family relationships.

6 Some drug takers reported how their parents permitted them to smoke cannabis in their bedrooms at home.

7 The significance of these transitions to adulthood for decisions about drugs will be explored further in the following chapter.

8 Such an understanding of drug taking cannot be achieved by cross-sectional or trend studies. They cannot capture the changing nature of drug journeys across the life course at the level of the individual and would categorize many of these interviewees as drug desisters when, in fact, their drug journeys have only temporarily ceased. The benefits of a qualitative longitudinal design will be discussed further in Chapter Six.

5 The journey to adulthood

1 Biernacki (1986) also reaches similar conclusions about the significance of chance for desistance from opiate addiction.

2 Traditionally, this has been referred to as the transition from school to work. However, in contemporary society, with young people more likely to remain in post-16 education, a more accurate moniker for this transition is education to employment.

3 It is acknowledged there are other transitions which affect young people's journey to adulthood. MacDonald and Marsh (2002), for example, identify transitions within drug careers, criminal careers and leisure time.

4 In contrast to Shiner's work, the significance of transitions to adulthood upon decision making are explored here using qualitative data. For an analysis which combines quantitative and qualitative data collected from female drug takers, readers are referred to Measham et al. (2011).

5 Some of the analysis presented in the remainder of this chapter also formed the basis of an update of the *Illegal Leisure* cohort (see Aldridge et al., 2011) and was originally presented in the author's PhD thesis (see Williams, 2007). Since then, the analysis has been developed further.

6 Some interviewees also expressed concern about the illegal status of drugs and presented this as a reason not to take them. They particularly emphasized the problem a criminal record could have for employment, however, this was not an issue discussed by drug takers.

7 Laub and Sampson refer not only to commitment to a spouse, but their family, friends and the very idea of marriage.

8 It is unlikely, however, that any of the interviewees would have wanted to present themselves as irresponsible parents.

9 Later in this chapter, the ways in which identity influenced their decision making will also be discussed.

10 It should be noted that not all drug takers viewed amphetamines or ecstasy as drugs only appropriate for teenagers. Many continued to take them in their twenties. Nevertheless, LSD did not feature in their adult drug taking repertoires.

7 Drug taking and risk assessment reconsidered

1 See Pearson (2001) for an enlightening account of the purpose and function of drug taking in older adulthood.

2 The ideas presented here focus on drugs research, however, they could equally be adapted for future research on risk.

3 For example, there have been locally designed harm reduction initiatives such as London's Safer Dancing Campaign in the 1990s.

4 This has occurred because those arrested for a trigger offence, which can include possession of drugs, must be drug tested at a police station for the presence of

opiates or cocaine. Although DIP was established to divert dependent heroin and crack cocaine users who were involved in crime, into treatment, the drug testing equipment cannot distinguish between crack cocaine and cocaine powder; therefore, cocaine powder users who are arrested are also referred into treatment.

5 Data collected from the overall NWELS sample at age 27 (n=217) indicated that 15.6 per cent of current drug takers had been cautioned and 3.8 per cent had been convicted of a criminal offence. The key offences related to their lifestyles and included: drugs possession, being drunk and disorderly, assault or wounding, drink driving, and drugs supply/intent to supply (see Aldridge et al., 2011).

6 Some of the interviewees in this study joked about phoning *Talk to Frank* the day after they had taken stimulant drugs and were experiencing a come down.

7 Non-attendance under the conditions of DIP can lead to arrest and a possible fine or custodial sentence.

References

Abbott-Chapman, J. and Denholm, C. (2001) 'Adolescents' Risk Activities, Risk Hierarchies and the Influence of Religiosity', *Journal of Youth Studies*, 4(3): 279–97.

Adams, J. (2003) 'Three Framing Devices' in R. V. Ericson and A. Doyle (eds.) *Risk and Morality*, Toronto: University of Toronto Press.

Advisory Council for the Misuse of Drugs (2010) *ACMD Response to Drug Strategy Consultation 2010*. Online. Available http:// www.homeoffice.gov.uk/publications/alcohol-drugs/drugs/acmd1/acmd-response-drug-strategy-2010?view=Binary (accessed 13 December 2011)

Aldridge, J. (2008) 'Decline But No Fall? New Millennium Trends in Young People's Use of Illegal and Illicit Drugs in Britain', *Health Education*, 108(3): 189–206.

Aldridge, J., Measham, F. and Williams, L. (2011) *Illegal Leisure Revisited: Changing Patterns of Alcohol and Drug Use in Adolescents and Young Adults*, London: Routledge.

Arnett, J. J. (2004) *Emerging Adulthood: The Winding Road through the Late Teens to Twenties*, Oxford: Oxford University Press.

Ashton, C. H. and Kamali, F. (1995) 'Personality, Lifestyles, Alcohol and Drug Consumption in a sample of British Medical Students', *Medical Education*, 29(3): 187–92.

Bachman, J. G. and Johnston, L. D. (1978) *The Monitoring the Future Project: Design and Procedures*, Monitoring the Future Occasional Paper 1, Ann Arbor, MI: Michigan University Press.

Bachman, J. G., Wadsworth, K. N., O'Malley, P. M., Johnston, L. D. and Schulenberg, J. E. (1997) *Smoking, Drinking and Drug Use in Young Adulthood: The Impacts of New Freedoms and Responsibilities*, Hillsdale, NJ: Lawrence Erlbaum Associates.

Banwell, C. and Bammer, G. (2006) 'Maternal Habits: Narratives of Mothering, Social Position and Drug Use', *International Journal of Drug Policy*, 17: 504–13.

Barnard, M. and McKeganey, N. (2004) 'The Impact of Parental Problem Drug Use on Children: What is the Problem and What Can Be Done to Help?', *Addiction*, 99: 552–59.

Beck, U. (1992) [1986] *Risk Society*. London: Sage.

——(1994) 'The Reinvention of Politics: Towards a Theory of Reflexive Modernization' in U. Beck, A. Giddens and S. Lash (eds.) *Politics, Tradition and Aesthetics in the Modern Social Order*, Cambridge: Polity Press.

Becker, G. S. and Murphy, K. M. (1988) 'A Theory of Rational Addiction', *Journal of Political Economy*, 96(4): 675–700.

Becker, H. S. (1963) *Outsiders: Studies in the Sociology of Deviance*, New York: Free Press.

——(1973) *Outsiders: Studies in the Sociology of Deviance*, New York: The Free Press.

Bennett, A. (2000) *Music and Popular Identity*, Basingstoke: Macmillan.

Berg, B. L. (2001) *Qualitative Research Methods for the Social Sciences*, London: Allyn and Bacon.

Biernacki, P. (1986) *Pathways from Heroin Addiction: Recovery Without Treatment*, Philadelphia, PA: Temple University Press.

Blackman, S. (2004) *Chilling Out: The Cultural Politics of Substance Consumption, Youth and Drug Policy*, Maidenhead: Open University Press.

Bourdieu, P. (1984) *Distinction: A Social Critique of the Judgement of Taste*, London: Routledge and Kegan Paul.

——(1990) *The Logic of Practice*, Cambridge: Polity.

Boys, A., Marsden, J., Griffiths, P., Fountain, J., Stillwell, G. and Strang, J. (1999) 'Substance Use Among Young People: The Relationship Between Perceived Functions and Intentions', *Addiction*, 94(7): 1043–55.

——, Marsden, J. and Strang, J. (2001) 'Understanding Reasons for Drug Use Amongst Young People: A Functional Perspective', *Health Education Research Theory and Practice*, 16(4): 457–69.

Braithwaite, J. (1989) *Crime, Shame and Reintegration*, Cambridge: Cambridge University Press.

——(1993) 'Shame and Modernity', *The British Journal of Criminology*, 33(1): 1–18.

Branigan, P. and Wellings, K. (1998) 'Dance Drug Education in Clubs: Evaluation of the London Dance Safety Campaign', *Health Education Journal*, 57: 232–40.

Byrne, B. (2004) 'Qualitative Interviewing' in C. Seale (ed.) *Researching Society and Culture* (2nd edition), London: Sage.

Calcutt, A. (1998) *Arrested Development: Popular Culture and the Erosion of Adulthood*, London: Cassell.

Cami, J. and Farre, M. (2003) 'Mechanisms of Disease: Drug Addiction', *New England Journal of Medicine*, 349: 975–86.

Caplan, P. (2000) *Risk Revisited*, London: Pluto Press.

Carroll, T. (2000) *Illicit Drugs Research to Aid in the Development of Strategies to Target Youth and Young People*, Report prepared for the Commonwealth Department of Health and Aged Care, Sydney: Blue Moon Research and Planning.

Caspi, A. and Moffitt, T. E. (1995) 'The Continuity of Maladaptive Behavior: From Description to Understanding in the Study of Antisocial Behaviour' in D. Cicchetti and D. Cohen (eds) *Manual of Developmental Psychology*, New York: John Wiley.

Charmaz, K. (2003) 'Grounded Theory: Objectivist and Constructivist Methods' in N. K. Denzin and Y. S. Lincoln (eds.) *Strategies of Qualitative Inquiry* (2nd edition), London: Sage.

Cloward, R. and Ohlin, L. (1960) *Delinquency and Opportunity: A Theory of Delinquent Gangs*, New York: Free Press.

Coffey, A. and Atkinson, P. (1996) 'Narratives and Stories' in A. Coffey and P. Atkinson (eds.) *Making Sense of Qualitative Data*, London: Sage.

Coffield, F. and Gofton, L. (1994) *Drugs and Young People*, London: Institute for Public Policy Research.

Cohen, S. and Taylor, L. (1992) *Escape Attempts: The Theory and Practice of Resistance to Everyday Life*, London: Routledge.

Coles, B. (1995) *Youth and Social Policy: Youth Citizenship and Young Careers*, London: UCL Press.

Connell, R. W. (1987) *Gender and Power: Society, the Person and Sexual Politics*, Cambridge: Polity Press.

Cote, J. and Allahar, A. L. (1996) *Generation on Hold: Coming of Age in the Late Twentieth Century*, New York: New York University Press.

Coveney, J. and Bunton, R. (2003) 'In Pursuit of the Study of Pleasure: Implications for Health Research and Practice', *Health*, 7: 161–79.

Crawshaw, P. (2004) 'The "Logic of Practice" in the Risky Community: The Potential of the Work of Pierre Bourdieu for Theorising Young Men's Risk-Taking' in W. Mitchell, R. Bunton and E. Green (eds) *Young People, Risk and Leisure: Constructing Identities in Everyday Life*, Basingstoke: Palgrave Macmillan.

Critcher, C. (2000) '"Still Raving": Social Reaction to Ecstasy', *Leisure Studies*, 19(3): 145–62.

Culpitt, I. (1999) *Social Policy and Risk*, London: Sage.

Dafters, R. I., Hoshi, R. and Talbot, A. C. (2004) 'Contribution of Cannabis and MDMA ("Ecstasy") to Cognitive Changes in Long-Term Polydrug Users', *Psychopharmacology*, 173: 405–10.

Dale, A. and Davies, R. B. (1994) (eds) *Analyzing Social and Political Change: A Casebook of Methods*, London: Sage.

Decorte, T. (2001) 'Drug Users' Perceptions of "Controlled" and "Uncontrolled" Use"', *International Journal of Drug Policy*, 12: 297–320.

Deehan, A. and Saville, E. (2003) *Recreational Drug Use Among Clubbers in the South East of England*, London: Home Office.

Dorn, N. and Murji, K. (1992) *Drug Preventions: A Review of the English Language Literature*, London: Institute for the Study of Drug Dependence.

Douglas, M. (1985) *Risk Acceptability According to the Social Sciences*, New York: Russell Sage.

——(1992) *Risk and Blame: Essays in Cultural Theory*, London: Routledge.

Duff, C. (2003) 'The Importance of Culture and Context: Rethinking Risk and Risk Management in Young Drug Using Populations', *Health, Risk and Society*, 5(3): 285–99.

——(2004) 'Drug Use as a "Practice of the Self": Is There Any Place for an "Ethics of Moderation" in Contemporary Drug Policy?' *International Journal of Drug Policy*, 15: 385–93.

——(2008) 'The Pleasure in Context', *International Journal of Drug Policy*, 19(5): 384–92.

Ettore, E. (2004) 'Revisioning Women and Drug Use: Gender Sensitivity, Embodiment and Reducing Harm', *International Journal of Drug Policy*, 15: 327–35.

Farrington, D. P. (2003) 'Key Results from the First 40 Years of the Cambridge Study in Delinquent Development' in T. P. Thornbury and M. D. Krohn (eds) *Taking Stock of Delinquency: An Overview of Findings From Contemporary Longitudinal Studies*, New York: Kluwer/Plenum.

Fendrich, M. and Macksey-Amiti, M. (2000) 'Decreased Drug Reporting in a Cross-Sectional Student Drug Use Survey', *Journal of Substance Abuse*, 11(2): 161–72.

Fergusson, D. M., Horwood, L. J. and Swain-Campbell, N. (2002) 'Cannabis Use and Psychosocial Adjustment in Adolescence and Young Adulthood', *Addiction*, 97: 1123–35.

Forsyth, A. (2001) 'A Design for Strife: Alcopops, Licit Drug – Familiar Scare Story', *International Journal of Drug Policy*, 12(1): 59–80.

Fox, N. (1999) 'Postmodern Reflections on "Risk", "Hazards" and Life Choices' in D. Lupton (ed.) *Risk and Sociocultural Theory: New Directions and Perspectives*, Cambridge: Cambridge University Press.

Furlong, A. and Cartmel, F. (1997) *Young People and Social Change: Individualisation and Risk in Late Modernity*, Buckingham: Open University Press.

——(2007) *Young People and Social Change: New Perspectives* (2nd Edition), Maidenhead: Open University Press.

Gamma, A., Jerome, L., Liechti, M. E. and Sumnall, H. R. (2005) 'Is Ecstasy Perceived to Be Safe? A Critical Survey', *Drug and Alcohol Dependence*, 77(2): 185–93.

Giddens, A. (1984) *The Constitution of Society: Outline of the Theory of Structuration*, Cambridge: Polity Press.

——(1990) *Consequences of Modernity*, Cambridge: Polity Press.

——(1991) *Modernity and Self-Identity: Self and Society in the Late Modern Age*, Cambridge: Polity Press.

Giordano, P. C., Cernkovich, S. A. and Rudolph, J. L. (2002) 'Gender, Crime and Desistance: Towards a Theory of Cognitive Transformation', *American Journal of Sociology*, 107: 990–1064.

Glaser, B. G. and Strauss, A. L. (1967) *The Discovery of Grounded Theory: Strategies for Qualitative Research*, Chicago, IL: Aldine.

Gottfredson, M. R. and Hirshi, T. (1990) *A General Theory of Crime*, Stanford, CA: Stanford University Press.

Graham, J. and Bowling, B. (1995) *Young People and Crime*, Home Office Research Study 145, London: Home Office.

Green, E. (2004) 'Risky Identities: Young Women, Street Prostitution and "Doing Motherhood"' in W. Mitchell, R. Bunton and E. Green (eds.) *Young People, Risk and Leisure: Constructing Identities in Everyday Life*, Basingstoke: Palgrave Macmillan.

——, Mitchell, W. and Bunton, R. (2000) 'Contextualizing Risk and Danger: An Analysis of Young People's Perceptions of Risk', *Journal of Youth Studies* 3(2): 109–26.

Hakim, C. (2000) *Research Design: Successful Designs for Social and Economic Research* (2nd edition), London: Routledge.

Hall, S. and Jefferson, T. (eds.) (1976) *Resistance Through Rituals: Youth Subcultures in Post-War Britain*, London: HarperCollins.

Hall, W. and Babor, T. F. (2000) 'Cannabis Use and Public Health: Assessing the Burden', *Addiction*, 95: 485–90.

Hammersley, R., Marsland, L. and Reid, M. (2003) *Substance Use by Young Offenders: The Impact of the Normalisation of Drug Use in the Early Years of the 21st Century*, London: Home Office.

Hebdige, D. (1976) 'The Meaning of Mod' in S. Hall and T. Jefferson (eds.) *Resistance Through Rituals: Youth Subcultures in Post-war Britain*, London: HarperCollins.

Henderson, S. (1996) '"E" Types and Dance Divas: Some Implications for Research and Prevention' in T. Rhodes and R. Hartnoll (eds.) *HIV Prevention in the Community: Perspectives on Individual, Community and Political Action*, London: Routledge.

——(1999) 'Drugs and Culture: The Question of Gender' in N. South (ed.) *Drugs, Controls and Everyday Life*, London: Sage.

Hinchliff, S. (2001) 'The Meaning of Ecstasy Use and Clubbing to Women in the Late 1990s', *International Journal of Drug Policy*, 12: 455–68.

Hirschi, T. (1969) *Causes of Delinquency*, Berkeley, CA: University of California Press.

HM Government (2010) *Drug Strategy 2010: Reducing Demand, Restricting Supply, Building Recovery: Supporting People to Live a Drug Free Life*, London: HMSO.

Hodkinson, P. and Sparkes, A. (1997) 'Careership: A Sociological Theory of Career Decision Making', *British Journal of Sociology of Education*, 18(1): 29–44.

Hunt, G. P., Evans, K. and Kares, F. (2007) 'Drug Use and the Meanings of Risk and Pleasure', *Journal of Youth Studies*, 10(1): 73–96.

Hutton, F. (2006) *Risky Pleasures? Club Cultures and Feminine Identities*, Aldershot: Ashgate.

Irwin, A., Allan, S. and Welsh, I. (2000) 'Nuclear Risks: Three Problematics' in B. Adam, U. Beck and J. van Loon (eds.) *The Risk Society and Beyond: Critical Issues for Social Theory*, London: Sage.

Jackson, P. (2004) *Inside Clubbing: Sensual Experiments in the Art of Being Human*, Oxford: Berg.

Joe, G. W. and Hudiberg, R. A. (1978) 'Behavioral Correlates of Age at First Marihuana Use', *International Journal of Addiction*, 13: 627–37.

Johnston, L. D. (1974) 'Drug Use During and After High School: Results of a National Longitudinal Study', *American Journal of Public Health*, 64: 29–37.

Johnston, L. D. and O'Malley, P. M. (1997) 'The Recanting of Earlier Reported Drug Use by Young Adults' in L. Harrison and A. Hughes (eds.) *The Validity of Self-reported Drug Use: Improving the Accuracy of Survey Estimates*, NIDA Research Monograph Series (167), Publication No. 97–4147, NIDA, Rockville, MD.

Jones, G. and Martin, C. (1997) *The Social Context of Spending in Youth*, Centre for Educational Sociology Briefing, University of Edinburgh, no. 11, June.

Jones, M. (2004) 'Anxiety and Containment in the Risk Society: Theorising Young People and Drug Prevention Policy', *International Journal of Drug Policy*, 15(5–6): 367–76.

Kandel, D. B. (1980) 'Drug and Drinking Behaviour Among Youth', *Annual Review of Sociology*, 6: 235–85.

——(1985) 'On Processes of Peer Influences in Adolescent Drug Use', *Advances in Alcohol and Substance Use*, 4(3–4): 139–62.

Keane, J. (1997) 'Ecstasy in the Unhappy Society', *Soundings,* 6 (Summer): 127–39.

Knowlton, J., Bryant, D. D., Collins, D. A., Noe, T. D., Strader, T. N. and Berbaum, M. (1998) 'Preventing and Reducing Alcohol and Other Drug Use Among High-Risk Youth by Increasing Family Resilience', *Social Work*, 43: 297–300.

Kushlick, D. (2007) 'Addicts Adventures in Wonderland', *Addiction, Research and Theory*, 15(2): 123–26.

Lash, S. (1994) 'Reflexivity and its Doubles: Structure, Aesthetics, Community' in U. Beck, A. Giddens and S. Lash (eds) *Reflexive Modernization: Politics, Tradition and Aesthetics in the Modern Social Order*, Cambridge: Polity Press.

Latkina, C., Forman, V., Knowlton, A. and Sherman, S. (2003) 'Norms, Social Networks and HIV-related Risk Behaviors Among Urban Disadvantaged Drug Users', *Social Science and Medicine*, 56: 465–76.

Laub, J. H. and Sampson, R. J. (2003) *Shared Beginnings, Divergent Lives: Delinquent Boys to Age 70*, Cambridge, MA: Harvard University Press.

Lupton, D. (1999) *Risk*, London: Routledge.

——and Tulloch, J. (2002) '"Life Would Be Pretty Dull Without Risk": Voluntary Risk-taking and its Pleasures', *Health, Risk and Society*, 4(2): 113–24.

Lyng, S. (1990) 'Edgework: A Social Psychological Analysis of Voluntary Risk Taking', *American Journal of Sociology*, 95(4): 851–56.

——(2005) 'Edgework and the Risk-Taking Experience' in S. Lyng (ed.) *Edgework: The Sociology of Risk-taking,* New York: Routledge.

MacDonald, R. and Marsh, J. (2002) 'Crossing the Rubicon: Youth Transitions, Poverty, Drugs and Social Exclusion', *International Journal of Drug Policy*, 13: 27–38.

MacDonald, R. Mason, P., Shildrick, T., Webster, C., Johnston, L. and Ridley, L. (2001) 'Snakes and Ladders: In Defence of Studies of Youth Transition', *Sociological Research Online*, 5.

Makhoul, M., Yates, F. and Wolfson, S. (1998) 'A Survey of Substance Use at a UK University: Prevalence of Use and Views of Students', *Journal of Substance Misuse*, 3: 119–24.

Malbon, B. (1999) *Clubbing: Dancing, Ecstasy and Vitality*, London: Routledge.

Manchester Evening News (2007) 'Interview with Shaun Ryder', *Manchester Evening News*, 4 July.

Marris, C. and Langford, I. (1996) 'No Cause for Alarm', *New Scientist*, 28 September: 36–39.

Maruna, S. (2001) *Making Good: How Ex-Convicts Reform and Rebuild Their Lives*, Washington, DC: American Psychological Association.

Massumi, B. (1993) 'Everywhere you want to be: Introduction to fear' in B. Massumi (ed.) *The Politics of Everyday Fear*, Minneapolis, MN: University of Minnesota Press.

Matza, D. (1964) *Delinquency and Drift*, New York: John Wiley and Sons Inc.

Matza, D. and Sykes, G. M. (1961) 'Juvenile Delinquency and Subterranean Values', *American Sociological Review*, 26(5): 712–19.

Measham, F. (2002) '"Doing Gender" – "Doing Drugs": Conceptualizing the Gendering of Drugs Cultures', *Contemporary Drug Problems*, 29(2): 335–73.

——(2004) 'The Decline of Ecstasy, the Risk of "Binge" Drinking and the Persistence of Pleasure', *Probation Journal*, 51(4): 309–26.

Measham, F. and Shiner, M. (2009) 'The Legacy of "Normalisation": The Role of Classical and Contemporary Criminological Theory in Understanding Young People's Drug Use', *International Journal of Drug Policy*, 20(6): 502–8.

Measham, F., Aldridge, J. and Parker, H. (2001) *Dancing on Drugs: Risk, Health and Hedonism in the British Club Scene*, London: Free Association Books.

Measham, F., Moore, K., Newcombe, R. and Welch, Z. (2010) 'Tweaking, Bombing, Dabbing, and Stockpiling: The Emergence of Mephedrone and the Perversity of Prohibition', *Drugs and Alcohol Today,* 10: 14–21.

Measham, F., Williams, L. and Aldridge, J. (2011) 'Marriage, Mortgage, Motherhood: What Longitudinal Studies Can Tell Us About Gender, Drug "Careers" and the Normalisation of Adult "Recreational" Drug Use', *International Journal of Drug Policy*, 22(6): 420–27.

Melechi, A. (1993) 'The Ecstasy of Disappearance' in S. Redhead (ed.) *Rave-Off: Politics and Deviance in Contemporary Youth Culture*, Aldershot: Avebury.

Melucci, A. (1996) *The Playing Self: Person and Meaning in the Planetary Society*, Cambridge: Cambridge University Press.

Merton, R. (1938) 'Social Structure and Anomie', *American Sociological Review*, 3: 672–82.

Messerschmidt, J. (1993) *Masculinities and Crime: Critique and Reconceptualization of Theory*, Lanham, MD: Rowman and Littlefield.

Miles, S. (2000) *Youth Lifestyles in a Changing World*, Buckingham: Open University Press.

Miller, J. (1996) *Search and Destroy*, Cambridge: Cambridge University Press.

Miller, M. and Neaigus, A. (2001) 'Networks, Resources and Risk Among Women Who Use Drugs', *Social Science and Medicine*, 52: 967–78.

Miller, R. (2000) *Researching Life Stories and Family Histories*, London: Sage.

Mitchell, W. (2004) 'Risk, Motherhood and Children's Play Spaces: The Importance of Young Mothers' Experiences and Risk Management Strategies' in W. Mitchell, R. Bunton and E. Green (eds) *Young People, Risk and Leisure: Constructing Identities in Everyday Life*, Basingstoke: Palgrave Macmillan.

Mitchell, W., Crawshaw, P., Bunton, R., and Green, E. (2001) 'Situating Young People's Experiences of Risk and Identity', *Health, Risk and Society*, 3(2): 217–33.

Moffit, T. E. (1993) 'Adolescence-Limited and Life-Course Persistent Anti-Social Behavior: A Developmental Taxonomy', *Psychological Review*, 100: 674–701.

Moore, K and Measham, F. (2008) '"It's the Most Fun You Can Have for Twenty Quid"': Motivations, Consequences and Meanings of British Ketamine Use', *Addiction Research and Theory*, 16(3): 231–44.

Muggleton, D. (1997) 'The Subculturalist' in S. Redhead, D. Wynne and J. O'Connor (eds.) *The Club Cultures Reader*, Oxford: Blackwell.

——(2000) *Inside Subculture*, Oxford: Berg.

Murji, K. (1999) 'White Lines: Culture, Race and Drugs' in N. South (ed.) *Drugs, Controls and Everyday Life*, London: Sage.

Murnane, A., Smith, A., Crompton, L., Snow, P. and Munro, G. (2000) *Beyond Perceptions: A Report on Alcohol and Other Drug Use Among Gay, Lesbian, Bisexual and Queer Communities in Victoria*, Victoria: The Also Foundation.

Mythen, G. (2004) *Ulrich Beck: A Critical Introduction to the Risk Society*, London: Pluto Press.

Newcombe, R. (2007) 'Trends in the Prevalence of Drug Use in Britain' in M. Simpson, T. Shildrick and R. MacDonald (eds) *Drugs in Britain: Supply, Consumption and Control*, Basingstoke: Palgrave Macmillan.

Nutt, D. (2006) 'A Tale of Two Es', *Journal of Psychopharmacology*, 20(3): 315–17.

——(2009) 'Equasy – an Overlooked Addiction with Implications for the Current Debate on Drug Harms', *Journal of Psychopharmacology*, 23(1): 3–5.

Nye, F. I. (1958) *Family Relationships and Delinquency Behavior*, New York: John Wiley.

Oakley, A. (1974) *The Sociology of Housework*, New York: Pantheon Books.

Parker, H., Aldridge, J. and Measham, F. (1998) *Illegal Leisure: The Normalization of Recreational Drug Use*, London: Routledge.

Parker, H., Williams, L. and Aldridge, J. (2002) 'The Normalization of "Sensible" Recreational Drug Use: Further Evidence from the North West England Longitudinal Study', *Sociology*, 36(4): 941–64.

Parrott, A. C., Milani, R. M., Parmar, R. and Turner, J. D. (2002) 'Recreational Ecstasy/MDMA and Other Drug Users from the UK and Italy: Psychiatric Symptoms and Psychobiological Problems', *Psychopharmacology* (Berl), 159: 77–82.

Pearson, G. (2001) 'Normal Drug Use: Ethnographic Fieldwork Among an Adult Network of Recreational Drug Users in Inner London', *Substance Use and Misuse*, 36(1&2): 167–200.

Pennay, A. and Moore, D. (2010) 'Exploring the Micro-politics of Normalisation: Narratives of Pleasure, Self Control and Desire in a Sample of Young Australian "Party Drug" Users', *Addiction Research and Theory*, 18(5): 557–71.

Percy, A., McAlister, S., Higgins, K. and McCrystal, P. (2005) 'Response Consistency in Young Adolescents' Drug Use Self-Reports: A Recanting Rate Analysis', *Addiction*, 100(2): 189–96.

Pilkington, H. (2007) 'In Good Company: Risk, Security and Choice in Young People's Drug Decisions', *The Sociological Review*, 55(2): 373–92.

Plant, M., Peck, D. and Samuel, E. (1985) *Alcohol, Drugs and School Leavers*, London: Tavistock.

Plant, M. and Plant, M. (1992) *Risk-Takers: Alcohol, Drugs, Sex and Youth*, London: Routledge.

Ralphs, R., Williams, L. and Seddon, T. (unpublished) *Cocaine Nights*, report prepared for Manchester Drug Service.

Ramsay, M. and Partridge, S. (1999) *Drug Misuse Declared in 1998: Results from the British Crime Survey*, Home Office Research Study 197, London: Home Office.

Reckless, W. C. (1967) *The Crime Problem* (4th Edition), New York: Meredith.

Redhead, S. (1993) (ed.) *Rave Off: Politics and Deviance in Contemporary Youth Culture*, Aldershot: Avebury.

Reilly, J. (1999) 'Just Another Food Scare? Public Understanding of the BSE Crisis' in G. Philo (ed.) *The Nation's Diet: The Social Science of Food Choice*, London: Longman.

Reissman, C. (1990) 'Strategic Uses of Narrative in Presentation of Self and Illness: A Research Note', *Social Science and Medicine*, 30(11): 1195–1200.

Reith, G. (2004) 'Uncertain Times: The Notion of "Risk" and the Development of Modernity', *Time Society*, 13: 383–402.

——(2005) 'On the Edge: Drugs and the Consumption of Risk in Late Modernity' in S. Lyng (ed.) *Edgework: The Sociology of Risk-Taking*, New York: Routledge.

Rhodes, T. (1997) 'Risk Theory in Epidemic Times: Sex, Drugs and the Social Organisation of "Risk Behaviour"', *Sociology of Health and Illness*, 19(2): 208–27.

Rhodes, T. and Quirk, A. (1998) 'Drug Users' Sexual Relationships and the Social Organisation of Risk: The Sexual Relationship as a Site of Risk Management', *Social Science and Medicine*, 46(2): 157–69.

Rietveld, H. (1998) *This is Our House: House Music, Cultural Spaces and Technologies*, Aldershot: Ashgate Publishing Limited.

Ritchie, J., Spencer, L. and O'Connor, W. (2003) 'Carrying out Qualitative Analysis' in J. Ritchie and J. Lewis (eds.) *Qualitative Research Practice: A Guide for Social Science Students and Researchers*, London: Sage.

Robbins, T. W. and Everitt, B. J. (1999) 'Drug Addiction: Bad Habits Add Up', *Nature*, 398: 567–70.

Roberts, K. (1995) *Youth and Employment in Modern Britain*, Oxford: Oxford University Press.

Roberts, K., Clark, S. C. and Wallace, C. (1994) 'Flexibility and Individualisation: A Comparison of Transitions into Employment in England and Germany', *Sociology*, 28(1): 31–54.

Rutter, M. (1996) 'Transitions and Turning Points in Developmental Psychopathology: As Applied to the Age Span Between Childhood and Mid-Adulthood', *International Journal of Behavioral Development*, 19(3): 603–26.

Sampson, R. J. and Laub, J. H. (1993) *Crime in the Making: Pathways and Turning Points Through Life*, Cambridge, MA: Harvard University Press.

Saunders. N. (1997) *Ecstasy Reconsidered*, Exeter: Nicolas Saunders.

Schifano, F., Oyefeso, A., Corkery, J., Cobain, K., Jambert-Gray, R., Martinotti, G. and Ghodse, A. H. (2003) 'Death Rates from Ecstasy (MDMA, MDA) and Polydrug Use in England and Wales 1996–2002', *Human Psychopharmacology Clinical Experience*, 18: 519–24.

Seddon, T., Williams, L. and Ralphs, R. (2012) *Tough Choices: Risk, Security and the Criminalization of Drug Policy*, Oxford: Oxford University Press.

Shaw, C. R. (1930) *The Jack-Roller: A Delinquent Boy's Own Story*, Chicago, IL: University of Chicago Press.

Shewan, D., Dalgarno, P. and Reith, G. (2000) 'Perceived Risk and Risk Reduction Among Ecstasy Users: The Role of Drug, Set and Setting', *International Journal of Drug Policy*, 10: 431–53.

Shildrick. T. (2002) 'Young People, Illicit Drug Use and the Question of Normalization', *Journal of Youth Studies*, 5(1): 35–48.

Shiner, M. (2009) *Drug Use and Social Change: The Distortion of History*, Basingstoke: Palgrave Macmillan.

Shiner, M. and Newburn, T. (1997) 'Definitely, Maybe Not: The Normalisation of Recreational Drug Use Amongst Young People', *Sociology*, 31(3): 1–19.

——(1999) 'Taking Tea with Noel: The Place and Meaning of Drug Use in Everyday Life' in N. South (ed.) *Drugs, Controls and Everyday Life,* London: Sage.

Sobel, M. (1991) *Lifestyle and Social Structure: Concepts, Definitions and Analyses*, New York: Academic Press.

South, N. (1999) 'Debating Drugs and Everyday Life: Normalisation, Prohibition and "Otherness"' in N. South (ed.) *Drugs, Controls and Everyday Life*, London: Sage.

Sumnall, H. R., Wagstaff, G. F. and Cole, J. C. (2004) 'Self-reported Psychopathology in Polydrug Users', *Journal of Psychopharmacology*, 18(1): 75–82.

Sutherland, E. H. (1939) *Principles of Criminology* (3rd edition), Philadelphia, PA: J. B. Lippincott.

Sykes, G. and Matza, D. (1957) 'Techniques of Neutralization: A Theory of Delinquency', *American Sociological Review*, 22: 664–73.

Taylor, I. (1999) *Crime in Context: A Critical Criminology of Market Societies*, Cambridge: Polity Press.

Thomson, R., Bell, R., Holland, J., Henderson, S., McGrellis, S. and Sharpe, S. (2002) 'Critical Moments: Choice, Chance and Opportunity in Young People's Narratives of Transition', *Sociology*, 36(2): 335–54.

Thornberry, T. P. (1987) 'Toward an Interactional Theory of Delinquency', *Criminology*, 25: 863–91.

Thornton, S. (1995) *Club Cultures: Music, Media and Subcultural Capital*, Cambridge: Polity.

Topp, L., Hando, J., Dillon, P., Roche, A. and Solowij, N. (1999) 'Ecstasy Use in Australia: Patterns of Use and Associated Harm', *Drug and Alcohol Dependence*, 55: 105–15.

Tulloch, J. and Lupton, D. (2003) *Risk and Everyday Life*, London: Sage.

Vervaeke, H. K. E. and Korf, D. J. (2006) 'Long-term Ecstasy Use and the Management of Work and Relationships', *International Journal of Drug Policy*, 17: 484–93.

Wallace, C. (1987) 'Between the Family and the State: Young People in Transition' in M. White (ed.) *The Social World of the Young Unemployed*, London: Policy Studies Institute.

West, D. J. (1982) *Delinquency: Its Roots, Careers and Prospects*, London: Heinemann.

White (2001) 'Heroin Use, Ethnicity and the Environment: The Case of the London Bangladeshi Community', *Addiction*, 96: 1815–1824

Wibberley, C. and Price, J. (2000) 'Young People's Ideas on Drugs and Drug Use – Implications for the Normalisation Debate', *Drugs: Education, Prevention and Policy*, 7(2): 147–62.

Williams, L. (2007) 'A Life Course Perspective on Drug Use from Adolescence to Adulthood: Onset, Continuity, Turning Points and Desistance', unpublished thesis, University of Manchester.

Williams, L. and Parker, H. (2001) 'Alcohol, Cannabis, Ecstasy and Cocaine: Drugs of Reasoned Choice amongst Young Adult Recreational Drug Users in England', *International Journal of Drug Policy*, 12(5–6): 397–413.

Winstock, A. R., Marsden, J. and Mitcheson, L. (2010) 'What Should Be Done About Mephedrone?', *British Medical Journal*, 340: 1605.

Wynne, B. (1996) 'May the Sheep Safely Graze? A Reflexive View of the Expert–Lay Knowledge Divide' in S. Lash, B. Szerszynski and B. Wynne (eds) *Risk, Environment and Modernity: Towards a New Ecology*, London: Sage.

Young, J. (1971) *The Drugtakers: The Social Meaning of Drug Use*, London: Paladin.

——(1999) *The Exclusive Society*, London: Sage Publications.

Zinberg, N. E. (1984) *Drug, Set and Setting*, New York: Human Sciences Press.

Index